EXTREME PURSUITS

EXTREME PURSUITS

Travel/Writing in an Age of Globalization

GRAHAM HUGGAN

The University of Michigan Press ✦ Ann Arbor

Copyright © by the University of Michigan 2009
All rights reserved
Published in the United States of America by
The University of Michigan Press
Manufactured in the United States of America
⊗ Printed on acid-free paper

2012 2011 2010 2009   4 3 2 1

A CIP catalog record for this book is available from the British Library.

Library of Congress Cataloging-in-Publication Data

Huggan, Graham, 1958–
    Extreme pursuits : travel/writing in an age of globalization /
Graham Huggan.
        p.   cm.
    Includes bibliographical references and index.
    ISBN 978-0-472-07072-5 (cloth : alk. paper) — ISBN 978-0-472-
05072-7 (pbk. : alk. paper)
    1. Travelers' writings—History and criticism.   2. Travel in
literature.   3. Literature and globalization.   4. Globalization in
literature.   5. Travel—History.   6. Travel writing—History.
7. Travel writing—Political aspects.   8. Travel—Philosophy.
9. Tourism—Philosophy.   I. Title.
PN56.T7H84   2010
808.8'0355—dc22   2009020596

Acknowledgments

This book has traveled a fair distance of its own, and thanks are due to the many people who helped me reach the destination. Included among these are LeAnn Fields and the editorial staff at the University of Michigan Press for their consummate professionalism, Shaun Tan for the book's startling cover image, and, particularly, Sabine Schlüter for her unfailing love and support throughout. Some sections of the book initially appeared, in modified form, in the following publications: "Australia, America, and the Changing Face of Nature Documentary," in *Imagining the New New World,* ed. Judith Ryan and Chris Wallace-Crabbe (Cambridge: Harvard University Press, 2004); "Derailing the Trans: Postcolonial Studies and the Negative Effects of Speed," in *American Studies in Transit,* ed. Brigitte Waldschmidt-Nelson (Heidelberg: Winter Verlag, 2006); "Going to Extremes: Reflections on Travel Writing, Death and the Contemporary Survival Industry," in *Seuils et traverses: enjeux de l'écriture du voyage,* ed. Jan Borm (Brest saint-Quentin-en-Yvelines: CRBC Sud d'Amérique, 2002); "'Greening' Postcolonialism: Ecocritical Perspectives," in *Modern Fiction Studies* 50, no. 3 (2004); and "Geography, Travel Writing and the Myth of Wild Africa," in my own book *Interdisciplinary Measures: Literature and the Future of Postcolonial Studies* (Liverpool: Liverpool University Press, 2008). Thanks to the publishers and editors of these volumes for allowing material from them to be reprinted here.

Contents

Preface: In Transit

This book begins, predictably perhaps, at the airport: two airports, to be precise, both in America but very much part of the wider world. The first is JFK, that decaying monument to continuous public underinvestment, with chronic overcrowding and inadequate facilities that "would not seem out of place in Lagos or Bombay" (Luttwak, 15). Here is Edward Luttwak's description of the airport in the early 1990s (and recent passenger feedback suggests that conditions have not improved much since):

> Instead of the spotless elegance of Narita or Frankfurt or Amsterdam or Singapore, arriving travelers at one of the several terminals that belong to near-bankrupt airlines will find themselves walking down dingy corridors in need of paint, over frayed carpets, often struggling up and down narrow stairways alongside out-of-order escalators. . . . The frayed carpets, defective escalators, and pervasive . . . dirt show that yesterday's capital is not being renewed but is rather consumed day by day—"deferred maintenance" is the most perfect sign of Third World conditions, the instantly recognizable backdrop of South Asian, African, and Latin American street scenes, with their dilapidated buildings, broken pavements, crudely painted hoardings, and decrepit buses. (16)

Now fast-forward to the turn of the millennium, and consider Pico Iyer's description of another of the world's biggest airports, Los Angeles International (LAX):

As I began to look around Los Angeles International Airport, walking around its terminals as I might a foreign city, I quickly realized that it really does have all the amenities of a modern metropolis. There is a fire station there, and a private hospital next door; the airport has its own $10 million post office. There is an airport police squad, cruising around in Crown Victoria patrol cars, another unit forms a Bicycle Patrol, and the Coast Guard also maintains a station there. There is a movie coordinator at LAX, a tow-truck service and a five-person Airport Commission (made up, not long ago, of a Chinese man, a Japanese man, a Hispanic woman, an elderly white man, and an African-American named Johnny Cochrane, Jr.). There is even a public-relations department, one of whose employees told me, casually, "FBI, Secret Service, CIA—everybody's here." (*Global Soul*, 45)

The contrast here is probably overdrawn, and anyone who has traveled through these airports knows the considerable inconveniences attached to both. What to make, though, of the international airport as a symbol of the Third-Worldization of the First World (JFK); or as its own micro-world, "an anthology of generic spaces" (Iyer, 43) replete with miniature models of itself (LAX)? Airports, it is clear, are figures for the process that is popularly—and often none too accurately—described as *globalization,* capitalism's renewed sense of itself as a world system, but also capitalism's untimely and inequitable reminder that "it has [historically] proposed a homogenisation of the world that it cannot achieve" (Amin, quoted in Lazarus, 26).

As figures for globalization, international airports are both global crossroads, in which people from all over the world are thrown together in a dizzying variety of cross-cultural mixtures, but also networked environments that testify to globalization's virtual command of a huge number of interconnected global flows. The international airport, meanwhile, testifies to the massification of tourism, itself nothing if not a global industry, and to the transition of air travel—travel itself—from a badge of the exotic to a marker of the everyday. Yet international airports, at the same time, provide reminders of the social inequalities off which globalization feeds, and which it in turn produces; reminders, too, of the anxieties and insecurities these global inequalities create. These anxieties are in part ontological, born out of the impossibility of knowing, amid the generalized disorientation and anonymity of airport spaces, where and who anyone is. But they also emerge out of the awareness that airports, particularly international airports, are potentially dangerous: microcosms of the anxieties produced by the knowledge of a world on red alert, they are social laboratories of global security risk. Nowhere more than at the airport do we find evidence of what Gearoid O'Tuathail calls the "normalization of paranoia" as a reaction to the unraveling of apparent certainties—of nationality, territory, identity—that no longer seem applicable in an increasingly deterritorialized world (254). Nowhere more than at the airport do we find proof that travel's contingencies of cultural encounter can bring pain as well as pleasure, and that the travel industries that like to promote world peace are often complicit in producing just the opposite: the ideological polarization rather than the inexorable "democratization-by-tourism" of the world (Goldstone, 49).

Recent figures suggest that there will be 1.6 billion arrivals at world airports by 2020, while the growth of tourism, already far and away the world's largest industry, more than tripled in 1999 (Goldstone). Tourism, it has been suggested, is a "learning instrument for forgetting national differences" (Goldstone, 258), yet it is also an instrument of division and a classic example of the confusion of democracy with "free trade." Tourism is both a conspicuous effect and a primary producer of the tangled cultural and economic processes of globalization. As such, it shares globalization's contradictions: consider the yawning gap between the part it plays in facilitating the free movement of people—in creating a world that is increasingly rootless and cosmopolitan—and the responsibility it carries for the "restless upsurging of uprooted populations" (Goldstone, 258)—for the creation of a world of destitute refugees. The cosmopolitan and the refugee are the reverse figures for today's conspicuously uneven global culture, a culture that provides abundant opportunities for the articulation of "privilege through movement" (Kaur and Hutnyk, 25), but also abundant evidence that movement is needed for survival, and is cruelly coerced. As Raminder Kaur and John Hutnyk argue in their 1999 collection *Travel Worlds*, enforced migration is the flip side of celebratory travel, giving "the lie to the myth of travel as a democratic cipher" (25). The modern travel industry, these authors maintain, involves a "colonization of pleasure and desire" that requires "the exploitation of labour in the production and travel of goods and people"; the outdated idea of travel as freedom thus flies in the face of "indentured trade projects, racialized exclusion, and orientalist cultural work" (25, 4).

This extremely negative but by no means unjustifiable view of tourism and travel poses a big problem for travel *writing,* the history of which is implicated in cosmopolitan privilege, and which has arguably proven none too successful in articulating the experiences of those who travel coercively: the victims rather than beneficiaries of modernity; the foot soldiers, not of global democracy but of "globalization from below" (Goldstone, 2). Nor is the problem merely one of inclusion. Let me briefly address two issues here, one tied to the production of *locality,* the other to the production of *anomaly.* While it is a myth to say that globalization has imposed a homogeneous view of a world subject to the management of capital, it has certainly affected the nature of locality on which many travel narratives have historically relied. As Arjun Appadurai asks rhetorically in his 1996 book *Modernity at Large,* "what is the nature of locality as a lived experience in a globalized, deterritorialized world?" (52). While the interpenetration of the local and the global need not spell an end to travel writing—that most resilient of genres—it implies the need for its adaptation to new conditions, as well as to what the anthropologist Edward Bruner calls the "model of entangled agencies" that these conditions create (10). Tourism now, according to Bruner, frequently involves staged scenarios in which tourists and "natives," well aware of their respective roles, perform their identities to each other in a kind of "touristic borderzone" (17). Travel writing, similarly, can no longer take refuge in the classic distinctions (tourist/"native," foreigner/local, etc.) on which it previously depended. For Paul Fussell, writing in 1980, "[a] travel book, at its purest, is addressed to those who do not plan to follow, but who require the exotic anomalies, wonders, and scandals of the literary form *romance* which their own place or time cannot entirely supply" (203). But anomaly requires an understanding of the normative conditions under which identities—personal, cultural, national—are constructed, and such conditions, already complicated thirty years ago, are almost certainly invalid today. Thus, while travel/writing remains an important "source for creating and maintaining cultural distinctiveness" (Bruner, 162), it relies increasingly on the "miscegenated" modes of cultural identity that are created under current conditions of globalization, modes that often reveal the complex patterns of transplantation and displacement embedded within the term *culture* itself.

A word is needed here, perhaps, on the compound term *travel/writing*. I am taking it as a given in this book that there is no meaningful distinction between the tourist and the traveler—an age-old debate that is forever being warmed up, not least by travel writers, but one that, like alienated (post)modern travelers still searching in vain for authenticity, has no place to go. However, the increasingly normative recognition that cultures are sites of travel, and are themselves constituted through different kinds of "travel practice," requires a rather different understanding of travel writing than has usually obtained until now. Like James Clifford, I intend to retain the term *travel* precisely because of its "historical taintedness, its associations with gendered, racial bodies, class privilege, specific means of conveyance, beaten paths, agents, frontiers, documents, and the like" (*Routes*, 39). But also like Clifford, I want to argue for the imbrication of travel *writing* with other kinds of travel practice, including some of those not previously counted as "travel" (Holocaust deportation, migrant labor) or "travel writing" (experimental ethnography, prose fiction), and including representations of travelers, travel practices, and "traveling cultures" in the popular audiovisual media, especially television and film. While such an expanded view of travel/writing runs the risk of collapsing travel into an undifferentiated, all-purpose metaphor—the impetus behind, say, Caren Kaplan's trenchant critique of Clifford—it shows that modern travelogs, as cultural documents of the present, are bound up in all kinds of movements that narrower, if still expansive, definitions of travel writing as "factual fictions" (Holland and Huggan) or "subspecies of memoir" (Fussell) have been unable to embrace. It also suggests that modern travel/writing is inextricably connected with the multiple ways in which tourism *engages* with, not *escapes* from, the unstable conditions of global modernity. Bruner puts this well when he says that tourism is emphatically not the handmaiden of a dystopic view of modernity in which "the utopian world of non-alienated relations is to be found where commodification and modernity are not, either among the unalienated 'primitive others' or through the recovery of past traditions and heritage" (164). But nor is tourism a compensatory mechanism for the ills of modernity; rather, it involves the appreciation and consumption of global modernity in its specific "socio-spatial forms" (169).

This self-conscious engagement with global modernity has resulted in several new, or at least reinvigorated, forms of travel practice. These include practices attached to specific forms of "responsible" tourism (ecotourism, humanitarian tourism, spiritual tourism) that emerge out of what I will be describing in this book as "global consciousness": the heightened ethical awareness of living in a socially divided but ecologically interconnected world. One particular form this travel takes might be encapsulated under the heading the "tourism of suffering," in which the modern cultures of confession and victimage are brought together in part-therapeutic, part-voyeuristic reminiscences of the traumatic experiences of disaster casualties and/or survivors of the recent (or, in some cases, more distant) past. Contemporary disaster writing, in all its different forms, enacts a tourism of suffering that trades on the compensatory currency of affect in the context of a "world risk society" (Beck) in which the normalization of disaster has inspired new and sometimes violent forms of capitalist opportunism and humanitarian interventionism, as well as producing its own distinct forms of emotional neutralization and compassion fatigue. But disaster writing also takes in a variety of other forms of extreme travel writing that seem to be the opposite of compassionate and responsible: the risk-filled adventures of endurance travelers gone troppo, or the deliberate courting of catastrophe that is a function of what the sociologists Claudia Bell and John Lyall call the "accelerated sublime." One of the central arguments of this book is that much of what passes for contemporary travel writing operates under the sign of the disaster; and that this disaster writing is, in turn, the epiphenomenon of a world perceived to be in a state of emergency as a result of the seemingly irresolvable conflicts embedded within it (endemic civil wars, emerging environmental crisis, the global terrorist threat). Contemporary travel writing, in this sense, is a paradoxical reaction to the perception of too much movement, or of movement that is the sign of intractable social disorder and potentially world-threatening unrest.

To what extent this writing, and the practices on which it draws, are really new is debatable. In one sense, this book is enthusiastic about the new; in another, it is profoundly suspicious of it. In this, as in other ways, it is of a piece with a number of recent critical studies on travel/writing, Debbie Lisle's *The Global Politics of Contemporary Travel Writing* (2006) and Marita Sturken's *Tourists of History* (2008) among them, that have attempted to review contemporary travel practices in the wake of ongoing globalization processes (neoliberalism) and allegedly world-changing historical events (9/11). Like both Lisle and Sturken, I am wary of making claims on the basis of a newness that might itself be considered the product of a divisive neoliberal consciousness. After all, no one likes the new as much as those who stand to make the most profit from it, whether in the paradoxical pursuit of commodified nostalgia in the face of hitherto unimaginable catastrophe (Sturken) or in the cynical demarcation of the latest "life-threatening" people and places for politically expedient ends (Lisle). As Naomi Klein puts it even more dramatically in her recent book *The Shock Doctrine: The Rise of Disaster Capitalism* (2007), the economy of disaster is capitalism's contaminated wellspring, the all-encompassing "shock doctrine" around which its opportunistic practitioners can "begin their work of remaking the world" (21).

If there is a danger, inherent in Klein's work, in merely rehearsing capitalism's self-revitalizing apocalyptic rhetoric, there is perhaps a similar danger in my own suggestion that there might be something new about current hypertrophic or mock-elegiac forms of travel/writing—all the more so given the shared propensity of otherwise markedly different travel practices to perpetuate reactionary ideologies in the service of putatively exploratory or innovating ends. It may well be that contemporary travel writing is ultimately condemned to reflect self-ironically on its own belatedness because there is precious little chance for innovation in the world it wearily reimagines, still less opportunity to explore. In this context, the extremist tendencies of contemporary travel, the sometimes bizarre death drives that appear increasingly to be sustaining it, might easily be seen as the latest epiphenomenon of an accelerated if, at the same time, a curiously attenuated postmodern consciousness turning increasingly to the body—turning destructively on the body—in a desperate attempt to purge itself of its own self-imprisoning knowledge of the banal. And the political manipulation of extremism might also be seen as further, unwanted evidence of this: of the vain attempt to rescue ideological certainties from historical contingencies, as if self-redeeming ideas can only be vouchsafed by the sacrifice of bodies, and as if only the spectacle of destruction might provide the self-accorded security of a morally superior life.

Such moral arrogance is part of the history of travel as both imaginative form and material practice. But moral arrogance is only part of the greater legacy of travel. Whether travelers in general and travel writers, more specifically, will ever succeed in cultivating a properly civic responsibility for the world(s) through which they travel is a moot point, and many would probably agree with Lisle's provocative suggestion that the history of travel writing as genre has been marked by a conspicuous absence of critical thought and political self-reflexivity, and that the more particular history of cosmopolitanism as travel is at one and the same time a history of the colonialism it conceals (265). This book will certainly affirm that travel writing continues to be haunted by its own imperial/colonial specters, not least because these are ghosts that the genre has always possessed the uncanny capacity to recreate. However, the largest and most frightening specter that stalks the genre is not imperialism or colonialism but their primary operating agent, *capital*. In a global era, travel practices of all kinds are necessarily shot through with the destructive logic of capital, or what I will describe in this book as the ideology of "globalism." Globalism, I will suggest, lies behind both the contemporary rise of high-risk travel and disaster tourism and what Sturken calls a hyper-commodified "tourism of history" that kitschifies atrocities past and present, shamelessly capitalizing on the memory of the dead. It even lurks behind more globally conscious forms of travel, such as cosmopolitan globe-trotting and ecotourism, that, themselves ensnared by late capitalism's apocalyptic rhetoric, suggest that the ratio of consumption to salvation continues to be carefully calibrated in the modern tourist industry's profitable marketing of moral angst.

The irresolvable clash between globalism and global consciousness provides the background for the book's opening discussion of travel in an era of globalization. Beginning with the argument that globalization enacts the often polarized struggle over conflicting definitions and interpretations of modernity, the first chapter goes on to look at the work of four quintessentially modern travelers—the Australian filmmaker Dennis O'Rourke and the Indian expatriate writers Pico Iyer, Amitava Kumar, and Suketu Mehta—who are acutely conscious of the complicities between the capitalist world-system that sustains them and the conspicuous injustices (corporate greed, economic apartheid, racial discrimination, caste and class hierarchy) of which their respective narratives relate.

Similar complicities are charted in chapter 2, which explores the symbiotic relationship between recent developments in ecotourism—now one of the most important niche markets in the tourist industry—and the rise in so-called eco-travel writing, which aims to promote an instructive, even interventionist approach to the threatened natural and cultural environments it narrates. While eco-travel writing, as the chapter suggests, is inevitably beholden to the consumerist ethos it attacks—as is perhaps most evident in its closest visual counterpart, nature documentary—it may still be effective at its best in drawing attention to the cultural ramifications of the various social and ecological struggles, many of them already or potentially extreme in their implications, in which Green movements across the world are actively engaged.

Chapter 3, probably the core chapter of the book, shifts its attention to the disasters, both natural and not, from which the contemporary tourist industry derives rich pickings, suggesting that world tourism is one of the primary engines of disaster capitalism itself. The chapter is less concerned to attempt a *psychological* explanation for what motivates disaster tourism, among other forms of extreme travel, than to show the *sociological* factors that underlie it, at least some of which are tied in with the aesthetic credos of what Bell and Lyall call the "accelerated sublime." The "accelerated sublime" and the physical, emotional, and, not least, ethical extremes toward which it aspires are both a direct effect of "world risk society" (Beck) and an indirect reflection of residual masculinist anxieties at a time of sexual role redistribution and nuclear family decline. As in other chapters, a wide range of contemporary examples is drawn upon to test this initial hypothesis, including the extreme adventure narratives of Sebastian Junger and Jon Krakauer, the war reportage of Philip Gourevitch, and the glamorized violence of such disparate works as Robert Pelton et al.'s lurid guidebook, *The World's Most Dangerous Places,* and Alex Garland's cynical anti-backpacker novel, *The Beach.*

Chapter 4, in some respects, is a continuation of chapter 3, but with an emphasis on *commemoration* as both a private and public means toward the containment of disaster as a spectrally indeterminate occurrence or catastrophically repeated form. The chapter considers a number of fringe cases of commemorative travel writing, from the maverick "ghost stories" of German expatriate writer W. G. Sebald to the elegiac post-Holocaust narratives of English historian Martin Gilbert and Canadian poet-novelist Anne Michaels, to the controversial, culturally riven memoirs of "Middle Eastern" cultural commentators Norma Khouri and Edward Said. Linking the whole is an argument around the continuing uses and abuses of nostalgia in a globalized cultural environment in which such necrological terms as *thanatourism* (Seaton) and *dark tourism* (Lennon and Foley) indicate a compromised desire both to acknowledge the legacy of atrocity and to assert an illusory authority over it by simplifying its social and political root cause.

The Postscript offers concluding, if perhaps necessarily inconclusive, insights into today's "Age of Extremes" (Hobsbawm) by way of media coverage of the post-9/11 Bali bombings, a discussion of the links between tourism and terrorism, a potted history of the Lonely Planet series, and an attempt to account for the shift from the "authenticities of endurance" that characterized earlier, life-affirming forms of travel/writing to the potentially life-threatening "authenticity of endangerment" that now holds increasing sway over the industry, and that provides the by-definition-unstable ideological mainstay for this book. While much of this commentary is speculative, the Postscript makes it clear that the book, in offering an extended meditation on both the physical and ethical dimensions of contemporary extremism, continues to have grave doubts about the moral capabilities of travel writing to provide viable alternatives to the sometimes excessive global realities it confronts. However, it is simply not true that travel writing, or indeed any other considered form of travel practice, has no critical capacity, or that its increasingly frenetic physical and imaginative activities are a sign of the lurking political *in*activity that is likely to presage its own eventual decline. On the contrary, travel writing is as politically engaged as ever, if considerably less likely to be politically correct. The nature of that engagement today is inescapably global, with the travel book showing all the signs of the "dissolution of sanctified literary boundaries" and "dissemination of the journey metaphor into other cultural forms" that are considered to be requisites for it becoming "a meaningful site for debates about mobility, location and belonging," both in the present conjuncture and times to come (Lisle, *Global Politics*, 268). Thus, while the extremes of travel writing—travel at large—

are part-responses to contemporary social, political, and environmental breakdowns, travel/writing itself appears to be in no imminent danger of collapse.

Let me end (and also make way for a beginning) by returning to the airport. As everyone knows, 9/11 has had irreversible consequences for the world's airports, prompted by the realization that air travel imbricates freedom with destruction, and that terrorism, which itself shares several important characteristics with tourism, is the "dark side of globalization," the unthinkable nightmare version of its dream for a freer, productively deterritorialized world (Powell, quoted in Urry, 57). If 9/11 has been the sign, but also the pretext, for a world considered to be terminally afflicted, then the post-9/11 airport, with all its "free-floating apprehension" (Iyer, *Global Soul,* 32), has become the terminus where the metaphysics of restlessness that informs travel/writing takes on a manic edge. The airport provides a gathering of many of the key themes of this book: the new conditions of global travel; the unease, even paranoia, that underlies them; the trying-out of alternative identities; the limbo between remembered and anticipated states. The airport is a preeminent site of volatile social inclusion; but perhaps, like the different possibilities of travel with which it is associated, it should be remembered for those it excludes, as a vigilant reminder that "the globe shrinks for those who own it, [but not] for the displaced or the dispossessed" (Bhabha, quoted in Urry, 62).

ONE

WTs and the WTO

Introduction

That the World Tourism Organization and the World Trade Organization share the same acronym can hardly be said to be a coincidence; tourism, after all, is nothing if not big business, and that business is conducted, increasingly, on a global scale.[1] Tourism is the product of a globalized modernity characterized by spiralling patterns of consumption, and by the rapid emergence of a system of cultural and economic interconnections that has actively contributed toward the creation of a single—global—"tourist space" (Meethan, 37). The impact of globalization on tourism has been, unsurprisingly, considerable. Critics have pointed out the homogenizing effect of globalization on tourism, leading to the establishment of a series of more or less interchangeable "packaged environments" (Goldstone) in which tourists can enjoy their leisure with a maximum of predictability and a minimum of risk. Yet it is also clear that globalization generates as many differences as similarities, and that these produce a suitably differentiated tourism. One example is the expansion of niche markets (e.g., within the range of "responsible" tourism) as a function of a deregulated post-Fordist political economy (Meethan, 56); another is the increasing privatization of the notion of the public heritage site. Globalization has been a driving force for the diversification of the tourist industry, which in turn provides a valuable resource for the creation and maintenance of cultural distinctiveness in many different regions of what still remains—and tourism admittedly contributes here as well—an unevenly developed world (162).

Two aspects of globalization have made a particularly significant impact on tourism over the last half century. These aspects can be loosely gathered under the headings the *economization of culture* and the *indigenization of modernity*. The economization of culture—its transformation into saleable commodity—is frequently considered to be one of the salient features of late-capitalist modernity, providing incontrovertible evidence of the worldwide commodification of all aspects of social and cultural life. Tourism is a test case for the conspicuous consumption integral to contemporary capitalism; it registers an immediately recognizable "extension of the commodification of modern social life" (Meethan, 4). The global branding of culture has obviously negative resonances, as in what Patricia Goldstone calls the "kitschification of cultural traditions" that results when local cultures are remodeled for global distribution, and when cultural authenticity—always a top tourist attraction—is refashioned for quick sale (224). On the other hand, there is evidence to suggest that such processes may be *beneficial*—and not just economically—to local cultures that, adapting swiftly to the "give-and-take of globalization" (Meethan, 128), are able to negotiate a favorable position for themselves within the global markets that increasingly, if by no means exclusively, regulate the modern dynamics of cross-cultural transaction and exchange. Tourism, in this context, acts as a catalyst for the transformation, not the dissolution, of locality; and for the strategic (re)indigenization of a global modernity no longer masterminded or monopolized—if it ever was—by the West. What this suggests is that it is far too simplistic to see tourism as a product of hegemonic Western supply-and-demand models, and non-Western peoples as happy/hapless consumers of imposed Western goods. Rather, tourism illustrates that "the process[es] of cultural commodification, like capitalism itself, [are] now played out on the global stage and in some cases . . . irreducibly associated with the dynamic interplay between politics and markets, or attempts to harness the[se] markets for political ends" (Meethan, 135).

Globalization involves the restructuring of space, not just the sum of its various (social/political/economic) interconnections; it also implies the development of a global consciousness, for example, in matters of the environment, social justice, and human rights (Meethan, 34). Global consciousness, or something like it, lies behind the development of new forms of sustainable tourism (ecotourism, agritourism, and so forth) although, as subsequent chapters of this book will illustrate, these forms are eminently co-optable by capitalism, characterized today more than it ever was by the relentless drive to create new markets and by the self-given right to use other people's rights to its own ends. Global consciousness is also the property of a relatively new kind of modern world traveler, both indulgent participant in and ironic analyst of marketed "cultures," both shocked witness to and shameless purveyor of global tourism's extensive range of retailed cultural goods. This type of traveler is less likely to go in search of unsullied local cultures than to enjoy—with strategic interruptions for tongue-in-cheek moral disapproval—the new transcultural hybrids thrown up by the impact of current processes of economic and cultural globalization on local tourist space.

An obvious example of this kind of world traveler is Pico Iyer, the epitome of the traveler as cosmopolitan speedster, globalization's accelerated equivalent to the modern urban flâneur. Iyer, in many respects, will be the key figure of this chapter, not least because his writing brings together several of the specific issues and concerns surrounding globalization that are a feature, more generally, of this book. These issues and concerns can be framed here in terms of a series of irresolvable dilemmas. One dilemma is *political*: how can the world be "made safe for tourism" (Goldstone) in an age of extreme instability? Globalization, after all, in unraveling the apparent certainties of state, territory, and identity, has arguably helped produce a climate of suspicion, even paranoia, in which ancient political enmities have been intensified, and (imagined) threats are countered by the increasing polarization of private and public space (O'Tuathail, 254). Another is *cultural*: how can tourism-as-commerce thrive when the very idea of otherness on which it depends is apparently endangered? If cultures are no longer seen as bounded entities but rather as relays chosen from a global-cultural repertoire, what future is there for "exotic" travel, in whichever corner of the world? When everyone is a traveler—albeit a different kind of traveler—then what future is there for the "exotic" travel book? Following on from this, another dilemma is *ontological*. Who, exactly, is a traveler? Is travel writing still defined by the privilege of movement—a privilege embodied in the capacity for world travel—or are there other possibilities for travel writing: counternarratives of modernity; travel narratives "from below"? And *where* is the traveler, for that matter? If travelers are increasingly seen as inhabiting a global space, how then are they to orient themselves? What happens when one global space stands in for another; when the city, for example, becomes a globe in itself, a microcosmic "travel world"? (Kaur and Hutnyk). Or what happens when the real and virtual spaces of travel intermingle, creating "fantasies of limitless choice" (Strain, 233) of the order provided by cyber-travel: not just where do I want to go, but who do I want to be today? Finally, there is an *ethical* dilemma posed by these choices, as perhaps there always has been for travelers. If, in an unevenly developed global culture, "the right to travel is only for those with the right credentials to travel" (Kaur and Hutnyk, 3), how should that right be exercised responsibly? How should it be shared? Should it be exercised at all?

Some of these questions resonate across the body of Iyer's writing, with several coming together in his ambitious 2000 travelog *The Global Soul.* I propose a close reading of this text before proceeding to analyze a different kind of late twentieth-century travel vehicle: the Australian filmmaker Dennis O'Rourke's ethically saturated ethnographic documentaries, *Cannibal Tours* (1988) and *The Good Woman of Bangkok* (1991). There are similarities, however; for in O'Rourke's work, as in Iyer's, the inescapable realities of globalization lead to an interrogation of the status of the cultural other in which otherness is dispersed but the problem of cultural voyeurism is arguably exacerbated rather than erased. The touristic consumption of the other is either filtered through the ubiquitous pseudo-anthropological trope of cannibalism (*Cannibal Tours*) or sublimated in repressed sexual desire (*The Good Woman of Bangkok*), allowing in both cases for an analysis of global tourism in terms of colonialist fantasies of containment and mastery in a post-colonial space. These fantasies are then applied to a set of readings of the modern global city, registered both from allegedly inside and outside perspectives, in which the boundaries are symptomatically blurred between the city as a "dwelling" and a "traveling" space. Cosmopolitanism provides the link between these spaces, with the worldly figure of the cosmopolitan being challenged by a consideration of its unwanted mirror-image, the refugee. Finally, in a coda I will examine another figure of global travel, the virtual traveler, whose "distanced immersion" (Strain, 233) provides an alternative model by which the increasingly disoriented global traveler can regain an illusory sense of mastery over culture and space.

Global Souls

In *The Global Soul: Jet Lag, Shopping Malls, and the Search for Home* (2000), Pico Iyer reproduces the slightly queasy combination of too-cool-for-school postmodernism and bleeding-heart sentimentality that were characteristic of much of his earlier travel writing, particularly his entertaining whistle-stop tour of South and Southeast Asia, *Video Night in Kathmandu* (1988). As in the earlier work, Iyer tends to replicate the shallow commercialism he claims to critique, both in the content of his writing and, especially, its form, an immediately identifiable mixture of up-market shopping catalog and glossy tourist brochure. It would be easy enough to see Iyer as one of his own spoilt "diplobrat[s]" (Iyer, 196), winging round the world on CNN and *Time* magazine's expenses, the corporate hack as global philosopher. Yet this would be to trivialize the deeper search underlying Iyer's expense-account cosmopolitanism, one identified in the opening chapter in terms of the unresolved effort to "preserve a sense of universality in a world that [is] apt to define unity in more divisive ways" (22). Globalism and universalism, Iyer insists throughout the book, are not the same thing, with the former often acting as little more than an alibi for the worst excesses of the free market and the latter defining, rather, a measured way of seeing and living "beyond petty allegiances and labels," in the free-floating manner of an Emersonian "universal soul" (17). "All the globalism in the world," he says ruefully, "does not add up to universalism"; indeed, globalism might be seen as an impediment to universalism insofar as it stunts the shared human aspirations on which universalism erects itself, turning the world into a playground for "those who have no one to play with" (244)—a "benign empire" in thrall to multinational capitalism and the media, dedicated to corporate commerce but still projecting the image of an "ideal Oversoul" (179).

Iyer's primary metaphor for this "benign empire" is the Olympic Games, which he sees as exemplifying the contradictory goals of mass-market globalism and human solidarity, these being fused in a festival of skin-deep patriotism in which the fact that "the flag is . . . eclipsed by the logo" (209) merely confirms a global order given over to corporate image-making—one in which an accumulation of brand names, "more and more a floating currency," have eventually succeeded in turning the Olympics from universal peace movement into global stock exchange

(193). Aptly, Iyer's sharp analysis of the "corporate optimism" and "bottom-line internationalism" (197) underlying the modern-day Olympic Games focuses on the much-criticized 1996 Games in Atlanta, a largely anodyne and unprepossessing venue that became, for two weeks, the unlikely setting for the "greatest planetary show on earth" (178). Atlanta, for Iyer, is a non-place, "a futuristic, globally linked web of terminals surrounded for as far as the eye could see by untamed wilderness" (206), a "would-be global city" (215) repeatedly betraying its own provincialism, and caught in the "empty space that lies between [corporate] globalism and true universalism" (214). Iyer's descriptions of Atlanta follow the pattern of contemporary anti-travel writing, which operates on the ironic principle that the best places to visit are often those in which there is nothing much to see:

> Atlanta at first sight looked like nowhere on earth: suburb led to interstate led to off-ramp led to suburb. I passed an Economy Inn, a Quality Inn, a Comfort Inn, a Days Inn; I passed a Holiday Inn Select, which gave way, soon enough, to a Holiday Inn Express. On every side of me were look-alike office blocks and landscaped driveways, mirror-glass buildings and office parks: all the interchangeable props of an International Style that could, in its latest incarnation, be called Silicon Neo-Colonial. (185)

If Atlanta is a global city at all, it is global by virtue of being featureless, "as if a city had been replaced by a scenic functional base as picturesque and not quite real as the forests you see on the background of personal checks" (186). Its globalism is a function of the rhetoric of corporate improvement, ironically aspiring to a grandeur of scale and a unity of purpose its segregated social system ensures will never exist. Far from embodying the dream of its most famous son, Martin Luther King, the city is racially riven and, in places, desperately impoverished, full of abandoned houses and boarded-up storefronts and "kids hawking T-shirts of the black-power salute at the '68 Olympics, and people [just] walking around and looking lost" (189). In a nice touch, Iyer, sitting on the porch outside King's home, looks down the street to the Ritz-Carlton, touted as the "tallest hotel in the hemisphere," and watches men "sashaying blearily down the side streets, in and out of their shotgun houses," near where Iyer's car is "precariously parked, a block beyond the sign that said FREEDOM WALK ENDS" (189).

Atlanta, for Iyer, parades its globalism as a gloss over deep-South intolerance and parochialism; as such, it is not an untypical Olympic venue, a not-quite-world-city riding the crest of its own pushy corporate image and "desperately attempt[ing] to prove itself a major global player" by shunting its own social problems temporarily offstage (183–84). The Games themselves are an example of "the global market hover[ing] over the global village" and threatening to swallow it whole, as emblematized in Atlanta's most famous corporate symbol, Coke (217). However, what is most striking about the Games is not their glib commercialism but the counterpoint they provide to an equally specious cosmopolitanism that, buoyed up by the "happy globalist" (During) ideal of living without attachments, provides Iyer's self-ironizing recipe for the unfettered Global Soul (140).

Perhaps the best example of this in the book is in the chapter on Hong Kong, which Iyer sees as a quintessential global city where just about everything—and, by implication, just about everyone—can be bought and sold from just about everywhere else. Hong Kong is a haven for the Global Soul in his (and it is nearly always "his") worldly avatar as mobile yuppie—a place apparently modeled after the postmodern "city-state as transit lounge" (96), and an ideal stopover for the class of roving "flexecutives"—another of Iyer's deliberately trite neologisms (85)—more than half of whose lives seem to be spent suspended in midair (84). An ideal opportunity, as well, for Iyer to stockpile some more postmodern/globalist clichés, as in the Worldwide Building, a faceless "shopping-mall-cum-conference-center-cum-world trade-center," which stands in metonymically for a city that is "less a capital of empire than an empire of capital," operating on the twin principles of fusion culture and free trade (96–97).

Bizarrely, Iyer is reminded here—not for the first time—of his privileged boyhood in Berkshire, the sugar-coated past of a well-off ex-colonial periodically susceptible to bouts of "imperial daydreaming," in which England is served up to its willing subjects "in a more open, friendly form" (93, 150). Interestingly, throughout the text Iyer suggests that cosmopolitan rootlessness is itself a form of benign imperialism, its reluctant adherents belonging to an "International Empire [where] the sense of home is not just divided, but scattered across the planet, and [in which] in the absence of any center at all, people find themselves at sea" (18). However, the self-indulgence such a vision of Empire might afford is temporarily offset by reminders of Empire's victims, one present-day equivalent being that itinerant underclass of global capitalism's cast-offs: the undocumented migrant worker, the unhoused boat person, the unwanted refugee. On his last day in Hong Kong, Iyer pays a visit to the Vietnamese boat people, diminished in number since the earlier waves of the 1970s and early 1990s, and now huddled together in an "open camp" at the far edge of the New Territories (108). Given his propensity for sentimentality, Iyer's portrait of the boat people is noticeably unromantic, but he still manages to point out the discrepancy between an official rhetoric of state protection and the continuing problems of official identity and citizen's rights. Reflecting on these problems, he picks up a copy of Simone Weil's classic *The Need for Roots,* in which the French Jewish writer, on being asked to write a report by de Gaulle on the situation facing the French after World War II liberation, famously warned that "no human being should be deprived of . . . those relative and mixed blessings (home, country, tradition, cultures, etc.) which warm and nourish the soul and without which, short of sainthood, a human life is not possible [at all]" (Weil, quoted in Iyer, 111). One might expect some kind of disquisition here on the fundamental difference between the illusion of cosmopolitan rootlessness and the realities of refugee expulsion; but instead, Iyer chooses to dwell on those who don't seem to have the gift for adapting to flight as "a way of being in the world" (80). Here as elsewhere in the text, Iyer blurs the boundaries between the beneficiaries and the victims of displacement, distracted as he is from the conspicuous material disadvantages of the impoverished by the—to him—equally intractable problem of the spiritual emptiness of the rich. (His host Richard, a high-flying businessman, has dealings with countless different countries, but Iyer notices that once he has taken down all Richard's contact details, "that left no room in my address book for his name" [113].)

To some extent, Iyer is quite right to draw a connection between refugees and cosmopolitans, whose alternative identity crises are linked by-products of the new global dispensation.[2] The central questions, though, are personal ones: whether to complain about deracination or to make a virtue out of it; and whether, when faced with a choice between potential homes and affiliations, to "claim or deny attachment when I chose" (21). These questions are couched in metaphysical terms—"how to keep the soul intact in the face of pell-mell globalism" (22)—yet their derivation is experiential:

> I know a little about the Global Soul in part because, having grown up simultaneously in three cultures, none of them fully my own [India, Britain, and the US], I acquired very early the sense of being loosed from time as much as from space—I had no history, I could feel, and lived under the burden of no home. . . . A person like me can't really call himself an exile (who traditionally looked back to a home now lost), or an expatriate (who's generally posted abroad for a living); I'm not really a nomad (whose patterns are guided by the seasons and tradition); and I've never been subject to the refugee's violent disruptions: the Global Soul is best characterized by the fact of falling between all categories (and at college, for example, I counted neither as a local, who could receive a government grant, nor as a foreigner, who was subject to a specially inflated fee). (22–24)

The Global Soul emerges, in passages like these, as a permanently transitional being, eternally poised between the cosmopolitan dream of multiple attachment and the existential nightmare of disorientation and disconnection (24). This transitional being is, strictly speaking, neither a local nor a foreigner, and is potentially relieved of the personal and social responsibilities that attach to each. Yet as Iyer suggests, lack of affiliation does not necessarily imply lack of accountability; instead, he seems to gesture toward something like a critical cosmopolitanism—a variation on the model of global consciousness—that steers a careful path between overcommitted loyalism, on the one hand, and underdefined internationalism, on the other (24–25).[3] All the same, this Global Soul seems at times to be remarkably soulless, growing so used to "giving back a different self according to his environment that he loses sight of who he is when nobody's around" (25). Despite the windy rhetoric that surrounds it, the supposedly enlightened figure of the Global Soul (GS) often seems to be little more than an unusually self-conscious version of the generic figure of the World Traveler (WT), with both global-market acronyms standing in for a perception, ironically itself market-driven, that there are "fewer and fewer [connections] in the classic human sense" in a technologically connected world (16).

This paradox is explored most fully in Iyer's chapter on LAX (Los Angeles International Airport), the first in the book's series of fully fashioned, self-sustaining micro-worlds. LAX, and airports like it, aren't just "intranational convenience zones" but anonymous spaces, fully equipped, that can easily be seen as "models of our future" (43). While they are spiritual centers in the sense that they offer a double life—"you get on as one person and get off as another" (42)—international mega-airports are better characterized by an empty functionalism that is, to all intents and purposes, spiritually bereft. Bereft of geography and history, too, insofar as airports tend to accommodate that strange race of deterritorialized human beings who have both entered a "stateless state of jet lag" (59) and succumbed to its temporal equivalent, amnesia—as if the airport served as a convenient safety valve for the "abolition of history, for people who sometimes had little else" (66). This floating condition invites a temporary suspension of hostilities that frequently turns out to be wholly illusory; in fact, international airports are by definition unsafe places, as much reminders of the distances as the correlations between the different cultures they temporarily accommodate, and shadowed by the violently interdependent histories that both working staff and traveling clients are always poised to reenact.

> One day, in the [LAX] Airport Sheraton, I asked my Ethiopian waitress how she liked LA. Well enough, she said in elegant, reticent English; she'd actually been here now for seven years. She must miss her home, I said, knowing that the shopping centers of LA are thick with places like the Homesick Bakery.
> She nodded sadly; she missed it bitterly, she said.
> "But I can't go home."
> "Why not?" I said, still smiling.
> "Because they killed my family. Two years back. They killed my father; they killed my brother." "They," of course, referred to the Tigreans, the friendly man down the street holding up fingers to show me how much I owed, the gracious woman collecting litter as I walked along the fourth-floor corridor. (77)

Like Atlanta, LAX is a largely featureless space—"a nowhere zone" (73)—despite its pretensions to being a multicultural conduit in a "global crossroads city" (75). Throughout the book, Iyer is as suspicious of the blandishments of multiculturalism as he is of the inflationary rhetoric of corporate globalism; both come together in his chapter on Toronto, aka "the city as anthology" (120), routinely touted as a "multicultural experiment with itself as guinea pig, . . . the most cosmopolitan city on earth" (123–24). Toronto, he suggests archly, is a city packed with Global Souls, a unique cosmopolis of professional "free agents" who double in their spare time as amateur ventriloquists and impersonators, and for whom the most haunting question is "who are you today?" (140). Toronto is also a haven for a happy globalism registered in the smiling faces of its multiethnic cab-drivers, evangelical in their conviction that the city is the world's best and safest place. This tongue-in-cheek sentimentalism applies to the doctrine of multiculturalism itself, neatly sent up in a dialogue between Iyer and his friends David and Alicia, the former of whom cringingly expatiates on two things that make him cry: "the new multiculture we've got here . . . [and] the lakes and wilderness . . . It's a beautiful thing, [this multiculturalism]: the glorious promise of it" (154). Interestingly, however, Iyer is ambivalent, rather than dismissive, about the promise of multiculturalism, quickly seeing through other people's cultural-pluralist clichés only to reproduce them in his turn: "[The world is] forming into tribes based on Web sites, communities of interest, affiliations described in nontraditional ways. The beauty of the present is that we can find ourselves in the company of the cultures that we never expected to encounter otherwise" (170).

The basis here for Iyer's only partly self-ironic sentimentalism is a perception of Toronto as a metropolitan confraternity of existential exiles, collectively fretting about their place in the world without necessarily having to worry about a roof over their own heads. Perhaps this is why his own chosen home is "alien" Japan, where he can live out his existential angst that much more authentically, and where the Global Soul—the "full-time citizen of nowhere" (277)—is almost automatically perceived with suspicion, or even as an outright threat. Japan affords Iyer a situation of what can only be described as comfortable alienation, in keeping with the country's stereotypically self-contradictory reputation as xenophobic "monoculture" and as welcoming amalgam of commodified cultures in which the response to globalism is a "promiscuous consumption of all the cultures in the world," and in which the world itself is presented in the image of a "giant souvenir store" (275, 280). There is a justice of sorts here, with Iyer's own bad faith being rewarded in a country that is conspicuously guilt-free about its own bad faith. This manufactured "Japan"—spiritually isolationist but materially internationalist—is perhaps the ideal spot for a bout of low-risk Global Soul-searching; meanwhile, all of this takes place in the larger context of a world made safe for precisely the kind of cultural tourism, acting in the consolidated interests of global consumer capitalism, that large swaths of Iyer's book had made it their business to contest.

Twisting Veblen, Martin Roberts has termed this particular phenomenon "conspicuous cosmopolitanism," and the phrase is certainly applicable, not only to Iyer's writing, but to an increasing number of contemporary, self-consciously globalist travel texts. These kinds of travel narrative are not just examples, or even primarily examples, of world travel; rather, they reflect on the impact of globalization on travel and on touristic perceptions of global culture itself. There is nothing particularly new about any of this. The history of travel writing reveals a much greater awareness of global interconnectedness than is often appreciated, even when writers claim to be reporting back from some previously untouched, or at least unfamiliar, site. *Global culture* is not a new term any more than *cosmopolitanism* is a new way of describing the sensibility of the world citizen; both terms have existed now for centuries, and their current reemergence, often under the rubric of a free-floating postmodernism, is more the sign of an alternative, sometimes seen as a second, modernity than evidence of some radical epistemological break. On the evidence of texts like *The Global Soul,* it is tempting to conclude that the globalist travel book has little to offer current analyses of either cosmopolitanism or global culture other than making the obvious point that both refer to, and are themselves often virtually indistinguishable from, locally inflected, individually oriented modes of cultural consumption in a technologically interconnected world. What is interesting about such texts is their recycling of globalist truths as self-ironizing clichés: a conspicuous feature of Iyer's writing, but also a staple in the recent history of the travel book. The master term under which these clichés shelter is not, as might be imagined, *globalization* but *tourism.* Tourism is the subject of *The Global Soul,* the motor force behind its reflections on contemporary global capitalism. Its rhetorical equivalent is tautology; in Iyer's text, the journey through (rather than to) a series of more or less interchangeable destinations provokes largely jaded reflections on tourism as tourism, as a seemingly inexhaustible supply of travel clichés projected back upon themselves. In this kind of touristic metatext, nothing very much happens; but nothing very much is learned about tourism either, other than its insatiable appetite to produce and consume semi-identical images of itself. There are elements of anti-travel narrative here: in the concentration on "non-places" and the banalization of the spectacular; in the emphasis on suspended movement and activity so frantic and apparently directionless it risks becoming the negation of itself.

In his back-cover pitch for Iyer's book, Richard Rodriguez suggests that "*The Global Soul* takes the genre of travel writing as far as it can go . . . [to] a world where no place is foreign and the most puzzling person one meets on the journey is oneself." This is standard back-cover fare, and an even more standard commentary on travel writing, which continues to flourish despite increasingly routine proclamations that it has no place else to go. Rodriguez's description might apply, in fact, to any number of recent travel narratives that, in accordance with many contemporary ethnographies, are much less interested in documenting the places and people they visit than in reflecting on the self-authored process of documentation itself. Self-reflexivity is the norm, so much so that it itself has become banalized (a different way of saying, possibly, that contemporary travel writing has no place to go). Travel writing, traditionally, has acted as a medium for personal opinion masquerading as considered sociopolitical analysis. What texts such as Iyer's suggest is that even the subjectivity of travel narrative—the element of personal quest that runs through an entire history of this particular kind of writing—has reached the point where it generates little penetrating insight or genuine novelty; little individualism, either, insofar as both traveler and "travelee" (Pratt, *Imperial*) exist within a well-thumbed catalog of readily identifiable travel types. To repeat: what is most characteristic about the figure of the Global Soul is its high degree of blandness, even soullessness; just as the figure of the traveler has historically tended to merge with its imagined nemesis, the tourist, so the Global Soul has little to distinguish it from the generic World Traveler (WT), the semiprofessional global tourist for whom labor is simply another form of leisure, and for whom leisure involves the consumption of ideas-as-clichés: ideas about "new" forms of travel/traveler: the "diplo-brat," the "flexecutive," and, for that matter, the "global soul." Iyer's neologisms are not just glib, they have an almost desperate ring to them, registering the desire for an innovation—a fresh perspective—

they are never likely to fulfill. A similar sense of wish-fulfillment informs what we might call the moral component of Iyer's narrative—his attempt to critique world tourism's symbiotic links with corporate globalism, and to gesture toward other, more civically responsible ways of looking at the self's relation to both local environment and the wider world. Neither attempt is particularly successful, but perhaps that's always likely to be the case given the ideological framework of the text, which assimilates both globalism and its more humane counterpart, global consciousness, to the master narrative of *tourism*—a term that applies as much to contemporary, dominant forms of social relations as to individual, culturally specific ways of seeing and experiencing the world.

That these social relations are structured primarily if not exclusively by consumer capitalism is a given; in this context, the Global Soul provides a moral alibi for the pleasures of consumption, just as critical cosmopolitanism offers a convenient cover for the addictive desire to voyage between real and imagined homes. This is in keeping with recent shifts in the ethnography of tourism, to which travel writing belongs and which is currently undergoing—like tourism itself—its own ethical turn. The choice here is not so much whether to consume or not, but how to consume responsibly and sustainably. In this sense, the conundrum of the Global Soul is not that of the anti-tourist tourist, that all-too-familiar pose of the contemporary traveler/writer. It is rather that of the antimaterialist materialist: not necessarily guilty about consumption but always conscious of its given limits; and equally aware of its effects, not always nefarious or even negative, on a world increasingly fashioned in the tourist image—a world in which touristic images circulate with the same degree of fluency, rapidity, and banality as that with which tourists themselves, in ever greater numbers, circumnavigate the globe. Global Souls are loath to exercise the kinds of licensed irresponsibility that are commonly practiced by world tourists, even in their more conscientious guise as globally conscious travelers; Global Souls, it might even be said, are loath to travel, at least in any conventional, destination-oriented sense, at all. But Global Souls are touristic consumers, too, and are not always as ethically sound as they pretend to be. They are perhaps best seen as morally ambivalent, and it is to the moral ambivalence of another globally conscious touristic figure, the tourist as humanitarian savior, that the chapter turns next.

Global Bodies

My second example of the staged conflict between global consciousness and globalism comes via the highly self-conscious ethnographic films of the Australian filmmaker Dennis O'Rourke. These films, reflecting on the moral slipperiness of their own cultural voyeurism, reveal an ethnographic project that is often indistinguishable from the capitalist-inspired global tourism it attacks. Anthropology and tourism, in any case, have long been seen at least as distant relatives; as Malcolm Crick ruefully observes in the contemporary context: "an anthropologist has no practical alternatives to being subjected to touristic rules in order to undertake [his or her] research; in that sense, an anthropologist simply is a type of tourist. In actual fact, irrespective of the particular topic of research one is doing, local people frequently experience and portray tourists and ethnographers in a comparable manner" (217). Anthropologists and tourists both travel, according to Crick, "to collect and expropriate what they value from the other and then [to] tell of their journeys"; and both are buoyed up, but also potentially compromised, by the stories they relate (210). Globalization provides the grounds for a further convergence between anthropology and tourism. As Edward Bruner suggests, tourism is "the quintessential transnational topic for anthropological enquiry" in the modern era (232). But this enquiry is complicated by the fact that anthropologists and tourists are increasingly viewed, not least by anthropologists themselves, as "alternative fieldworkers . . . journeying to the peripheries of modernity" (10)—a view that makes a mockery of the anthropological fantasy of working in a "tourist-free" cultural space (8).

Ethnographic film, according to several of its practitioners, is well placed as a medium to comment on the contradictions raised by representations of cultural difference that, while easily identifiable as belated, continue to be seen as the cornerstones on which the integrity of anthropology as an academic discipline, as well as the vitality of tourism as a commercial enterprise, are upheld. A brief aside on the history of ethnographic film might help explain this. While early ethnographic films were largely sustained by the impossible dream of the invisible camera, their latter-day counterparts are much more likely to bring the filmmaker, if not necessarily his or her technology, to the fore. Ethnographic film, in this sense, has evolved into a "visual dialogue between . . . filmmakers and their subjects" (Weinberger, 45) in which the conventional aim of ethnography, that of interpreting one culture for another, has been superseded by that of tracing the transcultural process of "looking itself, not as a line drawn between the subject and object of viewing, but as an artifact in which the two are inseparably fused" (MacDougall, 265). This shift, as David MacDougall among others has suggested, entails the move to a more fully self-conscious "transcultural cinema" that, while continuing to draw on many of the traditional devices of ethnographic documentary, places greater emphasis on ethnographic films as "repositories of multiple authorship, confrontation and exchange" (97). It also adds to what MacDougall calls the primary and secondary levels of ethnographic representation—"one cultural text seen through, or inscribed upon, another" (97)—at least a third, involving a self-conscious analysis of the limits of ethnographic (and, for that matter, other forms of cultural) representation itself. This third, metalevel is foregrounded in several of O'Rourke's movies, which use cross-cutting techniques and a variety of often conflicting narrative strategies to comment on ethnographic film's (in)capacity to register cultural difference at a time of globalization when such differences are artificially played up even as they appear to be naturally played out. Tourism plays a vital part here in what might be called the restorative staging of cultural difference, a willfully self-contradictory process in which tourists and anthropologists, effectively competing for the same territory, end up playing almost interchangeable roles.

This sets the scene for probably O'Rourke's best-known work, *Cannibal Tours* (1988), one in a series of wryly self-critical commentaries on the detrimental impact of world capitalism on the socially and culturally marginalized peoples of the global South. Ostensibly, *Cannibal Tours* is a travelog that follows the fortunes of a small group of European and North American tourists as they make their way up the Sepik River in Papua New Guinea, interspersed with grainy ethnographic photographs and talking-head interviews with both the tourists (in toe-curling form) and their long-suffering Iatmul hosts. But as O'Rourke has said of his own film, it describes not one but two parallel journeys: "The first is that [actually] depicted—rich and bourgeois tourists on a luxury cruise up the mysterious Sepik River, in the jungles of Papua New Guinea . . . the packaged version of a 'heart of darkness.' The second journey (the real text of the film) is a metaphysical one. It is an attempt to discover the place of 'the Other' in the popular imagination" (quoted in MacCannell, *Empty*, 25).

The place of the other in the film is largely occupied by the ubiquitous figure of the cannibal, that trope of otherness par excellence, routinely invoked to draw the line between civilization's defenders and their barbarian foes. While primitive modes of cannibalism have arguably died out with primitivism itself—as Dean MacCannell suggests, all that remains in the film of the primitive world are "performative primitives," staging their own backwardness for a complacent Western audience (26)—cannibalism certainly exists in the modern era on the symbolic and economic scale. To pick up here on MacCannell's useful distinction between symbolic and economic registers, *symbolic* cannibalism is a form of social solidarity in which the dead have been "honorably" slaughtered to increase the stock (spirituality, knowledge) of the living; while *economic* cannibalism is a form of capitalist accumulation, a "crude but effective method of producing capital gain through legalized murder, plunder, or inheritance, and compounding the gain by eating the dead" (53). What O'Rourke's film illustrates is the process by which cannibalism has effectively *merged* symbolic and economic registers under the conditions of (post)modernity, with global capitalism understood here as playing the crucial support role. Globalization, in fact, turns out to be at the root of the film's symbolic/economic cannibal fantasies, informing the fictions of reciprocity that bind WTs (World Travelers) and EPs (Ex-Primitives) in a pact of manufactured conviviality, but also the barely disguised hostilities that underlie staged touristic encounters with the other based on strategic incomprehension, controlled acquisitiveness, and the disavowal of imperial/colonial shame. An embodiment of all of these characteristics is the film's über-cannibal, a self-satisfied German tourist who sees himself as reliving former colonial conquests, and for whom world travel is itself a form of cannibalist/capitalist accumulation; as he boasts to the camera, "Yes, I have been to Lebanon, Iran, India, Thailand, Burma, China, Japan, the Philippines, Indonesia, the Pacific Islands, Australia two times, once to New Zealand, South Africa, Rhodesia, all of South America . . ." (quoted in MacCannell, *Empty*, 26).

For O'Rourke, the kind of cultural tourism undertaken in *Cannibal Tours* is both enabled by global capitalism and paradoxically outstripped by it. The (pseudo)anthropological search for cultural distinctiveness, driven back in time, reveals itself to be little more than a form of self-defeating nostalgia, as both seekers (WTs) and guardians (EPs) of authenticity are co-opted into performing their strangeness to each other in a variety of oddly familar roles. This is exoticism by numbers, and as such is both mutually reassuring and reciprocally delusive. Mac-Cannell puts it well again here when he refers to the different encounters in the movie in terms of a "shared Utopian vision of profit without exploitation, logically the final goal of a kind of cannibal economics shared by ex-primitives and postmodern [tourists] alike" (28). The point is clinched by describing a scene in which an Iatmul woman loudly complains that the whites have all the money, at which moment the camera drops down to show what she is selling: strings of shell money, which, taken by the tourists for mere trinkets, are obviously traded under massively unfavorable conditions of exchange (30). Extrapolating from the scene, MacCannell reaches this conclusion:

> There is so much mutual complicity in the . . . interactions between the postmodern tourist and the ex-primitive that the system comes close to producing the impossible economic ideal. The performing primitives claim to be exploited, but in so doing they take great care not to develop this claim to the point where their value as a "primitive" attraction is diminished. In short, they must appear as almost noble savages, authentic except for a few changes forced on them by others: they sell beads, they do not trade in currencies. They gain sympathy from the tourist based on the conditions of their relationship to the tourist. And the entire arrangement almost works. (31)

Almost, but not quite; for the rhetorical manipulation of exploitation is itself a sign of uneven development, of a predatory global system that thrives on conspicuously unequal relations of material/symbolic exchange. This tests the limits of what MacCannell elsewhere calls the film's condition of "globality": its ironic conversion of a discredited primitivism, shorn now of all attachment to locality, into the self-serving gestures of globalized postmodern pastiche (26). Granted, the *genres* of the movie are blurred, both visually and acoustically. The soundtrack, for instance, alternates between a Mozart string quartet and an Iatmul flute concerto, with garbled messages from the boat's shortwave radio—tuned, predictably perhaps, to World Service—thrown in. But the fact remains that while, in Bruner's words, there's not so much difference between the "closet ethnographer on tour" and the "closet tourist doing ethnography" (1), neither of these alternative WT-figures would wish, for all the world, to swap places with an impoverished EP.

The final, excruciating scene in which the tourists merrily perform a "tribal" mock-up confirms, not contradicts, this truism; and it does so by exhibiting the crucial difference between performative primitivism as a necessary opportunity for labor (EP) and as a voluntary outlet for play (WT). In terms of MacCannell's cannibal economics, one might describe this as the difference between "survival" and "recreational" modes of cannibalism; certainly, it further complicates models of entangled agency, like Bruner's, that describe activities in the "touristic borderzone" in terms of a theatrical performance in which tourists are always conscious of their roles as tourists, and natives always conscious of their roles as natives, but the former cannot be considered merely as exploiting the latter, nor the latter seen simply as the former's fool (17).

Bruner is right, nonetheless, to suggest that in touristic performances of this kind, material inequalities are symbolically suspended, allowing tourists to be presented reassuringly with their own "transnational media images of cultures and peoples in their primitive state" (92). This is primitivism, of course, of the "soft" rather than "hard" variety, in which the figure of the "colonial savage" has metamorphosed into that of the "pleasant primitive" (87), and in which nostalgia for cannibalism precludes the possibility of any active cannibal threat. (German tourist to Iatmul guide: "Where have you killed the people? Right here. People were killed right here? (he pats the stone for emphasis) Now I need a photograph of the two of us here before the stone for the memory" (quoted in MacCannell, 27). As MacCannell suggests, gestures such as these are both self-congratulatory and implicitly expiatory, providing a reminder of postmodernity itself as a "symptom of the need to suppress bad memories of Auschwitz, Hiroshima, and the other genocides on which modernity was built" (26).

If one of the aims of O'Rourke's film is to return Euro-American modernity to the scene of its own crimes (the "Heart of Darkness" theme), these crimes are now displaced onto the figure of a domesticated cannibal other—one well-adapted to the needs of a global tourist industry supplying anthropological entertainment to the seasoned cultural voyeur. This inevitably raises the issue of O'Rourke's own complicity in the exercise—a complicity he has been all too eager to accept. In an interview, O'Rourke makes it clear that *Cannibal Tours* is not simply an "anti-tourist" movie but a film about the capacity of an increasingly globalized commodity culture to turn us all into each other's voyeurs (Bayer, 6–8). If the anthropologist is a type of world tourist, so too is the globally conscious filmmaker, who is deeply implicated in the potentially destructive processes of objectification and commodification that both industries (cinema, tourism) create. O'Rourke volunteers one particular scene in *Cannibal Tours* as summing up the compromised position of the filmmaker. In the scene, O'Rourke is in the process of asking a young man what it is like to be filmed when a tourist suddenly steps into the back-frame, wishing to take her own picture of him. "One of them is looking at you now," O'Rourke says to the man half-accusingly. But the embarrassment is effectively shared: by the filmmaker who wants footage for his film, by the woman who wants her photograph even if she has to pay for it, and by the man who needs the custom of both, however demeaning the whole process is for him. Caught in the cross-fire of anthropological/touristic gazes, the man—or rather, the man's objectified "ethnic" body—becomes a symbol for the all-consuming cannibal economics that structures O'Rourke's film. Self-reflexivity is not a way out of this; in fact, moralizing self-consciousness is very much part of a system in which complicity itself circulates as a valuable commodity, and in which different forms of post-touristic knowingness are deployed to ensure that the tourist gets satisfaction, with just a frisson of anxiety, while the native gets fed.

In O'Rourke's later tourist vehicle *The Good Woman of Bangkok* (1991), the ethical stakes are raised much higher to include the emotional involvement of the filmmaker, which quickly overtakes the documentary material to become the main subject of the film. *The Good Woman of Bangkok* is an account of O'Rourke's nine-month involvement with a Thai prostitute, Aoi (Yagwalak Conchanakun), and of the light this involvement sheds on the two partners, the Thai sex-tourism industry, and the global-capitalist system that prostitution metonymically represents. That the film can be read on several different levels is made clear in O'Rourke's liner notes: "Like Brecht's play [*The Good Woman of Setzuan*], the film is an ironic parable about the impossibility of living a good life in an imperfect world. [It is also] about prostitution as a metaphor for capitalism, here played out across the borders of race and culture, and about prostitution as a metaphor for all relations between women and men."

As in *Cannibal Tours,* O'Rourke is also concerned to show the inherent voyeurism—what E. Ann Kaplan calls the "imperialist gaze"—of the Western film industry, a voyeurism merely enhanced by the reality effect of documentary film. Unsurprisingly, the film has been criticized for being manipulative, for lacking a feminist perspective, and for using sociological analysis as a smokescreen for the filmmaker's personal and professional desires. These criticisms miss the point insofar as the film doesn't so much critique what it rehearses as rehearse what it seeks, unavailingly at times, to critique. The film, in other words, is a multilayered dramatization of *complicity,* revealing through a process of almost pathological self-reflexivity the moral ambiguities of both sex tourism and the director as a sex tourist himself.

Some cursory reflections on sex tourism may help put these moral conundrums into focus. As Chris Ryan and C. Michael Hall observe in their book on the subject, "representations of sex and sexualities are . . . integral to contemporary tourism, as are the social and economic structures within which such representations and transactions take place" (x). Sex tourism—nominally, tourism the main purpose of which is the procurement and consummation of sexual relations—thus belongs to a much wider socioeconomic nexus, involving both a "legally marginalised form of commoditization" (paid sex) and the national/transnational leisure and entertainment industries (tourism) to which that form belongs (Thanh-Dam, quoted in Ryan and Hall, x). While sex tourism is not always associated with travel from "developed" to "developing" countries, it is often strongly linked to global economic inequalities. Indeed, there is a symbiotic connection between globalization and the trafficking of sex and sexual identities that highlights vast disparities within the global economy—those who travel in search of sexual freedom, for instance, versus those who travel in need of sexual work. As Jeremy Seabrook argues, perhaps too sentimentally in this instance:

> It is a savage irony that sex tourism should be one symptom of globalization, the "integration" of the whole world into a single economy, when both workers in the industry and the clients from abroad are

themselves the product of disintegration—of local communities, the dissolution of rootedness and belonging, the breaking of old patterns of labour and traditional livelihoods; and the psychic disintegration of so many people caught up in great epic changes, of which they have little understanding and over which they have less control. (169–70)

Seabrook underestimates the agency that both sex workers and their clients (tourists) exercise; he also overlooks the fact that the commercialization of sex belongs to a general process of "acceptable" commodification under the aegis of late-capitalist modernity, even though it still remains very much part of unequal, often racialized relations between "developed" and "developing" worlds. To sum up: sex tourism today is a product of the intersections between globalization, travel, and imperialism. It shows the unwelcome truth that tourism has become "the most significant and visible arena of global sexual inequality" (Altman, 106) in the modern era, and that this inequality is maintained through the discrepant movement of sexed/racialized bodies on a global scale. Sex tourism, in fact, provides a reminder that the focus of global consumer culture is the *body;* and that under the conditions of late capitalism, the body, in active search of other bodies, may well be up for sale. The sex-tourism industry thus brings tourists and sex workers together within a number of different but interconnected contexts: within the global context of consumer capitalism, in which sexed bodies circulate as commodities in an uneven world economy; within the local context of "marginal encounters" (Ryan and Hall), where the normal rules governing gendered social behavior are temporarily suspended or no longer apply; and within the ever-changing context of travel in a world increasingly defined by and through movement—a context in which sex workers may often be travelers as well.

The Good Woman of Bangkok offers an example of what Erik Cohen among others has called "open-ended prostitution": the type of relationship, involving both economic investment and emotional attachment, that develops—or, perhaps better, is imagined as having developed—between a Thai sex worker and a white-male foreign tourist or *farang*. The actual degree of emotional attachment on both sides is often highly questionable, despite the temptation—particularly on the part of the *farang*—to push the working relationship into friendship, or even to detect the first blossomings of love. O'Rourke's film both enacts and satirizes these self-delusive tendencies, exposing the (male) insecurities behind them and the myths of male chivalry and compassion that provide a moral alibi for his own sexual needs. At the basis of this behavior is the so-called white knight syndrome by which the *farang* imagines himself to be a humanitarian savior, rescuing his consort from her condition of servitude and offering her the possibility of another, better life. The portrayal of Aoi as a "good woman" feeds into this egregious white-male fantasy, further buttressed by O'Rourke's calculated offer to pay her way out of the sex trade by offering her and her family a rice farm (the attempt backfires, as the formula always suggests it might). O'Rourke's film can thus be seen as a performative engagement with the bogus moralism that surrounds those encounters in the sex-tourism industry that are characterized by a faux gentlemanly civility not to be found in much harsher—and less successful—relationships at home (Ryan and Hall, 29). According to this formula, female compliance is the reward for traditionally protective male behavior—a scenario also manipulated to her own profit by the sex worker, who is often skillful in appealing to her client's "Western perception of himself as a real man who knows how to take care of his woman" (Phillip and Dann, 68).

Complicities such as these also point to the colonial subtext underlying this particular type of hyper-commodified relationship: one marked by the desire not just for morally sanctioned patronage but for a kind of self-redemption in the name of the other—a further variant on the "white knight" myth. In this sense, *The Good Woman of Bangkok* enacts an ironic version of the ethically charged white salvation narrative that was a staple of late nineteenth-century colonialist literature, and that found a cinematic niche a century later in the ostensibly anti-colonialist heroics of the revisionist Western (e.g., *Dances with Wolves*). It is interesting to reflect here on O'Rourke's ambivalent status as an Australian, as a member of a formerly colonized society with its own continuing record of colonialism, both abroad (e.g., Papua New Guinea) and at home. Certainly, the "Australianness" of O'Rourke's films has not always been picked up on by their commentators, though the reverse might be said of their reception in his home country (Berry, Hamilton, and Jayamanne). Connected with this is the ambivalence inscribed into the investigative documentary, a genre arguably complicit with the social abuses and injustices it is designed to reveal. O'Rourke's movies, in this respect, might be described as anti-imperialist in intent but imperialist in method, with their predominantly visual authority being mediated by the self-contradictory figure of the globally conscious filmmaker as touristic consumer and cultural voyeur. In *The Good Woman of Bangkok,* this voyeurism is enhanced by the physical absence of the filmmaker from his own movie, even though he is obviously the central player in it, and by the conspicuous if paradoxically invisible act of "self-exposure" (O'Rourke's own term) he performs in order to highlight the moral ambiguities it explores. The film, in fact, wholeheartedly embraces its own condition of voyeurism: the "primary" voyeurism of the sex tourist, but also the "secondary" voyeurism of the would-be researcher of sex tourism, who both recognizes and rehearses the "scopophilic" and "ego libido" instincts of the voyeur (the pleasure of looking at a person as an erotic object; the various forms and processes of self-identification through which this pleasure is expressed and played out [Mulvey]). Further entanglements are produced by the affiliation between the tourist and the prostitute as "liminal people, people who occupy spaces between different worlds" (Ryan and Hall, 20). Sex tourism, according to Ryan and Hall, involves the encounter between two different but related sets of "sanctioned marginals": the socially stigmatized prostitute and the tourist, trying to "get away from it all." As they put it: "The tourist engages in a temporary escape from the world of work, but [eventually] returns to it. The prostitute exists more permanently on the edges of society, but also engages in processes of departure and return as she, or he, resumes non-prostitute roles" (20).

To see sex tourists and prostitutes as like-minded "partners" in this way masks the motives behind what always remains a commercial transaction between them; it also encourages a form of false friendship in which the former see themselves as helping the latter, as happens in several instances in the film. One such instance is when O'Rourke records a conversation with a fellow-Australian tourist, who cheerfully professes his belief that prostitution—while admittedly demeaning—is only a temporary measure, and that he is playing his own small part in building the Thai economy toward the day when prostitution will no longer be necessary and its workers will be liberated from their chains. This cynical view, repeated with variations throughout the film, implicitly satirizes O'Rourke's obligations toward the "virtuous" Aoi while also suggesting that *The Good Woman of Bangkok* effectively challenges its own status as a naive morality tale (Stone). *Travel* is the key term under which the film's various mystifications congregate, allowing its actors to exercise freedom from the ethical constraints of their routine working existence while experiencing fantasized attachments to a number of beautiful young women who would almost certainly be unavailable at home. The feeling of empowerment is crucial here, and is expressed not just in terms of race and gender but, equally important, in terms of class as well. While sex tourism, like most other forms of tourism today, cuts across conventional class boundaries, it arguably holds particular attraction for those who see themselves as being materially or symbolically disadvantaged at home. As Suzy Kruhse-Mount-Burton suggests, sex tourism is a form of play "which allows for the reconstitution of the individual both physically and mentally"; however, it has an "added rejuvenating potential for the worker in that the personal sense of power it provides may act as a compensatory behaviour for an individual unable to exercise any real authority within his daily existence" (197). In *The Good Woman of Bangkok,* several of the foreign tourists O'Rourke interviews (who include Europeans and Americans, as well as Australians) are visibly emboldened by their encounters with the local women, suggesting that a model of white-male authority is being reinstated that is perceived, for whatever reason, to be threatened at home. As Kruhse-MountBurton's research suggests, this model—essentially nostalgic—holds appeal for a certain category of *Australian* men, for whom sex tourism acts both as a "foil for their alienation in the workplace" and as a salve for their felt "loss, within the normal social environment, of the support audience for the conventional male role of financial support and sexual authority" (202). O'Rourke's film plays self-consciously on these myths of Australian masculinity in crisis, but, as has been argued, it is by no means rescued by its own self-consciousness; as Aoi tells him at one point, exasperatedly if more than a little disingenuously, "I think everything you do and say to me is to manipulate me for this film."

Global Cities

In both Iyer's and O'Rourke's work, the major distinction is that between tourism as a function of *globalism,* which functions almost exclusively according to the dictates of the world market, and tourism as an opportunity for the exercise of *global consciousness,* which remains largely complicit with the market but seeks to redress its structural tendency to exploit labor within the context of global social and economic flows. Tourism as globalism is more likely to support what Gayatri Spivak calls the "great narrative of [global] development" based on the supposedly liberating potential of the free market, and sponsored and monitored by such hegemonic agencies as the World Bank (*Critique,* 372–73). Tourism as global consciousness is more likely to draw attention to the social and economic divisions brought about by globalization processes and, counteracting the view of travel as the self-given right of the "enabled classes" (Kaur and Hutnyk, 3), to engage with the ways in which travel—both voluntary and enforced—effects a globalization "from below." In both cases, tourism/travel involves much more than the regulated movement between different, pre-designated places, but also has the capacity to encompass a wide range of often highly irregular activities within a single social space.

A good example of this interplay between controlled and uncontrolled movements is the contemporary global city, described by the social geographer John Rennie Short as a "competition in progress," in which the different forces underlying globalization and urbanization processes are brought together, creating or accentuating social exclusions as they do so, in the interests of "maintaining, securing, and increasing . . . economic competitiveness in a global world" (7). Global cities, according to Short, are not just "command centers" of the global economy and knowledge industries, they are also crucial cultural "switching points" in which "diversity is . . . managed [and] celebrated for maximum effect" (2, 83). This symbiosis of the economic and the cultural, which Short calls the "capitalization of culture" (72), is what distinguishes a global city from a world city: while in the latter, global *business* is conducted, only in the former can one speak of global *culture* being produced. As nodes in a global network of economic and cultural flows, global cities highlight the tension between "international connectivity and local livability" (72). In this sense, they complicate the distinction between a "native" and a "tourist." After all, it is quite possible, even desirable, to be a tourist in one's own city. As much places to be traveled through as traveled to, global cities are continually revisited even by those who live there. Dwelling places of the transient, they help generate the capital that drives the world's major travel industries while themselves operating as major tourist centers, attracting a variety of "ephemeral transnationals" (Hannerz): pleasure-seeking holidaymakers, job-seeking immigrants, high-flying business elites. The highly mediatized nature of the global city also blurs the boundaries between real and virtual travel, creating a whole class of shape-shifting cybertourists whose imaginary journeys are both facilitated and circumscribed by the new technologies they deploy. As Short puts it: "We have greater mobility but greater reliance on the grid of international communications. Globalization has both untethered us from the heavier constraints of international travel and has also tethered us to the circuits of telecommunication. Global cities are the points in the world where we can both travel and be connected" (130).

Global cities—to sum up—can be seen in terms of four, loosely interconnected functions. First, they are *transnational spaces* characterized by an almost constant flow of information, goods, and peoples. As such, the links between these cities may be stronger than those between the city and the nation, reinforcing "euphoric" notions of globalization in which new forms of transcultural ferment and technological interconnectedness convey the impression of a world without economic or cultural boundaries, a densely networked world that appears—especially to those most obviously benefited by it—to supersede the moribund ideology of the nation-state. Second, they are *cosmopolitan environments* insofar as they participate in the production and cross-fertilization of social and cultural differences, and insofar as their highly mobile, implicitly deterritorialized inhabitants dwell less in a fixed place or set of places than within the volatile space of global flows (Short, 116). Not all city dwellers, needless to say, can afford the signal privileges of the cosmopolitan lifestyle, which draws attention to a third property of global cities: their tendency toward a *polarization of social relations* marked by spaces of inclusion and exclusion, and witnessed at its most extreme in the state of "normalized paranoia" that accompanies the perceived separation of urban space into "wild" and "tame" zones (O'Tuathail, 254). (Global cities, as we should have not needed 9/11 to remind us, are also prime terrorist targets; if one of the impulses behind terrorism is the production of global spectacle, then the global city becomes the most obvious arena for a violent—spectacularly violent—exhibition of what happens when the cosmopolitan pleasures of deterritorialized urban living meet a wholly different, but in its way equally conspicuous, influx of peoples and ideas from the "outside world" [Short, 82].) Fourth, global cities—in both a positive and a negative sense—are *microcosmic "travel worlds"* (Kaur and Hutnyk). To an extent, this is the result of what some postmodern theorists call "time-space compression" (Harvey): the telescoping of time and space that is produced by the refined management of current transport and information technologies, but also by increasing media control (and corresponding urban bias) over the perception of global issues and events (O'Tuathail, 250). However, it is also a reflection of present global economic realities: the trans/national influx of workers into the city in search of better, or at least livable, futures; the creation of an entire underclass of "survival travelers" who are reliant on—and more often than not exploited by—the more privileged, self-consciously transient cosmopolitans with whose lives their own are inextricably enmeshed. Global cities, in this sense, are worlds-within-the-world that carry within them an entire vocabulary of defamiliarization and displacement—"exile," "diaspora," "immigration," "traveling cultures"—while providing a constant reminder that "travel, far from being some transgressive actuality of the postmodern condition, just as often serves as the conduit for redrawing the boundary between what is acceptable and unacceptable around the norm of the 'known'" (Kaur and Hutnyk, 16). They also act as reservoirs for the contradictions of a late-capitalist globalization that, while holding out the universal promise of free movement, has also proved instrumental in the uprooting of entire populations whose separation from their homelands is less a blessing than a curse.

In what follows, I will compare two quite recent travel narratives, Amitava Kumar's *Bombay London New York* (2002) and Suketu Mehta's *Maximum City* (2004), that explore some of the discrepancies and contradictions surrounding the multifaceted figure of the global city. These two accounts offer globally conscious, diasporically interconnected readings of what is fast turning into the world's biggest city, Mumbai (Bombay). Both are metatouristic, asking what it is to be a tourist in a city in which the already volatile relationship between insiders and outsiders is constantly being renegotiated; what it is to be a tourist in one's own city; and whether it is ever possible to escape from the condition of being a tourist in the world. By extension, then, they are also critical explorations of the myths underlying modern experiences of world tourism and travel: the myth of travel as a "democratic cipher" (Kaur and Hutnyk, 25); the myth of tourism as an exercise in international public relations (Goldstone); and the myth of the tourist/traveler as a free agent, "someone who has the security and privilege to move about [the world] in relatively unconstrained ways" (Clifford, *Routes,* 34). Finally, each account, in its own way, inquires into the changing relationship between tourism and global modernity. The city, in these texts, is a prime site for the playing out of competing narratives of global modernity, narratives not readily contained within even the most generous parameters of traveled urban space.

For both writers, the sprawling city of Bombay, fast becoming "the biggest city on the planet of a race of city dwellers" (Mehta, 3), embodies the contradictions of a global modernity (or, perhaps better, global modernit*ies*) that provide very different versions of what it is to be modern for the nation's rich and poor. This assertion of a plural modernity, particularly insistent in Kumar's narrative, complements the view, increasingly common in the sociological literature, that globalization is not just a shared instrument of financial control or a transnational effect of state dominance, but rather the sum total of quotidian encounters in which local experience is both mediated and transformed by the larger, global networks within which it is contained. The city is the locus classicus for such "glocalized" encounters;[4] it is also a testament to the notion, however stretched, of conviviality—the sense of joyfulness, as well as frustration, that comes from constantly battling it out with others in a crowd.[5]

The almost unimaginable congestion of Bombay exemplifies both the unending frustrations of conviviality and the paradoxical freedom conferred upon its inhabitants by the "pursuit of a life unencumbered by minutiae"—a life of daily struggle in which many people "don't pay taxes [or] fill out forms . . . [and few] stay in one place or in one relationship [for] long" (Mehta, 588). For Mehta, returning to the city where he grew up after a break of twenty years, Bombay is a city of extremes—a "maximum city"—in which private lives are exposed to the full glare of public scrutiny, and the daily battle for self-improvement or survival is an amplified version of the urban "battle of the self against the crowd" (589). This struggle is memorably described in the following paragraph, taken from the final pages of his narrative:

Bombay itself is reaching its own extremity: 23 million people by 2015. A city in which the population should halve, actually doubles. Walking alongside every person in the throng on the streets today will be one more person tomorrow. With every year Bombay is a city growing more and more public, the world outside gradually crowding the world inside. In the mad rush of a Bombay train, each one of the herd needs, as a survival mechanism, to focus on what is most powerfully himself and to hold on to it for dear life. A solitary human being here has two choices: He can be subsumed within the crowd, reduce himself to a cell of a larger organism . . . or he can retain a stubborn, almost obdurate sense of his own individuality. Each person in that train has a sense of style: the way he combs his hair, the talent he has for making sculptures out of seashells, an ability to blow up a hot-water bottle till it bursts. A character quirk or eccentricity, extrapolated into a whole theory of selfhood. I always found it easy to talk to people in a crowd in Bombay because each one had distinct, even eccentric, opinions. They had not yet been programmed. (589)

In passages like this one, Mehta seeks confirmation for his thesis that Bombay, foreshadowing "the future of urban civilisation on this planet'" (3), demonstrates the impossible necessity of living life both as an individual and as part of a larger collective in which individual dreams are inexorably merged into a "mass dream of the crowd" (589). This model for living, distilled in the twin epigraphs to *Maximum City,* presupposes that we are all "severally alone" and "individually multiple." It also suggests that all lives have importance, even if many go unnoticed in the global context; as one of Mehta's interlocutors, the would-be writer Babbanji, a homeless runaway from Bihar, tells him: "[My book, *Untold Life,* is] the life about which nothing is told. There is plenty of discussion about the lives of the rich, but nothing is spoken about the lives of the poor" (527). Mehta's own book goes some way toward articulating the untold lives of Bombay's impoverished masses, setting the celebrity world of the socially powerful—politicians, film stars, executives—against a counterworld of the socially marginalized—exotic dancers, hired assassins, small-time thieves. His temporary alliances with these different individuals and groups of people become the means by which he tries to reconcile himself to a once-familiar city, partly by recognizing a similarity between their impermanent condition and his own. Bombay thus becomes a city of "internal exiles: Parisian socialites in Colaba, London bankers in Cuffe Parade" (39), replicating their experiences of other cities, but also a city of transitory locals, whose "little lives, unnoticed in the throng, uncelebrated in the . . . movies," share with those of their more illustrious counterparts an incurable capacity for "restlessness, the inability or disinclination to stay still" (492). However, while Mehta seems ready to suggest that the slum- and pavement-dwellers of Bombay are, as he is, "happiest in transit" (492), there are worlds of difference between their condition, defined by an aggravated form of shifting entrapment, and his own, characterized by a heightened form of cosmopolitan prestige. In this sense, Mehta's view of Bombay as an "impossible" city, or even a case study in "urban catastrophe" (3), blurs the line between different degrees of urban hardship while making light of his own cosmopolitan privilege: "[J]ust when we get comfortable in Bombay, we prepare to move again—back to New York. But it's all right, because, after two and a half years [in Bombay], my question has been answered. You can go home again; and you can also leave again. Once more, with confidence, into the world" (586).

Like Iyer's, Mehta's confraternity of the restless is in part an exercise in wishful thinking, based on an overcapacious understanding of cosmopolitanism as a shared experience of "originary displacement" in the world (Porter). On the other hand, Mehta's narrative also points to alternative cosmopolitans not necessarily framed by, or phrased as, individual privilege or aggressive globalism: cosmopolitanisms based on the simultaneous experience of dwelling and travel—dwelling as travel—and enacted in the daily routines and rituals of urban living as an exemplary form of "planetary conviviality" or "globalization from below" (Mignolo, 721). These two phrases, drawn from Walter Mignolo's seminal essay on cosmopolitanism, require some differentiation here:

> The term *cosmopolitanism* [can be used] as a counter to *globalization,* although not necessarily in the sense of globalization from below. Globalization from below invokes . . . the reactions to globalization from those populations and geohistorical areas of the planet that suffer the consequences of the global economy. There are . . . local histories that plan and project global designs and others that have to live with them. . . . [G]lobalization is a set of designs to manage the world while cosmopolitanism is a set of projects toward planetary conviviality. (721)

Mignolo's assertion of a vernacular, implicitly counterglobalist cosmopolitanism is central to Amitava Kumar's lively account, part impressionistic literary study, part autobiographical travel narrative, *Bombay London New York* (2002). An expatriate Indian like Mehta, whom he knows personally, Kumar shares his compatriot's cosmopolitan dilemma of attempting to reconcile intermittent feelings of nostalgia with the strong desire, expressed irrespective of place, to "belong elsewhere" (19). This dilemma, while deeply personal, opens out onto a metaphysical discussion of the "stations of . . . displacement" (8) that entertains alternative, nonelitist understandings of what it means to be a citizen of the world. These understandings are distilled into the notion of a vernacular cosmopolitanism grounded paradoxically in local experience, and through which the linked lives of both resident and nonresident (N.R.I.) Indians show evidence of local connections to the wider world. Such are the alternative cosmopolitanisms of the slum dweller, relocated to the city from the village; or the street seller, "hawking the fragments of another world" (71, 213–14). These proletarian cosmopolitanisms don't share the attitude of worldly sophistication usually contained within conventional understandings of the term *cosmopolitanism;* but this isn't to say that the often highly localized experiences upon which they are based have no place in the world. Cosmopolitanism, on the contrary, is no more monopolized by the privileged than the modernity to which it is umbilically attached is automatically sanctioned by the state (55). Nor is it even necessarily metropolitan; hence Kumar's rapt attention to the (literary) lives of India's towns and villages, which show that the provincial can also be worldly, and that the "small town, [as well as] the city, is already part of a global planet" that contains them both (70).

In this sense, *Bombay London New York,* a book that looks as if it is about the connections between three global cities, turns out at least in part to be an apology for nonurban contributions to a pluralized modernity that is both local and global in a number of different, conflicted ways. At the same time, the book seeks to recapture the embodied truths of metropolitan openness and cosmopolitan hybridity, intrinsic to global modernity, that have been compromised in Bombay and throughout India by the unchecked ascent of a ruthlessly competitive consumer capitalism, and by an equally divisive "ideology of purity, of religion and region, [that] has taken [a powerful] hold" (56).

Kumar's portrait of Bombay thus celebrates the promiscuous mixing of cultural influences that characterizes Indian metropolitan popular culture while showing, at the same time, that such forms of vernacular cosmopolitanism implicitly resist the attempted hijacking of the nation's future by fundamentalist groups (56). Nationalist and/or religious fundamentalisms, according to Kumar, are a flip side to the conspicuous inequalities of globalization (162). Not that he is against globalization per se; rather, he is opposed to the view of globalization as a machine for disembodied financial management—a putting into practice of the corporate ideology of globalism—or as a sign of the inevitable spread of social systems based on narrow notions of individual freedom and democracy, and on the imagined superiority of the West.

Such systems, Kumar suggests, tend to champion freedom of movement while simultaneously restricting it, an irony explored most fully in his nuanced meditation on the conflicting meanings contained within the word *flight*. These different meanings—freedom, escape, air travel, and so forth—are in turn connected to the (self-)destructive tendencies bound up in the promise of a better life. "There are many in the poorer countries of the world," he says, "for whom the plane in flight represents the journey that, when undertaken in the future, will take them to the promised land" (228). A pathological version of this, he goes on to suggest, were the events of 9/11 in which the suicide hijackers, seeking entry into the garden of heaven, removed their earthly chains and "claw[ed] their way into the air [to] wreak havoc from on high" (229). Still a different version of this is the sad story of the Pakistani stowaway Mohammed Ayaz, who, desperate to clear his debts and to help his ailing family, died in midair after climbing onto the wheel bay of a departing Boeing at the international airport of Bahrain. Hidden behind figures like Ayaz, says Kumar,

> are the untold millions in countries like India or Pakistan who dream of a different future. Often, these young men and women have been turned into migrants in their own land because of poverty, or famines, or wars waged by others in the fields where their families have toiled for generations. How removed is the pathos of the stowaway from the rage of the hijacker? (234)

The conclusion Kumar draws is equally plangent:

The body falling out of the sky is the other and silent half of the story of international travel and tourism. We are reminded that not everyone crosses borders alive, despite the cheerful acceptance of globalization by many governments of the world. Standing near his son's unmarked grave, a mound of brown earth ringed by stones and covered with a plastic sheet, Mohammed Ayaz's father said, "My son was as strong as four men but he died in search of bread." (234)

"There are new stories of travel, and now terror touches all," suggests Kumar somewhat melodramatically in this episode (229); offset against these are the equally important narratives of "what is suffered as well as celebrated in the most ordinary of ways by those who do not leave, those who stay behind, whether because they want to or simply because it cannot be otherwise" (223). For Kumar, then, the idea of travel necessarily contains its opposite; narratives of travel—including imaginary travel—encompass those who never actually leave home.

Literature is the primary vehicle in Kumar's text for both the recording and the imagining of travel. Reading and writing, Kumar suggests, are means of understanding displacement in terms other than those of severance and alienation; literature also acts as a comforting mirror, allowing him to see parallels between his own experience and others' transplanted lives. The Bombay-London-New York continuum, in this sense, is as much a product of the author's literary activities as a filter for his private memories; literature plays a formative role in the creation of an affective geography that first removes the reader/writer, then returns him to the world:

> Writers are caught in the contradictory tasks of building imaginary worlds that are removed from the everyday life and, at the same time, establishing how the imagination is not detached from the quotidian world and very much a vital part of it. To realize the truth of this condition is to know that books not only offer refuge from the world, they also return you *to* it. (15)

This dialectic of detachment and reattachment is particularly acute for the diasporic reader/writer, as Kumar—a self-styled diasporic—suggests in his affectionate readings of Indian literature in English, itself often a product of readers/writers based abroad. This diasporic condition is also explored during the course of Mehta's narrative, helping to ex-

plain both his ambivalent attitude toward Bombay and his extreme
view that, like all great cities, it is "schizophrenic . . . Bombay suffers
from multiple-personality disorder" (50). The condition of the diasporic, Mehta suggests, is similar to that of the "internal exile" and the
"adulterous resident," living in one place but desiring another:

> My father once, in New York, exasperated by my relentless demands
> to be sent back to finish high school in Bombay, shouted at me,
> "When you were there, you wanted to come here. Now that you're
> here, you want to go back." It was when I first realised I had a new na-
> tionality: I was an exile. I am an adulterous resident: when I am in one
> city, I am dreaming of the other. I am an exile; citizen of the country
> of longing. (33)

Like Kumar, Mehta sees literature as a means to come to terms with the
dividedness of the city while confronting his own feelings of internal
fracture and displacement. (As Kumar puts it ironically: "Who is an
N.R.I.? The one who goes back—with many suitcases instead of that
single one that he or she had brought on the first journey. The tourist
citizen" [21].) Hence the double meaning in the title of the last section
of *Maximum City*, "Passages," which refers to the many journeys undertaken by those who are officially or unofficially resident in the city,
but also to the episodic style of Mehta's own narrative, which moves
breathlessly from one journey to the next. "Passages" thus establishes
Bombay as an occasion for, and an exercise in, writing: it is writing that
allows Mehta to thread together the various stories of Bombay's seemingly always impermanent residents; and most of all, it is writing that
allows him to rediscover the city for himself. Similarly, it is writing that,
for Kumar, helps create the myth of London in particular as a literary
city—a place of artistic beginnings where the provincial writer can
finally make a head start (107). Writing joins places, enhancing the con-
ciliatory work of personal/cultural memory and engaging head-on, as
writers must, with the "worldliness of the world" (15, 32). But writing
also divides them; for the worldliness of books and libraries, so important to Kumar, also becomes a reminder of the distance that separates
him from the vast majority of India's people, only 5 percent of whom
are literate in English, and that separates the cosmopolitan traveler-
writer from the created subjects of his or her chosen "travel world."

This separation is felt most acutely in Bombay, despite the city's multiple forms of vernacular literacy (films, music, food, etc.). Such is the dilemma of the "tourist citizen" (Kumar, 21): the part-time resident who, caught between a multiplicity of alternative (imagined) homes and places, seems destined, for all the choices, to be a foreigner in each. As both Kumar and Mehta experience on their travels, it is relatively easy for their interlocutors to exclude them: "It is different for you," says one to Mehta, matter-of-factly, "[because] you are not from here" (517). Such is the dilemma, too, for the tourist as surrogate anthropologist, temporarily engaging with, then subsequently recording, the tangle of other people's lives. Still, Bombay is so vast that it can turn everyone into a tourist in their own city; while popular vehicles such as, particularly, the Bollywood movies cast touristic perspectives on a city in which "people have been living . . . all their lives; even those who have never actually been there" (Mehta, 382). Bombay is an object of touristic myth, both for its numerous visitors and for its innumerable inhabitants; Kumar playfully recognizes this when, in one of his self-ironic epigraphs, he quotes Kai Friese from the *Voice Literary Supplement*: "And if you simply must read a book about India, buy the *Lonely Planet* guide." In any case, as Mehta suggests, myths and dreams form a basis for people's lives in *any* city: "a city is an agglomeration of individual dreams, a mass dream of the crowd" (589). These myths and dreams might stretch far beyond the fleeting pleasures of touristic satisfaction, yet they provide a powerful mechanism by which the lives of both outsiders ("travelers") and insiders ("dwellers") in the city are enmeshed. And, as both Kumar and Mehta make clear, these roles are continually in flux; such is the volatility of the city that "dwellers" are never far away from becoming the next "travelers," while self-designated insiders are never secure in their sense of their own local ownership for long. Impermanency is a constitutive feature of city life, whether driven by large-scale immigration (New York, especially, and London), or by the relentless influx of people from small towns and villages, all in search of a better life (Bombay). The modern metropolis, argues Mehta,

> is a collection of transients, on their way from somewhere to somewhere else. New York is a collection of migrants from other cities; Bombay is a collection of people from villages, who come into the city and seek to re-create the village. The anxiety of the city dweller is the

anxiety of transience; he does not know where he will be next year or
where his children will be. He cannot form lasting friendships, because sooner or later his friends will be scattered. . . . The city dweller
has no . . . trust in the permanency of relationships. (557)

Within this context, the status of the world traveler, much of whose
time is spent shuttling between cities, is symptomatic; still, there is
something very distinctive about Kumar's and Mehta's Iyeresque ruminations on the city-hopping global soul. For one thing, both writers'
generalizations about Bombay reflect their own mixed feelings as returning visitors to India; for another, their ambivalent status as NRIs
inevitably shapes their attitude toward what Kumar calls the "traveler-
translator": the "commuter between cultures," writing "from a space
of in-betweenness," whose own characteristic form of committed restlessness joins his or her experience to that of other global souls (178).
Ironically, the expansive world of the global soul starts to look suspiciously cozy, defined as it is by admittedly transnational alliances with
other like-minded, and almost exclusively city-living, global souls. It
seems the global soul is shaped as much by the specific experience of living in and across the distinct localities of global cities as by some
heightened sense of "originary displacement" (Porter), or some speculative understanding of the general condition of being a tourist in the
world. If the global soul, as I have been suggesting, is a product of the
collision between globalism and global consciousness, then the global
city is the place where the impact of that collision is most likely to be
felt.

   Cosmopolitan, perhaps, is the most fitting adjective to describe the
self-consciously worldly condition of the global soul—a condition
poised between the nagging fear of urban alienation and the idealistic
urge to support practices of conviviality, however trivial or transient,
that are most likely to be found in the everyday activities of city life.
Cosmopolitanism, in this sense, inhabits the space between an awareness of individual privilege—the characteristic awareness of the world
traveler—and an attempt to articulate new visions and versions of community, "new theories of sharing which value the partial allegiances
and unassimilated communities that for many constitute home"
(Walkowitz, 10). This notion of cosmopolitanism gives the lie to the
idea of the traveler as free agent; instead, it implies responsibility and

commitment, a distaste for all forms of bigotry and xenophobia, and a preference for attachment to more than one community or place. Rebecca Walkowitz, on whose work I am drawing here, likens this kind of cosmopolitanism to "itinerant ethnography" (31): the ability to reflect on different processes of travel, and to move away from a detached appreciation of a more consistent engagement with the world. Not that travel in itself automatically supports the idea of a freer world—it may do just the opposite—but it certainly provides an opportunity for the "productive estrangement from one's own culture" that mutual encounters, however fleeting, with difference produce (Gilroy, 78). *Maximum City* and *Bombay London New York* are good examples of travel writing as itinerant ethnography, and are driven idealistically by the cosmopolitan desire to generate mutual understanding and goodwill. Cosmopolitanism's own particular form of global consciousness, however, does not rescue it from the charge of residual elitism—a charge not altogether inapplicable to Mehta's and Kumar's well-intentioned accounts. Perhaps what Paul Gilroy calls "the globalized mindset of the fortunate, unrestricted traveler" (83) is never that far from the global consciousness of the responsible world tourist, and it falls upon the worldly travel writer to take on the qualities of each.

Coda: Thinking Globally, Acting Virtually

For both Mehta and, especially, Kumar, Bombay is a hub city within a "digital meritocracy" based on the globalist language of IT entrepreneurs (Kumar, 189). IT, in fact, is the most obvious basis for Bombay's globalism—and an obviously unequal basis, too, with most of both the management and the workforce being men (195). While the digital revolution has been enabling for the diffusion of a vernacular cosmopolitan culture (digital sampling, technopolitics, etc.), it has also reinforced the kinds of corporate greed and aggressive managerialism for which globalism is known (215). This raises the question of the role of IT in the spread of a more responsible global consciousness that deploys technological means to broaden cultural horizons, and to faciliate the kind of global citizenship needed to address common problems in the world. While the evidence suggests that IT is more than capable of doing this, it also encourages the development of empowering forms of cybertravel (CD-ROM travel games, virtual-reality tourism) that stimulate and reward colonialist fantasy without perpetrating its ruinous side effects. In her analysis of the role of video games in virtual-reality (VR) tourism, Ellen Strain calls the spaces that these games model examples of "distanced immersion, those behaviors designed to counteract disorientation and culture shock by giving travelers a sense of mastery over space and culture" (233). VR tourist sites, while highly diverse, are often versions of hyper-documented spectacle, in which the world's cultures—world culture—become a set of more or less readily decodable ciphers, a puzzle to be worked out (234–35). Simulated travel of this kind potentially counteracts the realities of touristic loss and despoliation, supporting the positive view of VR as "replacement tourism," a convenient and relatively inexpensive way of saving a fragile world from marauding tourist hordes (Pinney). Yet VR tourism is as likely to avoid global problems as to confront them, either by realizing impossible attempts at environmental control or historical recovery, or by giving travelers/players the opportunity to speed up time, or carve up space, for themselves (Strain, 246).

Virtual reality flirts with the idea of culture shock, only to control it through "strategies [of] epistemological mastery" and "mechanisms of visual distantiation" (Strain, 272). Similarly, it offers "the fun of embodied experience without the threats that embodiment brings" (262). Thus, while the range of corporeal experience opened up by VR—"embodied tourism," Strain calls it (252)—is potentially enabling, it is also profoundly self-deluding, as the technology repeatedly permits the temporary illusion of becoming someone else. VR's thrilling journeys through virtual spaces/bodies borrow freely from the language and conventions of travel narrative, converting its rhetoric of escapism into the total fantasy-vision of a world without conflict or, perhaps more accurately, a world whose conflicts can be simulated, recreated, and controlled. Such is the ideology behind "global" digital games like "Around the World in Eighty Days" or "Mondo 2000," an ideology most comprehensively captured in the 1993 establishment of the first Virtual World site. The Virtual World site is the culmination of classic VR games like "Civilization," a digital rendering of postmodern "time-space compression'" (Harvey) in which space becomes infinitely contractable and time is just as readily reversed. Not that the process is effortless; as the guidebook to "Civilization" dutifully informs us: "As a general rule, the larger the world, the longer the game will take to complete." And, as if our own world weren't enough, there are other, invented worlds to civilize and conquer, from "archipelago worlds," which consist of "many small areas of land completely isolated by surrounding oceans," to "terra worlds," which are much more "similar in layout to Earth." Sören Johnson's Afterword to the guide is suitably enthusiastic, referring to the game's capacity to take in the totality of world history and geography and to make something new of it, to create "a new world from scratch."

VR tourism's relationship to globalization generally falls into the category of "planetary management," Andrew Ross's multifaceted term for the range of mostly top-down sociopolitical and environmental processes by which the world's material resources are appropriated, distributed, and controlled. Despite its often startling technological innovations, VR is often less a case of creating a new reality than of falling back on older paradigms of epistemological mastery and control (Strain, 272). Future travel, in this sense, may prove to be technologically advanced but ideologically outdated, presenting VR tourists with the opportunity to reenact, visually and acoustically, some of the most leaden attitudes expressed by traveler-writers in the past. It would be a pity if VR, for all its educative potential, turned out to be the culmination of the objectifying tourist gaze rather than a revolutionary alternative to it, producing gunfire as its most meaningful vehicle for cross-cultural exchange (Strain, 278).

TWO

Going Green, Saving Nature

Introduction

Anticapitalist resistance has intensified over the last couple of decades, much of it orchestrated by broad-based environmental organizations in many ways as global as the multinational corporations whose human rights and ecological abuses they address. These "popular ecological resistance movements," as Bron Taylor calls them, have been to varying degrees effective in drawing public attention to global conditions of environmental decline and degradation (2). Some of the more radical groups subscribe to forms of "environmental apocalypticism" (Buell)[1] seemingly confirmed by the current extinction crisis and by increasing worldwide evidence of systemic ecological collapse. This chapter assesses the extent to which these catastrophist scenarios have given rise to new, or significantly modified, forms of ecologically sensitive travel writing that reflect less on the wonders of the natural environment (a staple of so-called nature writing) than on the wider social and cultural implications of global environmental crisis. Two questions immediately press forward here: first, what are the dimensions of contemporary *eco-travel writing*; and, second, how far does this new subgenre (if it can be agreed upon to exist) reflect current movements within the global tourist industry, notably the expanding niche market in ecotourism and other forms of environmentally responsible travel?

Eco-travel writing belongs first and foremost to the wider field identified by Lawrence Buell as *environmental writing,* a field for which

Buell, in his groundbreaking study *The Environmental Imagination* (1995), provides the four following criteria:

(1) "The nonhuman environment is present not merely as a device but as a presence that begins to suggest that human history is implicated in natural history";

(2) "The human interest is not understood to be the only legitimate interest";

(3) "Human accountability to the environment is part of the text's ethical orientation";

(4) "Some sense of the environment as a process rather than as a constant or a given is at least implicit in the text." (7–8)

These criteria suggest, in turn, a reversal of the traditional hierarchy of fictional and nonfictional writing that has often been invoked, explicitly or implicitly, to relegate putatively nonfictional forms such as nature writing to secondary or peripheral status (8). But is eco-travel writing coextensive with nature writing? Yes, insofar as it works toward conferring a degree of agency on the natural environment, recognizing nature and its actors as bona fide narrative subjects rather than illustrative vehicles for human action or expedient objects for scientific analysis or meditative thought. Yes, insofar as it tends to combine the three main ingredients of what has alternatively been called "the literature of nature" (Lyon) or, more problematically, "landscape writing" (McDowell): documentary information about the natural environment and natural history (the field guide); a personal response to nature (autobiography); and the philosophical interpretation of nature (the environmental essay). And yes, insofar as it is committed to the cause of promoting greater ecological awareness and responsibility, drawing attention toward possibilities of acting *in*, rather than merely *upon*, the natural environment, and emphasizing the need both for specific strategies of conservation and protection and for a general attitude of respect.

Unlike most forms of nature writing, however, eco-travel writing does not necessarily downplay the movements or achievements of the traveler-writer. Its ratio of narration to description is often weighted heavily toward the former, while the perceived need for documentation—for the self-effacing, more or less accurate recording of the traveler-writer's experiences of the environment—exists in almost constant tension with travel writing's traditional counterimpulses toward entertaining fabulation and self-glorifying myth. This might suggest, in eco-logical terms, that contemporary eco-travel writing is residually "an-thropocentric" (human-centered) rather than committedly "bio-" or "ecocentric" (life-centered; Earth-centered);[2] or even that, in keeping with other forms of the modern travelog, it has failed to lay the ghosts of travel writing's imperial past. Such a view underestimates, however, the valuable role played by eco-travel writing in critiquing the egocen-trism of more conventional forms of travel writing, and in providing modes of thought and vision other than those dictated by the Western traveler's "imperial eye" (Pratt). It also fails to appreciate the ideo-logical work performed by eco-travel writers in counteracting historical legacies of "ecological imperialism" (Crosby),[3] as well as in critically analyzing contemporary instances of human exploitation and environ-mental abuse. In both cases, it is clear that human and environmental issues are inseparable, reconfirming the usefulness of travel writing as an instrument of social and cross-cultural critique. Eco-travel writing, moreover, tends to emphasize the social constructedness of "nature," providing an antidote to those less considered forms of nature writ-ing—and, it could also be argued, ecological criticism—in which a cer-tain culture blindness becomes the counterpart of Western romantic ex-cess.[4] This is not to say that eco-travel writing has always managed to avoid the familiar rhetorical pitfalls of romantic nature writing—the pathetic fallacy, anthropomorphism—nor is it to suggest that its Green political stance has guaranteed a bulwark against romantic individual-ism or the delusions of arcadian escape. In any case, eco-travel writing, like the Green movement(s) it serves, is remarkable for playing across the political spectrum, accommodating a variety of sometimes self-con-tradictory ideological positions ranging from the implicitly reactionary to the overtly revolutionary; from "light Green" liberal conservation-ism to "dark Green" radical ecologism; from a recalcitrant disdain for all forms of technological development to an up-to-the-minute enthusi-asm for the global media machine.

This chapter does not aim to produce a taxonomy of contemporary eco-travel writing, nor does it intend to give an overview of the rapidly expanding range of environmentally oriented travel texts. Instead, like other chapters in this book, it considers how the traditional concerns of travel writing have been adjusted to contemporary needs and interests, and the extent to which these genre modifications intersect with recent developments in the modern tourist industry. The most obvious set of connections to be traced here is that between eco-travel writing and the burgeoning ecotourism business, which has emerged over the last twenty years or so as a major player in what is now the world's largest and fastest growing industry. Ecotourism, in David Fennell's definition, is

> a sustainable form of natural, resource-based tourism that focuses primarily on experiencing and learning about nature, and which is ethically managed to be low-impact, non-consumptive, and locally oriented (control, benefits and scale). It typically occurs in natural areas and should contribute to the conservation or preservation of such areas. (43)

Fennell's definition begs several questions. How, for instance, can ecotourism be thought of as "nonconsumptive" when the wider tourist industry to which it belongs is without doubt the paradigmatic example of modern consumption on a global scale? How can it be "ethically managed" without significantly compromising profits, and when recent patterns of ownership and investment clearly indicate that transnational corporate interests continue to be placed over and above local social concerns?

As Deborah McLaren argues provocatively in her revisionist study *Rethinking Tourism and Ecotravel* (1998), it may be merely utopian to see ecotourism as serving to promote "environmental and economic conservation, international understanding and cooperation, political and economic empowerment of local populations, and cultural preservation," when there is ample evidence to suggest that it is "environmentally destructive, economically exploitative, [and] culturally insensitive" (97–98). Other critics agree: Joe Bandy, for example, views ecotourism as a function of neocolonialist relations between the First and Third Worlds, contributing to a revitalized set of global conditions "under which [historically] marginalized peoples are subject to a new dependency and a new colonialism" (541); while Helen Gilbert sees it as being based on "specific modalities of travel that reflect, and even consciously replay, aspects of European imperialism, especially as manifest in the exploration and subsequent domestication of distant natural environments and their native populations" (249). These criticisms seem rather harsh, overlooking significant differences within the ecotourist industry and preferring to rush to judgment on tourism (after all, in spite of obvious structural inequalities, a valuable source of revenue for many impoverished countries) as a whole. The fact remains that tourism, however conservation-oriented, is simply "not eco-friendly" (McLaren, 98), and that even the most democratically organized and best-intentioned of (eco)touristic ventures is likely to be disruptive of the local communities it claims to serve. It is also clear that ecotourism, far from being a saving grace, often represents little more than an extension of the mainstream tourist industry, indicating that industry's "concentrated attempts to capture a niche market by selling a (fantasized) dissociation from the rituals of mass tourism" (Gilbert, 250), and helping in some cases to manufacture the paradoxical conditions under which national and regional governments can liaise with international development agencies to create an often expensive form of "acceptable" tourism that caters largely to free-floating global elites.

It would be tempting, but also inaccurate, to insert eco-travel writing into this incriminating context as another brand-name alternative that seeks to profit by reworking the compromised history of Western travel writing into superficially palatable, and eminently marketable, forms. This view, though not without a certain validity, seems unduly cynical. After all, eco-travel writing, while it shares at least some of ecotourism's constitutive contradictions, often aims to produce a concerted critique of it—and of the tourist industry at large. Eco-travel writers such as Barry Lopez and Peter Matthiessen—to cite two of the best-known current examples—have been instrumental, both in celebrating the Earth's biodiversity and in showing how prevailing material conditions and practices, not least those produced by the tourist industry itself, place that diversity under threat. Such writers—again, Lopez and Matthiessen are good examples—have sometimes been given to lapse into evangelical antitechnologism or portentous pseudomysticism, to some extent reflecting the romantic tendencies already inherent in the Green movements they support. However, at their best they have been remarkably effective, both in drawing attention to continuing histories of environmental exploitation and in reaffirming the potential of the "environmental imagination" (Buell) to envision alternative worlds, both within and beyond the realm of everyday human experience, that might reinvigorate the ongoing global struggle for social and ecological justice.

Eco-travel writing, in this last sense, combines the utopian dimensions of nature writing with the travel writer's imaginative capacity to explore other worlds. While this might suggest, perversely, that the "greening" of travel writing merely increases its potential for escapism, its more usual intention is to gesture toward the conditions under which our own (Western, late-capitalist) world might be creatively transformed. The practical implications of eco-travel writing vary widely. Some writers might choose to undertake that celebrated version of the romantic quest, the life-changing spiritual odyssey; others, less individualistic and/or more pragmatic, might wish to draw attention to a specific ecological dilemma or to subscribe to a particular environmental cause. Similarly, eco-travelogs can be located at several points along travel writing's fact–fiction continuum. In several cases, documentary evidence is called upon to rationalize an emancipatory politics, while information is supplied, not only about the workings of Green movements, but also about the means by which such organizations might be best supported and the procedures by which they might be joined. (Facts, to a greater extent than in most other travelogs, are an integral part of eco-travel writing, whether these are marshaled in the interests of a collective, as in the Green call-to-arms or manifesto, or whether they are intended more to support individual observations and criticisms, as in the environmentally oriented investigative report.)[5] Finally, contemporary eco-travel writers—though most, as I have suggested, see themselves as responding to global conditions of environmental crisis—may choose very different forms of ecological advocacy in their work. Some, adopting what the environmental philosopher Deane Curtin calls "weak anthropocentrism," might wish to emphasize social conflict and the human fallout of environmental destruction, while others might prefer to look for representational means of empathizing with the phenomenal lifeworld; still others, seeking to produce concrete evidence of ecological collapse—spiralling increases in man-made disasters, accelerated patterns of wildlife extinction, and so on—might insist on a proper appreciation of the environment, and a drastic turnaround in human attitudes toward it, before many of our most precious natural assets, and perhaps we ourselves with them, disappear.

In what follows, I will consider some of the different forms of, and ideological presuppositions behind, contemporary eco-travel narrative, looking first at three self-consciously activist eco-travel texts that draw extensively on factual sources to engage with specific environmental crises; second, at two conservation-oriented writers whose work imaginatively confronts the condition of "wildness" in an effort to produce an intuitive relationship with the natural environment; and third, at two (eco)touristic television series that attempt, not so much visually as voyeuristically, to salvage a diminishing world for a mass audience before it disappears. Finally, I will critically reassess the relationship of eco-travel writing to ecotourism, gauging the degree to which the salvationist discourses attached to both have been able to support and, ideally, to further the twin ecological causes of environmental protection and sociocultural critique.

Acting

"Ecuador's Oriente is now on a course toward destruction and disaster," warns the American environmental lawyer Judith Kimerling at the end of an uncompromising 1991 study, commissioned by the U.S.-based Natural Resources Defense Council for which she works:

> Within our lifetimes, the day could come when oil reserves are exhausted, the lush tropical forests are gone, and rainfall is less frequent. Clean water, wildlife, and fish could be scarce and uncounted species extinct. Indigenous people could be landless, poor, and hungry and impoverished colonists close to starvation. Migrants from the Oriente could flood already crowded cities in the coastal and highland regions. (103)

While the wholesale human/ecological catastrophe predicted by Kimerling might have held off, at least for the moment, environmental conditions in the Oriente—one of the world's richest biotic zones[6]—can hardly be said in the two decades since her study was first published to have improved. The principal source of environmental destruction, now as then, is oil development, spearheaded by a number of large multinational companies, most of these based in the United States. The story of oil pollution in the Oriente, and the threat it poses to traditional indigenous lifeways, is of course hardly a new one, having spurred a large number of environmental action groups worldwide into producing a series of protest statements and consciousness-raising investigative reports. The American journalist-explorer Joe Kane's *Savages* (1996) can be inserted into this context as a classic example of what Clifford Geertz has called "blurred genres": part adventure-travelog, part anthropological treatise, part firsthand environmental report.[7] Kane's text turns around a conspicuous instance of human/ecological abuse in the Oriente: the forcible attempt to open up the traditional homelands of one of the region's least populous but most combative indigenous peoples, the Huaorani, to oil development. Who are the Huaorani? "All that could be said with certainty about [them, says Kane,] was that American oil companies coveted their land, American missionaries their souls, American environmentalists their voice. But no one knew what [they] wanted. No one really knew who [they] were" (10).

These, accordingly, are the tasks Kane sets himself: to familiarize himself with the Huaorani; to attempt to give voice to their concerns without necessarily speaking for them; and, in crossing the street from workaday journalism into environmental activism, to play his part in saving the rain forest as well (11). But as he is soon forced to admit, the Huaorani, talismanic objects of other people's desires, are "his" people too. Symbolic victims of a world left behind, they are his very own noble savages: an isolated people, besieged from all sides, "forced to leap from [the] Stone Age to [the] Petroleum Age" (20), and determined to defend their rights—even if defending them means to kill. The central figure in this unashamedly romantic ecological fable, in which a handful of the People (the "traditional" Huaorani) are pitted against the massed ranks of the Company (corporate interests, the forces of modern industrial development), is the redoubtable Huao tribesman Moi. Impressively captured in stock "native warrior" pose on the cover of the Vintage edition of *Savages,* Moi fights the good fight with considerable skill, and on several different fronts. Caught between "modern" and "tribal" worlds, shuttling between his remote forest home and urban appeals courts in Quito and Washington, Moi stands astride a bewildering array of competing multinational corporations, missionary societies, human rights organizations, environmental advocacy groups, and government agencies, several of which appear to have little in common other than that they are unknown to the Huaorani themselves (9–10, 21).

However, as the plot thickens, the black-and-white outlines of

Kane's fable, even while it retains its moral intensity, become increasingly blurred. For one thing, it emerges that the Huaorani, in keeping with other Amazonian indigenous peoples threatened by oil development, are no more united or unambiguous in their intentions than the giant offshore corporations who manufacture their endorsement in order to pursue their own ambitions; and for another, even those well-intentioned groups—often confusingly reduced to a jumble of acronyms—that wish to rally behind the Huaorani frequently have uncertain motives, with internal rivalry and one-upmanship proving to be as much the rule as adversarial solidarity, and with deals being struck behind the Huaorani's backs that provide more evidence of top-down "environmental imperialism" than grassroots ecological support (73, 76–77).[8] Indeed, environmental advocacy itself—significantly, "environment" is seen by Moi and other Huaorani as a Western word (199)—is treated with a degree of ironic suspicion throughout the narrative, as in the skeptical view taken up toward local environmental lobbying groups such as the feminist-activist "ecochicas" (206–7, 223), or in the spectacle of well-paid American development workers, custodians of USAID's $15 million budget for ecotourism and "sustainable resource extraction" in Ecuador, dining in Quito's most expensive restaurants or billeted at its premier hotels (175–76).

The self-irony with which Kane greets the environmentalist aspect of his own particular mission is symptomatic of a text that is not so serious that it forgets how to be playful, and that is well attuned to the contradictions of the various salvationist discourses it brings into conflict with one another, making these in turn the source of play. These ironically interconnected discourses—each associated, in its way, with the production of "savagery" on which its claims to redemptiveness depend—include both secular (environmentalist) and religious (evangelical) versions, bringing together a colorful band of would-be supporters whose liberationist ambitions provide a means not so much of delivering the Huaorani from their enemies as of capturing them to their own particular cause (84, 87, 138–39). There is no shortage, then, of individuals and groups eager to tell the Huaorani how to steer a path toward self-determination; even oilmen like the religious-minded general manager of Maxus, the company that poses the most direct threat to Huaorani sovereignty, appear to want to "save" them, educating them to the complexities of living in the "modern" world and "equip[ping] them to deal with what people call civilization" (121).

While critical of the self-interest, or at best mixed motives, of those who have pledged themselves to helping the Huaorani, Kane freely acknowledges his own complicity in profiting from their cause. He is also well aware of his own investment in romancing a threatened indigenous people, an investment best demonstrated in the ironic manipulation throughout the text of clichéd primitivist motifs. His partner-in-crime here is the self-deprecating Anglo-Iranian aid worker Ali Sharif, much beloved of stock Conradian phrases that resonate in his own particular Heart of Darkness, and quick to take the wind out of Kane's sails by pointing out that they are both at best mock-saviors whose media-conscious activism might well be seen as indirectly contributing to the further commodification of the traditional people they wholeheartedly support (96, 132). The Huaorani, in this context, exhibit most of the "standard commodities" (Goldie) of indigeneity, including bravery, superstition, a quaint ingenuousness in the face of modern technology, and traditional survival skills (36, 47, 99). Most of all, they are endowed with an equally commodified authenticity as the only "true warriors of the forest" who, in their own eyes, "had never been conquered and never would be, because they were the bravest people in the Amazon" (200, 218). While this comic-strip view of the Huaorani is counterbalanced by a more nuanced appreciation of their encounters with modernity, Kane never quite manages to purge his text of the stereotypical romantic embellishments that its own particular variant on the Amazonian quest narrative—the Lévi-Straussian cautionary tale—traditionally supports.[9] Thus, it is no surprise to find cannibalism serving as the indexical sign of the Huaorani's alleged savagery, nor is it any less unusual to discover that both of these signs ("cannibalism" and "savagery") are reversible, applying less to the Huaorani themselves than to the nexus of foreign corporations and government agencies that seek to control the People's interests in order to consolidate the Company's power and serve its material ends. A typical response is that of one of Kane's most trustworthy informants, the moralistic Capuchin missionary José Miguel Goldáraz, who tells him solemnly: "'When the Huaorani kill, there is a spiritual discipline to it.' . . . 'Americans kill without knowing they are doing it. You don't *want* to know what you are doing it. And yet you are going to destroy a whole way of life. So you tell me: Who are the savages?'" (75).

The success of Kane's narrative lies in the extent to which it is able to mark ironic distance from the kind of travel writing that, wearing its bleeding heart on its sleeve, energetically traffics in such banalities, without necessarily diminishing the importance of ecological action or trivializing a valid indigenous cause. The combination of adventure-travelog and investigative journalism also allows Kane to make a plea for a "hands-on" approach to environmental issues, and to issue a reminder of the limitations of, and limited audience for, more formal scholarly analyses and statistical reports (58). Thus, while Kane's book is certainly well researched, liberally deploying facts and figures to confirm the extent of corporate greed and environmental destruction (49, 70, 111), it retains the modern travelog's frequent suspicion toward set rules and its mischievous spirit of creative play. Moving freely between apparently incompatible discourses, unafraid to exhibit its own amateurism, *Savages* makes skillful use of travel writing's characteristic mix of popular anecdote and nonexpert analysis, combining these in the attempt to draw in and entertain its readers, as well as to engage their sympathy and support.[10]

A similar combination can be found in another environmentally oriented travel narrative, the English ecologist Charlie Pye-Smith's colorful account of his wanderings through the Himalayan region in the mid-1980s, *Travels in Nepal* (1988). While Pye-Smith, like Kane, is by no means averse to using the conventional tools of the Anglo-American travel writer—thrills-and-spills, self-deprecating humor, snappy dialogue, and sentimental descriptions of the native landscape can all be found in abundance in the narrative—he also shares Kane's moral concern for the impact of large-scale foreign intervention on geographically isolated local communities, and for the human/ecological fallout that has resulted from an impoverished nation's "opening up" to the wider world. Pye-Smith's more immediate aim in the text is to show the largely negative effect of foreign aid on the country, which he depicts as a happy hunting ground for aid agencies from all over the world. As he remarks at one point early on in his travels, "virtually every road, bridge, hospital and college had been built, or was about to be, with the help of a grant or loan from one of a score of countries which had set up shop here since Nepal opened its doors to the outside world in 1951"

(19). More specifically, his focus is on Western development aid for local environmental projects, the prevailing if oversensationalized view being that Nepal has fallen into a state of potentially cataclysmic environmental decline (31, 162–63). While Pye-Smith will not go so far as to dismiss all forms of foreign aid as intrinsically imperialist, he does suggest that the "continued interference of central government and foreign aid agencies" has generally had a damaging effect on Nepal, providing at worst a displaced form of European colonial rule (17, 30).[11] He goes on to cite the usual sources for continuing aid failures: technological gigantism and top-down approaches to international development; obstructive bureaucracy; widespread incompetence and corruption; distributional problems inherent not only in the recipient country but in the uneven capitalist world-system at large; and, not least, the cultural arrogance of donor countries that have persisted in imposing often ill-thought-out schemes without considering the possible consequences of their actions, still less understanding the changing needs of those whom their projects were originally intended to support. These errors are writ large in a number of failed agrarian projects Pye-Smith visits as he makes his way across the country, several of which seem to have succeeded only in intensifying the very environmental problems they were designed to tackle, or in driving a further wedge between the nation's rural poor and its urban ruling elite (83, 102–4, 159).

Pye-Smith's assertions, while extrapolated from what is little more than a series of temporary, impressionistically rendered visits, are lent a degree of authority by the evidence of background research and by the author's repeated, if generally understated, reminders that he has professional training as an ecologist in the field. Pye-Smith may well be right to be suspicious of institutions such as the World Bank and the Overseas Development Administration, huge international bodies that have sometimes seemed to thrive on creating and perpetuating the "problems" and "crises" they are designed to redress (166). And he is surely right to point out that foreign aid policies often spring from confused or contradictory motives, helping to create dependencies that exacerbate already acute conditions of poverty, or endorsing paternalistic attitudes toward the Third World that are a legacy of European imperial myths (151–52, 157–59). It seems worth asking, however, whether these confusions and contradictions might not also apply at other levels to the narrative. Pye-Smith seems torn, for instance, between his professional desire to criticize one form of Western "interference" (foreign aid) and his personal awareness of another (tourism), drawing ironic attention at several points in the text to the touristic luxuries and preferences that are an integral part, however disguised or downplayed, of almost every modern travel book. Thus, while—entirely predictably—he has little good to say about tourists, especially comfort-loving European trekkers, he is well attuned to his own privileged status, taking several opportunities to articulate that most generic of modern travel-book sentiments, white-liberal "tourist shame" (61).[12] A second source of contradiction in the text, well captured in Tim Brennan's resonant phrase "the aestheticization of underdevelopment" (185), is played out in the tension between Pye-Smith's conscience-stricken impulse to document conditions of extreme poverty and the imaginative capital he generates from, say, his voyeuristic descriptions of near-starving hill tribes on Nepal's northern borders or his almost visceral fascination with the disease-ridden slum quarters of "untouchable" Kathmandu (14, 62–63, 74–75). Finally, the text's ethical imperative to provide empirical evidence for continuing human/ecological abuses is counteracted to some extent, as can also be seen in works like *Savages,* by travel writing's tendency to cultivate its own inconsequentiality—by the relative ease with which it seems able to substitute high jinks for high moral seriousness, or to seek a compensatory refuge in the playful deconstruction of familiar triumphalist myths.

These counterimpulses are perhaps best demonstrated in one of the book's most instructive but also most entertaining sequences, when Pye-Smith visits the Gaida Wildlife Camp and other conservation-oriented areas in the environmentally vulnerable region of Terai in central Nepal. Here, he finds himself shuttling between those who have a stake in protecting nature (National Park staff, visiting ecologists from the Smithsonian) and those who shamelessly exploit it (a rambunctious American crew commissioned to make a pulse-quickening television special on tiger hunting in Nepal). While his professional sympathies lie with the former, he finds himself equally attracted to the latter—fast-talking adventurer-types with large physiques and even larger egos, whose staged nostalgia for the glory days of adventure-travel to some extent matches his own (39, 42–43). Yet if Pye-Smith's attitude toward what might facetiously be called the "100-years-too-late" school of travel writing is ambivalent, so is his response to the political correctness of environmental concern.[13] Reflecting, for example, on a common area of dispute within environmentalist circles, he claims that "in many different parts of the developing world the success or failure of a national park is measured solely in terms of whether its wildlife flourishes or declines, and little or no thought is given to the fate of the people displaced by the parks or living next to them" (50). Too often, he contends, national parks and other conservationist ventures are "imposed willy-nilly on people who already find it hard enough to make a living" (50); too often "Western conservationists . . . spend more time telling people of other countries how to look after their wildlife than they do worrying about their own" (49). At moments like these, Pye-Smith adds the liberal-minded travel writer's cautious defense of cultural relativism to the ecologist's responsible concern for a balanced environment, bringing both together to provide a corrective to the tacit ethnocentrism that sometimes lurks behind Western-radical "ecocentric" views.[14]

Eco-travel writing, in this last context, has less to do with the specific practices of environmental (mis)management than with the general cultural attitudes that underpin them, attitudes that tend to reflect the assumed superiority of Western import technologies and the universal applicability of European philosophical/ethical precepts. Pye-Smith's primary target, then, as in his attack on foreign aid, is cultural arrogance—an arrogance evenly distributed throughout the text in the figure of self-serving foreign experts, among them academic advisers, industrial consultants, and, worst of all, anthropologist "peeping Toms" (29, 91–92). (This last group has long since become grist to the mill of a certain kind of critically savvy travel journalism that has ironically taken over many of its duties, with traveler-writers taking on the mantle of eager amateur ethnographers even as they seek to convince their readers of the "interfering" designs of professional anthropologists and their "anachronistic" views. Pye-Smith cannot be accused here of being unaware of his own bad faith, tempering his negative judgment with a grudging admiration; even so, the apparently mutual disregard of the travel writer and the anthropologist, which has a well-documented history, is allowed at several junctures in the text, as is also the case in the more deliberately self-ironic *Savages,* to kick in.)[15]

Arrogance is linked throughout the text to a continuing history of imperialism. Here, travel writing and environmentalism alike have found themselves uneasily poised between the desire to be critical and the awareness of being complicit.[16] As if to register this awareness, *Travels in Nepal* sets out to record a number of contemporary instances of what might be described, loosely following Crosby (1986), as "ecological neocolonialism." Such instances not only include those recrudescent forms of exploitation that operate under the cover of modern industrial development but also, more contentiously, the authoritarian tendencies of certain strands within the Western environmental movement itself. Modern-day versions of environmental imperialism, in fact, may assume a variety of unexpected guises, lying hidden for example behind the pseudophilanthropic gestures of a wealthy entrepreneurial elite. Take the Varja, Pye-Smith's hotel in Kathmandu, which turns out to be part of a network of environmentally friendly projects financed by an eccentric Texan businessman with a theatrical and ecological bent (5). While acknowledging the elegance of his surroundings, Pye-Smith is justifiably uncertain about the wider ecological benefits of these parallel ventures, among them a giant biospheric bubble in Arizona "containing marshes, forests, grasslands and room for half a dozen people to live" (5). And he is equally suspicious of the philanthropic leanings of their donor: "Philanthropy implies an interest in the general welfare of mankind. Mr Bass is simply a rich man who spends his money as he wishes. To spend $1 million on a hotel which houses a few Thespians and caters for visitors like me, when a few minutes' walk away there are people living in the depths of misery, is not the action of a philanthropist" (5).

Pye-Smith's liberal anxieties are once again apparent. Humanitarian projects, he implies, often act as conduits for political and business interests; while the environment presents an opportune site for competitive commerce (ecotourism) or rival conservationist factions (national parks services, international environmental aid agencies), even as each of these would-be benefactors claims to act in local communities' own best interests for a worthy global cause. Sensibly, however, he proposes no immediate solution to these dilemmas: First World environmentalism, he rather suggests, will always be likely to betray the strategic interests behind its own attempts at altruism, just as in matters of Third World aid political will is always likely to override humanitarian concerns (168). In this context, eco-travel writing becomes not so much a stimulus for environmental action as the ambivalent medium for a crit-

ical inquiry into the prescriptivism of First World environmental debate. After all, as Pye-Smith implies, the relationship between ecology
and travel/writing is never likely to be an easy one. At best, it might be
said, eco-travel writing succeeds in balancing curiosity with conscience,
producing a blueprint for the kind of responsible travel that both
reflects and actively promotes environmentalist attitudes and concerns.
At worst, it falls an easy prey to those displaced forms of "imperialist
nostalgia" (Rosaldo) to be found in romantic fantasies of attachment
or in elegiac tributes to "vanishing" indigenous traditions that Western
modernity and its exemplars, foremost among them the tourist industry, have done their best to destroy.[17] Aware of all this, Pye-Smith turns
the expansionist history of European travel/writing against itself to examine the fault lines in contemporary First World environmentalist discourses. In the process he succeeds, partly in spite of himself, in uncov-
ering the contradictions inherent in his own professional field: ecology.
In the roving figure of Pye-Smith, the accidental tourist meets the conscientious ecologist. This convergence is instructive: a pragmatic, in
many ways thoroughly modern discipline, dedicated to the maintenance of complex biological and social interdependencies, is discovered
surreptitiously to harbor nostalgic visions of lost wholeness and misty
romantic-individualist ideals.[18]

Like *Savages* and *Travels in Nepal*, the American journalist Mark
Hertsgaard's *Earth Odyssey* (1999) is something of a genre hybrid, fus-
ing the event-filled travelog with the fact-based environmental report.
This fusion, as Hertsgaard explains, aims at producing "a different
kind of environmental book"—one in which, rather than resorting to
"the dry bureaucratic prose [to be] found in most such volumes," the
author attempts a firmer grounding of the narrative in stories about the
people and places he has encountered during his travels (vii). These
travels, immodestly framed as an environmental odyssey, take our hero
far and wide in search of possible answers to his apocalyptic questions:
"Would human civilization still exist one hundred years from now? Or
would our species have been wiped out, partially or completely, by ecological disasters of its own making?" (15). The ecological outlook, he
discovers, is unimaginably bleak. A harrowing journey through southern Sudan reveals that Africa's enormous environmental problems—
soil erosion, desertification, lack of clean water—are inextricably
linked with globally produced conditions of underdevelopment and

acute poverty; an extended tour through China and the former Soviet Union unfolds a litany of environmental horrors, including extreme air and water pollution and a whole host of potentially lethal health-hazards unleashed by carbon emissions, industrial toxins, and nuclear waste; while briefer trips to Brazil, Thailand, and, in the book's final chapter, the Czech Republic ("Europe's worst polluter") confirm that recent efforts in several "emergent" countries to deploy less environmentally damaging forms of sustainable development have fallen far short of their objectives, and that for many people in the world "the environmental crisis is no mere abstraction [but] is rather a punishing reality they live with every day" (vii).

Hertsgaard's book is undoubtedly effective in appealing to its target Euro-American readership to lead the way in creating the global, as well as local, conditions for much-needed environmental reform (27, 77, 195). The book functions, that is, as an "environmental wake-up call" (88) in which worsening conditions in the South and other so-called developing regions act as vivid reminders of the need to rethink attitudes toward consumption in the postindustrial societies of the (over)developed world. These attitudes are perhaps reflected most clearly in Hertsgaard's home country, the United States, where—in then Czech president Václav Havel's suitably baleful terms—an "omnipresent dictatorship of consumption, production, advertising, commerce, [and] consumer culture" has only succeeded in creating the latest "well-spring of totalitarian thought" (quoted in Hertsgaard, 315). *Earth Odyssey* is much less effective, however, as a variant on the cautionary eco-travelog, frequently lapsing into the finger-wagging preachiness and florid overwriting that, in more obviously self-conscious texts like *Savages* and *Travels in Nepal,* are either scrupulously avoided or implicitly sent up. Some purple passages are embarrassing, emanations from a dim-and-distant National Geographic era: "Here in the village of Pochala, on the eastern edge of southern Sudan, deep in the continent of Africa, the daily cycle had begun anew" (19); "[I]n eastern Africa one could still sense the deep past of life on this planet—in the bloody maw and languid gaze of a lion fresh from a kill, in the perfect stillness of the endless rolling plains of Masai Mara at sunrise, in the stoic endurance of tribespeople like the Dinka and Masai, whose daily lives are more similar to those of their Stone Age ancestors than not" (59). Others, meanwhile, simply press too hard in championing the cause of "ecological salvation," this latter term being understood not so much in the hackneyed sense of saving the planet as in our doing what it takes to rescue ourselves from the increasing likelihood of our own destruction (15–16).

A more general problem of the book is that its overwhelming temptation to moralize interferes with its stated goal of empirical observation (vii, 7).[19] Hertsgaard the travel writer clashes here with his alter ego, Hertsgaard the environmental activist. The former's impressionistic renderings of local people and customs are so fleeting as to be virtually invisible, quickly giving way to the latter's Gradgrindian enthusiasm for hard facts: "In 1950, the United States had three-quarters of the world's cars; today, its share is only one-third. While the world's population has doubled since 1950, the number of cars has grown by a factor of ten, to five hundred million" (108); "Because similar disparities pertain to many commodities and activities, a baby born in the United States creates thirteen times as much environmental damage over the course of its life-time as a baby born in Brazil, and thirty-five times as much as an Indian baby" (196). *Earth Odyssey* emerges in this light as a travelog without travel or, at least, without the recorded evidence of movement, Hertsgaard's world journey functioning rather as the pretext for an assemblage of environmental disaster reports. Nor is there much evidence in the text of the travel writer's alleviating humor. This is partly due to the fact that Hertsgaard has little interest in sweetening his cautionary tale with the customary diet of traveler's anecdotes and antics, appearing to view such inconsequentialities as characteristic of the type of self-serving travel narrative that disclaims responsibility for the misadventures its writer helps to bring about.[20] Instead, *Earth Odyssey* dedicates itself to documenting *other* people's misfortunes, producing a powerfully cumulative account of often extreme circumstances of human deprivation in which suffering is made to appear simultaneously unavoidable and self-induced.

For all the work of conscience in his text, Hertsgaard is arguably more interested in the fate of humanity as a whole than in individual people. The semiformal interview substitutes, by and large, for the impromptu conversation; and even when Hertsgaard's less articulate interlocutors—never really more than shadowy figures—appear to want to say something, he is often all too quick to drown out their voices with his own. These particular instances of the "silenced subaltern"

(Spivak)[21] are exacerbated by Hertsgaard's tendency toward condescension, as registered in his amazement that local peasants cannot understand even the simplest of environmental issues or in his parroting
back of their rustic English, a common feature of the colonialist travel
writing he allegedly deplores. In his impatience to get his point across,
Hertsgaard sometimes simply fails to listen, thus laying himself open to
the accusation he is otherwise so keen to counter—that his environmentalist agenda is above all a wealthy foreigner's privilege, out of
touch with local realities and immediate socioeconomic concerns (262).
Predictably, however, Hertsgaard projects this particular failing onto
others, accusing his Chinese guide Zhenbing of not paying attention to
his arguments, or expressing frustration when a Kenyan shopkeeper
with whom he has been exchanging idle banter cannot be brought to
talk about the environment, "despite a number of conversational gam-
bits on my part" (295). Similarly, the narrative often seems reluctant to
articulate the immediacy of its vision, either seeking refuge in stock
phrases about embattled indigenous cultures or adopting the distanced
tone of the official guidebook: "Combine the flair of Florence, the fairy-
tale charm of Vienna, the elegance of Stockholm, and the grandeur of
Paris, and you begin to approach the magnificence of Prologue" (314).
As Hertsgaard observes at the end of his preface, "Travel is like knowledge. The more you see the more you know you haven't seen" (16). But
for much of his journey, he seems just as keen to impart knowledge as
to acquire it; and that knowledge appears, at times, to be almost uncannily dissociated from the particular places he has visited, the various
people he has encountered, and the specific things he has seen.

It seems ironic, in this context, that a narrative consciously designed
to avoid abstraction should so often fall back upon it (vii). Time and
again, Hertsgaard emphasizes the relevance of his accumulated statis-
tics or insists on extrapolating general theories from a relay of specific
historical facts. For all that, *Earth Odyssey* is less skillful than either
Savages or *Travels in Nepal* in moving between the specific and the general, partly because it is less likely to inquire into the ideological contradictions—not least, the moral ambivalence—inscribed into the
travel-writing genre. Perhaps the greatest problem of a heartfelt text
like *Earth Odyssey* is its demonstrable impatience, as manifest in the
overwhelming earnestness with which it insists on its environmental
warning being delivered, even before the story has a chance to be prop-

erly told. Related problems, familiar to didactic genres, are those of making virtue interesting and of finding ways of giving political activism, however worthy its cause, a patina of aesthetic appeal. Here, *Earth Odyssey,* as its title implies, appears burdened by the magnitude of its own efforts. The text labors under the weight of its own political convictions; as if seeing the world were the necessary precondition for saving it, and traveling light the catalyst for going Green.[22] Above all, perhaps, Hertsgaard's is a travel book that forgets the *vagaries* of travel and the immediate sensory pleasures that travel writing, even at its most socially concerned and environmentally committed, affords.

Feeling

Earth Odyssey, with its sentimental Thoreauvian undertones, never quite manages to uphold its author's felt conviction that "Third World travel . . . cautions one against romanticizing the nontechnological life" (334). This seems equally true of any number of contemporary Third World-oriented travel narratives. The African continent, in particular, presents a site of contradiction, as the traveler-writer struggles to reconcile the conspicuous hardships of local people's daily existence with the self-serving European myth of Africa as "a refuge from the technological age" and "a glorious Eden for wildlife" (Adams and McShane, xii). East Africa, especially Kenya, bears the brunt of this particular colonial legacy, as captured in such familiar tropes as the "great white hunter," later turned enthusiastic conservationist, and the Janus-faced vision of the African wilderness as both artificial paradise and area beyond human control (Adams and McShane, 6). Wilderness narratives of this type frequently engage with the contradictions of colonial Africa as a field for the free play of European conquistadorial fantasy (Hammond and Jablow) and as a site to be reverentially protected, "held in trust for future generations . . . as a reminder of our savage past" (Adams and McShane, 8). Two narratives to battle with these contradictions are the Italian expatriate Kuki Gallmann's emotion-soaked memoir of her rise to prominence as a Kenyan landowner, *I Dreamed of Africa* (1991), and the American adventure-traveler Rick Ridgeway's account of his risk-filled journey through Tsavo National Park on foot, *The Shadow of Kilimanjaro* (1998). Both narratives can be read, in part, as postcolonial homages to the Euro-American literary myth of "Old

Africa" (Ridgeway, 236): Kenya duly emerges as a stirring place inhabited by a variety of latter-day Ernest Hemingways and Karen Blixens, all apparently intent on impressing their authority on an uncompromising landscape eventually made to submit to the equal ferocity of their own desire for control. But they are also self-consciously environmentalist texts in which the desire to achieve what Ridgeway describes as a "visceral feel" for the condition of wildness is balanced by an awareness of the need to protect it, both for others and themselves (199).

Protection, however, means very different things for the two writers. In Gallmann's case, the eventual establishment of her own conservationist foundation, centered on the vast freehold ranch she acquired shortly after moving to Kenya, is inextricably connected with an ideology of proprietorship through which she is able to rationalize her own privileged class position as a powerful expatriate landowner, a self-appointed "guardian" or "trustee." The protection of the environment, for Gallmann, entails a "balance between the wild and the tame," bridging the apparently incompatible principles of noninterference and domestication (189, 252). Such a balance in turn provides the justification—mediated by that quintessentially domestic form, the memoir—for an expatriate community of controlling European families entrusted not only with the responsible day-to-day management of their own commercial properties but also with the quasi-metaphysical stewardship, apparently vouchsafed by their rich colonial forebears, of the land as a whole. This unashamedly self-privileging version of the white (wo)man's burden is very different from Ridgeway's much more modest, if similarly ambivalent, protectionist mission, which consists in offering moral support to the conservationist cause in East Africa while doing his best, within the time-honored tradition of extreme adventure-travel writing, to remove the protective barriers around himself, thereby placing his own physical safety at maximum risk. The *untamability*, rather than the *taming*, of the wild is Ridgeway's operating principle, and it is backed by a relatively orthodox travel narrative in which the specific encounter with danger, as well as the generalized apprehension of endangerment, reveals varieties of affective response. To some extent, Ridgeway's narrative is an attempt not just to account for but to aspire to the condition of wildness; by mimicking "the perpetual alertness of . . . wild animals" (260), he seeks to minimize the distance between himself and the animal other, going beyond mere recognition to risk the absorption of the other into himself. Gallmann's and Ridgeway's may be described, then, as narratives united in their self-conscious, partly self-ironic exploration of the myth of wild Africa, but divided by their ideological attitude toward it, as well as by the specific rhetorical strategies they adopt. It is time to look more closely now at some of these strategies and their ideological underpinnings, gauging their effectiveness in conveying either the fiction of attachment (Ridgeway) or the fantasy of entitlement (Gallmann) to the natural world.

Of the two books, Gallmann's *I Dreamed of Africa* is the more obvious crowd-pleaser, situating itself squarely in the European romantic-colonial tradition upheld by such writers as Beryl Markham, Elspeth Huxley, and Karen Blixen—a tradition tapped more recently by such commercially viable subgenres as the nostalgic blockbuster (e.g., *Out of Africa*) and the New Age spiritual quest (e.g., the metaphysical travelogs of Laurens van der Post). (The tradition, for Gallmann, amounts to more than the observed rites of intertextual deference: Gallmann's range of friends in Kenya encompasses distant relatives of Blixen's, while she has a brief affair with an English filmmaker whose credits include *Out of Africa*.) Ostensibly a family memoir taking in the early years of Gallmann's transplantation from neoaristocratic northern Italy to postcolonial East Africa, *I Dreamed of Africa* owes both its tone (melodramatically intense) and its structure (cyclically repetitive) to exotic romance. Africa, as the title of the book implies, is the epitome of the exotic, conjuring up the dreamlike backdrop of "unbounded freedom, . . . wild open horizons and red sunsets, [and] green highlands teeming with wild animals" (17) against which the domestic dramas of expatriate life, itself conceived as an expression of freedom, are played out. After a succession of disasters, foremost among them the untimely deaths of her husband Paolo and her son Emanuele, we might conclude that Gallmann eventually learns to live in Africa rather than merely to love it. But in keeping with the spirit of exotic romance, Africa never quite sheds its aura of manufactured mystery. Both spatially and temporally other (predictably, Gallmann's nostalgic preference is for the Old Africa), the Kenyan plains can be turned into a home precisely insofar as they are displaced. Local knowledge, in a paradigmatic rehearsal of colonial displacement, is held in check by an imported European poetic sensibility, with the Kenyan landscape, in particular, acting as a conduit for European neoclassical and romantic myths. The customary tropes are all present and correct: "untouched" landscapes are dramatically unfurled before the panoramic gaze of the new settler (57); wild animals abound; while people, their poverty carefully disguised, their fealty uncritically acknowledged, disport themselves in front of the delighted European spectator in a sequence of resplendent *tableaux vivants:*

> [The Pokot] women were dressed in long skirts of soft hide, greased with a mixture of goat fat and red ochre like their faces and hair. They looked like terracotta statues, agile and feminine with their rows of brass bangles clasping thin wrists and ankles, and with brass rings hung from pendulous ears. . . . Their breasts were greased and bare. Their heads were shaven at the sides, but reddish ringlets sprouted on top, like the crests of exotic birds or manes of wild animals, which gave a suprisingly feminine effect. . . . They snaked their way through the garden and sang as they danced. Their beauty and wildness silenced my European guests, and long into the night the guttural cries mixed, without interference, with the whooping cry of the hyena calling to the moon from the hills. (84)

The effortless control implied in staged ethnic spectacles such as this one reconfirms the host's (Gallmann's) naturalized authority, not just over her awestruck guests, but over "primitive" peoples she seems able to summon up, and whose "wildness" she can domesticate, at will. Similar patterns can be traced in the Gallmann family's encounters with wild animals. Paolo, a latter-day version of the great white hunter (56, 93), plays the role of the noble warrior, his worldview apparently encapsulated in the febrile love-letter he writes his wife in which he imagines their unborn child being brought "to the centre of an horizon from which one can dominate the world" (130). Emanuele, meanwhile, Gallmann's son by her first marriage, is the inveterate collector, catastrophically killed by one of the snakes he mistakenly believes he has it in his power to control. Kuki herself, finally, is—as one might expect within this transparent romantic structure—the survivor: the nurturing maternal figure who translates the tragic losses of her husband and son into a salvationist mission to protect indigenous wildlife; and whose ranch, a beacon of conservationist goodwill in an increasingly resource-depleted country, is ceremonially transformed into a "living monument to the memory of the men I had loved" (252). This gesture of creating a "living monument," however worthy, characteristically assimilates the collective practice of *conservation* to an individual act of *possession,* an act signed and sealed, like the ranch itself, in the Gallmann family name. The link between conservation and proprietorship had already been clinched at an earlier point in the narrative when Gallmann, contemplating whether to return to Europe to have Paolo's baby, decides to stay on at the ranch to fulfill her self-accorded responsibility as an environmental "trustee":

> More than anything, I wanted to prove that I deserved my guardian-ship. . . . Sitting on the top of the hill at Mugongo ya Ngurue, looking down at Baringo through the intact cliffs of the Mukutan Gorge, I touched the rough trunk of the old twisted acacia growing there at the edge of the world, as a sentinel to the silent, vast, majestic scenario. That landscape had been there long before our advent. It would still be there after I left. Not only had I no right to spoil it, but I had to be actively involved in protecting it. Special privileges come at a price: and this was my inheritance. (147)

Here as elsewhere, the obligation to protect rationalizes Gallmann's sense of her own entitlement, an entitlement she also ascribes to the tight-knit community of wealthy European expatriates, most of them substantial landowners, whose company she often shares (38). The bonds that form within this community are used to establish a patrician lineage confirmed in the nobility of Italian bloodlines and played out in nostalgic colonial rituals, like the quaint anachronisms of the Club (85–86). Inherited privileges, however, are not enough to sustain Gallmann, who must persuade herself, in an alien land, that she somehow belongs. Hence the importance of "guardianship" over the land, a motif invoked in sweeping panoramic vistas (57), as well as in linked images such as the totemic acacia—envisioned by Gallmann, in oracular New Age mode, as an atavistic soulmate—with which the memoir begins: "There, on the extreme edge of the Great Rift Valley, guarding the gorge, grows an acacia tree bent by timeless winds. That tree is my friend, and we are sisters. I rest against its trunk, scaly and grey like a wise old elephant. I look up through the branches, twisted arms spread in a silent dance, to the sky of Africa" (xvii).

Episodes like this set up what Gallmann later describes as "a wonderful feeling of being part of the landscape" (80, 145), a reassuringly mutual recognition that reconfirms her natural calling as a "trustee" (149, 183). "Trusteeship" comes in hand with a sense of loss, reinforced by Gallmann's own domestic tragedies; and with the heartening conviction that conservation has emerged as a new burden for the post-independence period, as registered in the white (wo)man's "commitment to keep the balance between the wild and the tame" (189). This modern-day version of the civilizing mission is a similarly educative enterprise, ridden with residual colonial condescension:

> The average urban African has never seen an elephant; how could these people make a policy which would enable them to protect the environment and at the same time ensure their survival? Was all the wilderness destined to disappear through lack of knowledge and planning? I certainly could not change everything, but I could not tolerate the thought of this happening to Ol Ari Nyiro [her own ranch]. (251)

The mission thus revolves around the establishment of a harmonious micro-environment, overseen by the figure of the benevolent white proprietor, and encompassing "the ranch and its animals, wild and domestic, and its plants, cultivated and indigenous, and its people, living in a changing Africa but still remembering—just—their traditional skills" (252). Needless to say, this microcosmic space reembodies the wisdom of inherited colonial hierarchies. A conservation system of a different kind, it represents a mapping of the Old Africa onto the New, represented in the iconic figure of the white hunter turned conservationist (262–63), and ritually accompanied by the destruction of the ivory pyre—centerpiece of the opening ceremony for Nairobi National Park that Gallmann and her friends have helped prepare, and to which they have been invited as guests of honor—that symbolically consigns "man's thoughtless destruction of the environment" to the past (302). For Gallmann, the burning pyre takes up its place in a wider romantic cycle of purification rituals, not just for the Kenyan nation, but for her own immediate family in whom the fate of the nation itself is symbolically intertwined: "It was another ending, another beginning, and it summarized, purified, and made sense of all that happened so far in all our combined lives" (303). Yet this latest death/rebirth is significantly followed by a further ceremony in which, returning home to the ranch, Gallmann and her daughter Sveva are greeted by a band of local Pokot warriors, come to pledge allegiance to the Musungu (white European) and her new conservationist cause:

> Before we knew it, the warriors stopped around us in an almost perfect circle. Sveva and I waited in the middle, on the manicured lawn carved out of the wilderness, among the flowers, our large dogs surrounding us. Our fair skin and hair stood out, and I realized that she and I were the only females present at this ceremony. Our European origin, my position as guardian of this land, gave us, I supposed, the status of men. (308)

Through these two parallel ceremonies, Galimann achieves the audacious (some might say outrageous) step of ushering in a new enlightened era, in which a combination of sound leadership, mutual trust, and cooperative effort will be conscripted to correct the environmental abuses of the past. The overriding sense of Gallmann's entitlement, once again, is simply staggering, the self-perpetuating structure of romance being used to shore up and reinvigorate white patriarchal authority in a new conservation-minded Kenya that looks suspiciously like the Old Africa conserved.

A rather different kind of elegy to the Old Africa is the Californian adventure-traveler Rick Ridgeway's *The Shadow of Kilimanjaro* (1998). The text, played out against the spectacular backdrop of Tsavo National Park in Kenya, is an unashamedly nostalgic tribute to an earlier (colonial) era of white park wardens and their antagonists, indigenous hunters, these two groups being brought together in "the warp and weft of predator and prey" that characterizes nature "in its wildest state" (247, 194). As Ridgeway suggests, both of these groups were to play their part in maintaining precarious equilibrium in a social/ecological system since irreversibly disrupted by the modern technologies that accompanied the emergence of the postcolonial nation-state (247–48). The apparently contradictory impulses to conserve and to hunt are similarly intertwined throughout the narrative, as in the triumphal invocation of a rogue's gallery of notorious great white hunters, "who celebrated Africa's wild game, who argued for its preservation, who mourned its decline, while, at the same time, hunted it and shot it and each in his own way—directly and indirectly—contributed to its unsustainable harvest" (194). Ridgeway recognizes his own belatedness with respect to these originary mythologies. Yet he still chooses to see his guided journey on foot through East Africa—a variant on the modern ecological safari—as an impossible attempt to recapture the "oneness with the bush" experienced by the earliest hunter-gatherers, as well as by later generations of white settlers whose sympathies were divided, as are his own, between the "attraction to hunt" and the "compulsion to conserve" (256, 246).

Unlike Gallmann, Ridgeway—a temporary visitor to Africa, after all, rather than a permanent settler—has no proprietorial claim to make over the territory through which he travels. He does share her fantasy, however, of a visceral connection with the landscape: "'Contact!' That is what I was looking for on this walk. That is what I came to one of the few remaining sections of wild Africa to experience. To see it, to smell it, to taste it, to feel it. To be part of it, not apart from it" (262). And contact, distilled through a heightening of the senses, is at its purest when involving *danger*. The exposure to danger, in this case, entails a willed encounter with wild animals in which the tourist's camera is imagined as being interchangeable with the hunter's rifle, and the distance between human and animal is minimized in the reciprocal acknowledgment of hunter and hunted, predator and prey. A charging elephant, for instance, produces an onset of adrenaline rush that borders on elation: "This danger, this possibility of approaching death, is a closing of a distance between two animals, one intent on damaging the other, and it has produced in me an exhilaration that contains neither fear nor regret, and as a consequence it is an exhilaration that feels clear and pure" (193). By projecting himself into the mindset of the big-game hunter, as well as engaging with the sympathies of the modern-day conservationist, Ridgeway aims to produce a travel text that moves beyond sentimentalized empathy for African wildlife—a text that, in positing the historical connection between contemporary forms of "animal-endorsing" ecotourism and earlier versions of "animal-destructive" safari (Soper), simultaneously succeeds in unraveling the puzzle of the "apparent irreconcilability between [the] veneration and [the] destruction of wild game" (193). In this context, travel takes the form of a series of proximate experiences and movements, registering the vertiginous effects of what the anthropologist Michael Taussig calls "mimetic excess."[23] In an alternating sequence of historical identification-fantasies, Ridgeway imagines what it must have been like to be a colonial game warden, a traditional indigenous hunter, a Victorian adventurer-explorer (104–5, 218–19, 92).

More than any of these, however, Ridgeway aspires to the "timeless" condition of a wild animal. It is not enough, he implies, for the traveler to mimic "the perpetual alertness of the wild animals" (Ortega y Gasset, quoted in Ridgeway, 260); rather, his goal must be to "travel light and unfettered . . . to live wild off the land . . . like a wild animal [itself]" (190). In Deleuze and Guattari's hypertheoretical terms, we might liken this goal to the radical project of "becoming-animal," a movement beyond the human representation of animal drives and instincts to challenge the boundaries between human and animal and, in so doing, to question the very nature of identity and representation itself. Yet it is the emotional experience, rather than the intellectual apprehension, of "becoming-animal" that most interests Ridgeway. Here is his attempt, one of a number of italicized dream-sequences in the text, to close the gap between himself and the animal other by producing a slow-motion replay of events in which ostensibly opposed human and animal consciousnesses converge to the point of being enmeshed:

> *Her legs trot forward massive yet weightless yet setting down with a force that would break the bones and back and ribs of every great animal that walks this wild land and she deserves her name, the matriarch. This monumental weight coming straight at us has slowed time so that each second is . . . a minute and so in one of these long seconds I consider how she is different from the other elephant who have charged us, that she has a different intent. I run backward at an angle so I am behind Danny as he spins and drops and in the same motion raises his rifle toward his shoulder. All with this same slowing of time, all within this one or two seconds that seem to stretch and stretch and stretch . . . (192)*

The imaginative connection Ridgeway draws between himself and the charging elephants illustrates his self-confessedly anthropomorphic view of "the personalities of wild animals" (143), while also lending support to his firm conviction that "we have as much to learn about animal behavior from approaching them emotionally—from relating to them as one animal to another—as we do from quantified scientific observation" (142). Yet, as throughout the narrative, the sympathetic imagination compensates for the fact that the actual point of contact is not reached. Nor can it be, for the physical contact between humans and animals in the text is imagined as being almost invariably fatal, the space of encounter between the two being one in which a life abruptly taken acts as the reverse image of a life arbitrarily preserved. Ridgeway's professional pursuit of extreme adventure, as previously evidenced in such high-risk sporting activities as mountain climbing (vii–viii), is translated here into the desire for a brush with death with the animal other. Human and animal (in what amounts, perhaps, to another version of "becoming-animal") are willed to come together, with the result that the human subject, converging with and absorbed into its animal counterpart, risks being physically destroyed.

Hence the voyeuristic fascination in the text with images of eating and being eaten, as in the scene when Ridgeway, imagination inflamed by having recently heard the legendary story of the man-eating lions of Tsavo, transfers the image of a dead buffalo found en route onto "the remains of a human, partly devoured" (108). Self-irony, as befits the modern self-conscious travelog, often accompanies these fanciful imaginings. A good example comes in an early scene, when the wildlife photographer Peter Beard is given pride of place at the center of a family album in which the masculinist heroics of Old Africa have mutated into a parodic exhibition of accumulated battle scars:

> There was a photo session with Danny after he'd blown his thumb off in a hunting accident, on the veranda, with the head of a dead cobra we'd chopped off: Peter had Danny hold the snake head next to the remains of his thumb. I have this potpourri of images, all mixed together: old Elui, Dad's Wakamba guide with his scars from leopard attacks and rhino gorings, Dad, with one squint eye, gaunt from his cancer, and Peter, in the middle of it all, pleased by the extremes. (74)

In episodes like this one, Ridgeway's mythicized Africa, closer in spirit to Chatwin's than to Hemingway's, presents an imaginary museum dedicated less to the wonders of the wild than to the enduring curiosities of human wildlife (52, 175, 179). Chatwin's trademark combination of crackpot wisdom and tongue-in-cheek aestheticism can be found, in fact, at several junctures in Ridgeway's narrative, as in the mock-epiphanic moment when, as his party slowly tracks across the boundless Kenyan landscape, he suddenly recognizes that his pastoralist desire "to wander in wildness across open spaces is [somehow] connected to some even deeper urge to follow the herds between their seasonal pastures" (83). Moments like these, registered with an almost comical solemnity, appear to indicate that Ridgeway's text is slyly disabused of the tendencies toward romantic nostalgia it apparently works so hard to affect. The text demonstrates similar ambivalence in its attitude toward sentimental European conceptions of unpopulated wilderness. Its leisurely discussion, for example, of the history of conservation policy in East Africa eventually mounts a convincing challenge to the implicitly self-serving Eurocentric opposition between people and wildlife. As one of Ridgeway's highest-profile interlocutors, David (Jonah) Western, the white African director of the Kenyan Wildlife Service, explains: " 'Wilderness is not an African concept' . . . 'Where I grew up in southern Tanzania, it was more remote even than Tsavo, but there were always a few people there, no matter how vast the land, and the people never understood the concept of pure wilderness. To them, nature and people go together. So I believe we have to be compatible' " (173).

Like Western, Ridgeway favors the development of more inclusive, democratically organized conservation programs—those connected with ecotourism, for instance—through which local communities might reap economic benefits from the wildlife they have chosen to support (173–77). However, being an ecotourist himself, Ridgeway is equally interested in his own benefits, and these include the temporary living out of a fantasy, not so much of *wilderness* as of *wildness*. As he suggests in his introduction:

> A wildness is intact. In wildness, all the original pieces are there. My own backyard mountains in California, from the Coastal Range through the Sierras, are in many places wilderness, but none of it is wildness because the grizzly is gone. . . . The last grizzly in California was gunned down in 1922, and as it died so did an essential element of our relationship with our land and the animals we are designed to share it with . . . So I was eager to visit on foot a wildness that still had all the predators in place. (ix)

Ridgeway's text, for all its playful skepticism, never loses this belief in the healing power of wild Africa, a belief perhaps not so divergent after all from Gallmann's more ostensibly colonialist projections of a patrimonial territory to be guarded, a white-European heritage to be protected, and an atavistic contact with the land to be recovered, even as the land itself is increasingly domesticated and "tamed." However, the two texts confront the impossibility of this salvage operation in different ways. In *I Dreamed of Africa,* exotic romance becomes the necessarily imaginary vehicle for a rehearsal of displaced colonial mastery, an ecological vision of "balance" and "natural harmony" that seeks to reinstall the social hierarchies that once legitimated colonial rule. *The Shadow of Kilimanjaro,* on the other hand, uses the conventions of twentieth-century travel writing—self-irony, parody, deflated adventure-heroism—to register its own sense of belatedness toward an Old Africa that can be imaginatively remembered but not historically reborn. In this sense, and in several others, Ridgeway's text condemns itself to search for a wildness it can never find, an originary contact it can never rediscover. Wildness, in fact, is the very image of escape to which the text, generically linked to a tradition of domesticated escapism, wishes to attach itself. This attachment, Ridgeway suggests, can only be achieved in the release of death; risk is its nearest approximation. But even danger, in Ridgeway's text, is for the most part vicariously experienced. Like so many other contemporary traveler-writers, Ridgeway must live in the shadow of the people he would most like to become. The text inhabits this shadow space, alternating between breathless expectation and inevitable disappointment. And relief, in the end, that the ordeal has been successfully overcome:

> I hit the water and taste the salt in my mouth and come up and dive in again and come up and think, This is the hardest I've ever worked in my life for a swim in the ocean. . . . I grab Iain and give him a bear hug and drop him in the surf, thinking that someday on some future adventure we will be bivouacked on a high, cold ledge . . . and recall the warm water of the Indian Ocean. (263)

Finally, then, as he had known all along, the traveler must save himself—for further adventures, for more writing. An ecological glimpse of human/animal interconnectedness, paradoxically grounded in the mutual respect that accompanies the mutual fear of destruction, is eventually traded for the safe knowledge of another journey completed, and the security of another human life conserved.

Watching

The conservationist sympathies of works like *I Dreamed of Africa* and *The Shadow of Kilimanjaro* are allied to a conservative ideology intent not so much on rescuing endangered animals as on rehabilitating a threatened way of (colonial) social life. This nostalgic impulse is also common in television nature documentaries and wildlife movies that, more than any other vehicle, have come to shape the way in which their modern Western viewers think about and experience the natural world today. As Alexander Wilson suggests, such "[nature and] wildlife films are [in part] a record of lost species, a memento of times and places we once have felt close to in the natural world" (128). Paradoxically, they use modern cinematographic techniques to retrieve largely imagined connections with preindustrial landscapes and the traditional peoples that inhabit them, such elegiac gestures acquiring an added poignancy insofar as the same technology that rescues is acknowledged as having the power to destroy (134). Nature documentaries, as several commentators have pointed out, abound in paradoxes of this kind, expressing "deeply contradictory ideas about nature and its relation to human culture" (117). "Disappearing" wildlife magically reappears, often in abundance, before the camera; biological rhythms are dramatically enhanced, and the natural world speeds up (Armbruster, 222–23). Such vehicles, in common with certain types of ethnographic film, elaborately stage the world that they present to us as natural.[24] We are brought close, but not too close: artful camerawork helps convey the illusion of intimacy without involvement, either by presenting "empty" landscapes disjoined from the human cultures that have historically shaped them, or by performing a variety of "disembodying tricks" (Kerridge, 182) that allow the spectator to take voyeuristic pleasure in observing, say, the secret nocturnal activities of an animal whose features, usually invisible, are now enchantingly displayed. This "technical clairvoyance," as John Berger calls it, has an accompanying ideology, bolstered by the myth of scientific objectivity, in which "animals are always the observed. The fact that they can observe us has lost all significance. They are the objects of our ever-extending knowledge. What we know about them is an index of our power, and thus an index of what separates us from them. The more we know, the further away they are" (14).

The genre of the nature documentary/wildlife movie, in highlighting the technical expertise that makes its own discoveries possible, effectively reconfirms the gradual disappearance of animals from the everyday world to which they once belonged (Berger, 9–14). In the recent history of the wildlife movie industry, Alexander Wilson suggests, we can see "the slow recession of animals into history, [where they] begin to merge with all that we call primitive in the world: primal landscapes, indigenous peoples, and a displaced human biology. The archaic becomes synonymous with everything that we understand to be lower on the evolutionary ladder" (127). This combination of nostalgic elements, although increasingly treated in the industry with a degree of critical irony, can be found in those many contemporary nature documentaries that seek to join an amateur-anthropological curiosity for traditional (often indigenous) cultures to a popular desire for scientific knowledge about the environment, bringing both demands together in the service of a liberal conservationist cause. Tourism provides the link between these two not always compatible imperatives. For nature documentaries are arguably driven less by the need to increase knowledge about the natural world than by the desire to maximize its consumption. They are a form of armchair tourism in which, at worst (as has been sometimes argued for travel writing), the commodified demand for wonder, drama, and varieties of anomalous experience is met with a seemingly endless supply of verbal and visual stimuli designed to engender a quasi-automated response. Bill McKibben wearily puts it this way:

> Like urban living, TV cuts us off from context—stops us from understanding plants and animals as parts of systems. . . . We are pulled toward [the] natural world, with a tug so strong it must be primal, but TV helps turn it into a zoo; hence most of our responses are artificial. Animals amble across the screen all night and day—I saw the same squad of marching flamingos twice during the day on different networks. ("They're stupid," said the handler on one of the programs. "It took me six months to get them to walk in formation.") (80)

McKibben's own response, no doubt colored by his deep-ecologist's distaste for the numbing effects of modern mass technology, is in its way equally artificial, appearing to subscribe to a sterotypical view of the passive television consumer that is embarrassingly out of date. Still, he illustrates the crucial point that nature programs are consumed by many, though by no means all, of their viewers in ways that undermine their conservationist motives or, perhaps better, in ways that expose the contradictions of a conservationist ideology entirely complicit with the consumerism it sets out to attack. McKibben's view that such programs have largely failed to fulfill their environmentalist agenda also points to the ambivalence inscribed in nature movies as an outgrowth of the booming adventure-travel genre. As Wilson suggests, nature and wildlife movies often feature a variety of competing elements and interests: "Their discontinuous history includes such genres and approaches as animal stories, science journalism, conservationism, ecological advocacy, social anthropology, adventure stories, and tips on hunting and fishing. Often a single TV program will be a hybrid of different documentary forms" (117). Generic hybridity may also point to ideological confusion, as in the type of program that promotes the spirit of free-wheeling geographical adventure in an environment simultaneously considered to be threatened by human expansionist resolve. Such programs come close at times to delivering the mixed message of the "anti-conquest"—an oxymoronic term defined by Mary Louise Pratt as that congeries of representational strategies "whereby European bourgeois subjects seek to secure their innocence in the same moment as they assert European hegemony" (*Imperial Eyes*, 7). The main protagonist of the "anti-conquest," for Pratt, is the "'seeing-man' . . . the European male subject of European landscape discourse . . . whose imperial eyes passively look out and possess" (7).

Contemporary nature documentaries continue to struggle with this European imperialist legacy, even though many of the best of them are only too well aware of their own ideological insufficiencies, the gap that separates their desire to increase scientific knowledge about, and thereby to help protect, the environment and their reliance on ways of seeing and thinking about the environment that mystify historically specific interactions between nature and culture, the human and non-human worlds. A particularly good example of this is in movies/programs that present a primitivistic portrait of indigenous peoples that reinforces stereotypical Western nature/culture dichotomies by equating the "tribal" with the "natural," compounding the error by misunderstanding indigenous cultures as essentially "static and unchanging and thus doomed in a modern industrial world" (A. Wilson, 149). Such movies/programs, though no longer as popular as they once were, persist in cultivating the anachronisms other travel vehicles have long since begun to parody, routinely producing a pastiche of nature mysticism and pseudo-ethnographic knowledge, and casting their producers in the role of liberal apologists for the "exotic" cultures they often crudely misrepresent.

In the rest of this section, I will briefly examine a late 1980s documentary, National Geographic's "Australia's Twilight of the Dreamtime," which falls into this resolutely antimodern category; I will then compare it with a much more up-to-the-minute, certainly much more openly commercialistic program, also focused on Australia, and featuring the self-parodically life-defying exploits of the telegenic Queensland naturalist Steve Irwin, aka The Crocodile Hunter. While the two programs, and the series to which they belong, are worlds apart in terms of their respective strategies of representation, they share a conservationist imperative that seems ill-served by their portrayal of the natural world as an endlessly replenishable resource. Both foster a voyeuristic appreciation of natural phenomena and, in the case of the National Geographic program, of "foreign cultures" as recyclable commodities, a view out of keeping with their ecological commitment to nature as both a finite, necessarily fragile, entity and an educational source. Both back off, finally, from the political issues raised by their environmentalist message, either by retreating into what Wilson calls "neocolonialist laments for 'a vanishing culture'" (151) or by foregrounding the role of the Western scientist-as-savior, even in circumstances where the salvation trope itself is obviously mocked.

"Far away, in an ancient land of mystery, live the Gaguju people . . . a part of the longest unbroken culture the world has ever known." Thus begins the standard trailer for a National Geographic Special on Kakadu National Park, "Australia's Twilight of the Dreamtime," solemnly narrated by presenter Richard Kiley in what McKibben has derisively described as nature-TV announcers' Churchillian wartime mode (70). This first utterance, effortlessly absorbing Aboriginal history and culture into a Western fairy-tale structure, already hints at the paternalism to follow, which will consist in simultaneously celebrating the ecological awareness of a people who "have built no monuments" other than the land, which "*is* their monument," and mourning the passing of a people, monumentalized in their turn, who seem ill-adapted for "survival in the modern world." The program closely follows the National Geographic formula of presenting the Fourth World in terms of interchangeable "peoples of nature" (Lutz and Collins, 109), whose ancestral (meta)physical union with their environment has been violently disrupted by their contact with the modern world. This is a "fatal contact" scenario with an ecological twist, in which traditional indigenous peoples, co-opted into the role of proto-environmentalists/conservators, are called upon to provide nostalgic visions of "an imagined condition of humanity before the industrial revolution and environmental degradation broke the link between humans and nature" (Lutz and Collins, 110).

As with other National Geographic vehicles, the world's "exotic" peoples become a conduit for displaced Western middle-class anxieties (Lutz and Collins). The Gaguju's reward for bearing the white man's environmental burden is to be offered a premature obituary. Cast as upholders of traditional values Westerners cannot afford to lose, they are turned before their time into (pre)historic artifacts, living museum relics whose continued existence invokes a "golden age that seems to have little connection to anything akin to contemporary life" (Goldie, 17). Not only are they viewed through the filter of the curatorial gaze as valuable collector's items, they are also seen as inhabiting a primeval landscape presented as part cultural treasure-house ("deep in the bush, the [Aborigines] created some of the world's greatest art treasures"), part natural-historical zoo. "Australia's Twilight of the Dreamtime" cross-cuts, accordingly, between the historical narrative of the Gaguju's bitterly contested custodianship of the land (now Kakadu National Park, a state-protected enclosure) and National Geographic's trademark photo-safari depiction of abundant, eternally regenerating natural life (A. Wilson, 141). The implications of this juxtaposition are clear: Kakadu will survive the onslaughts of modernity; the Gaguju may not. And even if they do survive in the modern world, the narrator dolefully informs us, "there will be no more true Gaguju people."

The point is clinched in the closing scene when, as the sun sets over the latest of the Gaguju's self-rejuvenating rituals, we are informed that one of the few remaining elders of the tribe died shortly after the program was completed. This elegiac gesture, although intended to mark respect, is distinctly double-edged. As Karla Armbruster suggests, National Geographic's message of ecological advocacy is often undercut by the apocalyptic visual symbolism it diffuses:

More often than not, the end-of-the show pleas for conservation are accompanied by an image of various animals [in this case, humans] against a setting sun, as if to warn viewers that they may be witnessing the end of the species as well as the end of the day. However, the sense that the sun's setting is inevitable, and that it will just as inevitably rise the next morning, may give viewers a false sense that the eradication of a particular species or its habitat is only "natural," in fact inevitable, and won't make much difference in the grand scheme of things anyway. (223)

This ambivalent view of the Gaguju appears in keeping with National Geographic's dominant social-evolutionist ideology, which consists in paying tribute to a passing way of life while implicitly celebrating the achievements of the Western modernity that has superseded it (Lutz and Collins, 24). The Gaguju will survive, it is implied, only if they adjust to the rapidly shifting expectations of modernity. Hence the program's focus on one of the tribe's younger members, currently employed as a Kakadu national park warden, who is constructed as a sympathetic intermediary figure, tentatively straddling the ancient traditions of the elders and a variety of modern Western interests and needs. This figure assumes the learner's role with which the program's spectators are encouraged to identify, as in several sequences where, listening intently, he absorbs the ancestral wisdom passed down to him by the elders he reveres. These sequences, while presented naturalistically, are obviously concocted. The camera freezes the performers in postures of almost surreal intensity, zooming in for close-ups that avoid the potential embarrassment of a directly confrontational gaze. "The story of Kakadu, as seen through the eyes of its last traditional inhabitants," is thus presented through the detached eye of the camera—a distancing mechanism enhanced by the use of voice-over, which ensures that the Gaguju's own version of the story, even as it is appropriated, is never told. The Gaguju, instead, are both (literally) silenced and (metaphorically) objectified within the context of a Western "salvage narrative" (Clifford, "Ethnographic") that uses fading memories of the Aboriginal Dreamtime to reinforce its own authorizing power. Gaguju culture, instrumentalized in this way, is only capable of being rescued insofar as it is embalmed as the ensemble of its own aesthetic practices—cherished, in itself, as a work of art. The key role is given here to the readily identifiable type of the tribal painter. This particular artist works on bark; his prehistoric ancestors worked on rock. But the art of both, stretching across the ages, symbolizes a desire to imaginatively represent, and thus preserve, the seamless continuity of all life-forms in the face of repeating patterns of technological disruption and environmental decline.

Needless to say, it is a white, rather than an indigenous, ecological vision that is being proposed here. Terry Goldie summarizes the paradigm well in his study of images of the indigene in Canadian, Australian, and New Zealand literature: "[White] texts which represent the indigene as an emissary of untouched nature and fear the ecological dangers of white technology turn to the indigene as environmentalist. . . . The embrace of the indigene is thus presented . . . as a return to a whole, before the 'abstracting and splitting' of civilized life" (36). "Australia's Twilight of the Dreamtime" combines at least three of the standard commodities Goldie associates with indigeneity: *nature, mysticism,* and the *prehistoric.* It would be a mistake, however, to assume that the program, and others of its kind, should only be read in this dismissively critical manner. National Geographic, after all, has undergone a series of significant transformations during its hundred-year-plus history, replacing its earlier, largely escapist view of non-Western peoples with a more nuanced appreciation of their—and our—social and environmental problems, and engaging more critically with the ideological implications of its own voyeuristic photography, its glamorized science, and its complacent Western-centered, predominantly white male middle-class view of the world. While National Geographic photographs, magazines, and films are still very much in the tradition of Eurocentric photojournalism, the arresting images they provide increasingly allow for alternative readings that challenge the self-privileging view of the "photographer as supertourist, an extension of the anthropologist . . . visiting natives and bringing back news of their exotic doings and strange gear" (Sontag, quoted in Lutz and Collins, 231). National Geographic's approach, however, remains touristic in the basic sense that it confirms the mobility and privileges of its First World readers/spectators over and against its Third and Fourth World subjects, these latter being presented all too often as historically out of touch and geographically rooted in place. National Geographic's conflicted attitudes toward the environment persist in its apolitical tributes to the beauty of "unspoilt nature," while its ambivalence toward modernity

continues to be played out in its aestheticized representations of indigenous peoples and their symbiotic connection to the natural world (Lutz
and Collins, 95). As Wilson insists, the popular study of nature in National Geographic films has become an "object of a much larger investigation of the world that goes under many names, among them science,
colonialism, and tourism" (148). This investigation continues apace today in works that, even as they endorse "the holistic cause of indigenous ecology" (Goldie, 37), breathe new life into old colonialist myths
about the place of non-Western "peoples of nature" in a changing modern world.

A very different type of nature program, though one that lays claims
to a similar conservationist mission, is Animal Planet's popular *Crocodile Hunter* series, hosted by the flamboyant Australian naturalist Steve
Irwin (who died in 2006) and Terri, his equally voluble American wife.
The series, which has attracted hundreds of millions of viewers since its
inception in the early 1990s, features a highly marketable blend of ge-
nial storytelling and ingenuous machismo, both of these embodied in
the larger-than-life figure of Irwin, a latter-day incarnation of the well-
known topos of the fieldworking scientist-as-buffoon.[25] Irwin's croco-
dile-catching exploits, combining the melodramatic athleticism of mud
wrestling, bullfighting, and rodeo-style gymnastics, are inserted into the
framework of a family-oriented education vehicle that aims to show its
international audience the value of respecting and protecting native
wildlife. Paradoxically, "wildness" is defined here, not by removal from
but rather exposure to human interference. Priding itself on bringing its
audience "up close to nature in the raw," the series uses hand-held cam-
eras and a variety of other low-tech equipment to convey the deliberate
encroachment on these animals' fiercely protected territory, the staged
invasion of their private space. Thus, while the series can provisionally
be placed at the extreme end of the participatory documentary spectrum, in which the audience expects "to witness the . . . world as represented by someone who actively engages with, rather than obtru-
sively observes, poetically reconfigures, or argumentatively assembles
[it]" (Nichols, 116), it also capitalizes on a dual formula well known to
other contemporary commercially successful nature documentary-
makers: the putatively educational attempt to win respect for animals
by commandeering them for entertainment ends.

Crocodile Hunter, in this context, operates on the sound commercial
principle of provoking the animals it promotes. In a scene from "Steve's

Most Dangerous Adventures," for example, Irwin steals up on a group of basking crocodiles, inviting them to attack him.[26] One duly does, sinking its teeth into his hand, but the unabashed Irwin claims later to have "learned from [this] mistake." Obviously not much, though, for in subsequent scenes we find him all over the globe, running the rapids with a herd of stampeding hippos, mixing it up with predatory Nile crocodiles, and—seeking out trouble where none exists—insistently poking a fugitive Egyptian cobra with a stick. Not surprisingly, the terrified snake makes a series of defensive lunges at Irwin and the camera, finally persuading its aggressor to wonder aloud whether it might not be better to "just leave this guy on his own." A further sequence in the same program sees Irwin chasing, and then being turned on by, a pack of enraged Komodo dragons, one of these taking a chunk out of his boot, which, he winningly tells us, is now a souvenir back home. In this relentless manner, the series accumulates the trophies of its presenter-hero's recklessness, even as he gamely attempts to convince us that he "is putting [himself] on the line to save the animals" he pursues.

Despite these occasional—and hardly persuasive—self-rationalizations, *Crocodile Hunter* is usually too glib, and nearly always too impatient, to fall into the patterns of the ponderously oracular and the dreamily sentimental that arguably define several of its best-known global-market competitors in the thriving nature-documentary genre. Its aesthetics, in any case, are those of postmodern pastiche, not romantic melodrama. Its cheerful triumphalism—part P. T. Barnum, part Crocodile Dundee—is undercut by the fatuousness of its protagonist's exhibitionist antics, while its staged excitements are often comically inept, taking on a farcical edge. (A good example of the latter is another scene from "Steve's Most Dangerous Adventures," when Irwin is invited to make a speech to the "fearsome" U.S. Rangers in Florida about the dangers posed by allegedly man-eating alligators in the wild. Irwin claims to be intimidated, but the Rangers themselves look less belligerent than bored. Their knuckle-headed response to Irwin's feeble attempt to butter them up ("you're the toughest blokes on earth") says a lot about the educational experience Irwin has in mind for this particular audience, while the strained atmosphere of mutual bravado provides another instance of the self-mocking machismo that has characterized several successful Australian export products such as, probably most notably, Peter Faiman's 1986 film *Crocodile Dundee*.[27]

While *Crocodile Hunter* is global in scope and certainly targets a worldwide audience, it also aims to create a familiar down-home feeling by including family footage (e.g., in the episode "Steve's Story")[28] and by focusing on regional conservation measures involving the rescue and relocation of "rogue" crocodiles considered to pose a threat to local farmers and other riverine wildlife. As might be expected, however, the emphasis falls not so much on the ecological intricacies of modern animal husbandry as on the stirring drama of physical capture—the traditional thrill of the chase. "Steve's Greatest Crocodile Captures" (1995), for example, offers a colorful variety of rudimentary capture methods. The standard drug-and-tag option is avoided, not because it is less humane but because it provides less interest for the camera.[29] Instead, crocodiles are trip-wired, encircled in nets, dragged around on ropes, loaded blindfolded into homemade, coffin-like boxes. In one scene, a particularly recalcitrant croc is finally pinned down and eight burly Australian men pile in on top of the thrashing body. (Irwin sits, appropriately, on the head.) Meanwhile, crocodile capture, both in the wild and at the family-run Australian Zoo, is transformed into a highly lucrative public spectacle.[30] Some of the best specimens, released into captivity at the zoo, become instant family favorites, provoked from time to time by Irwin and his band of eager helpers into performing for the ever-present camera and in one case, gratifyingly, destroying it. ("You see," explains Irwin, "Charlie really hates people"—which is presumably why he's in a zoo, stared at all day by tourists and watched in turn by millions on TV.)

Crocodile Hunter is aware, even crudely so, of its own commercial basis. Documentary information—on the specificities of animal habitat, the history of human-animal conflict, the practical implications of conservation ethics, and so on—is never allowed to get in the way of a good rollicking adventure. Little knowledge is conveyed, in fact, about the animals whose interests the series claims to be representing. (Irwin in a cage surrounded by marauding sharks: "I have no idea what species they are, but I do know they're big!") Rather, animals are seen and judged largely in terms of the—possibly mortal—danger they pose to humans, a danger the programs themselves are designed to court, so that the conflicts they claim to be defusing are the same ones they continually recreate. The commercial success of Australia Zoo, and other Irwin-financed conservation ventures, suggests that publicity—even the negative publicity Irwin inevitably attracted—is an important part of the global drive for conservationist support. The even greater success of the *Crocodile Hunter* series suggests that knockabout comedy may be a more appropriate vehicle than moralizing anthropomorphic sentiment in generating sympathy for animals and a greater desire to understand the delicate ecological systems to which they, and we, belong.[31] Notwithstanding, *Crocodile Hunter* to some extent inherits the mantle of the older, "anti-conquistadorial" National Geographic-style nature documentary it ostensibly replaces (Pratt). For even as it exuberantly engages in one kind of conflict (individual, physical), *Crocodile Hunter* does its level best to avoid another (social, political). Displacement is the order of the day; as if the dangerous encounter with wild animals were the ironic guarantee of a certain ideological detachment, a sanctioned refusal to acknowledge the social conflicts and political entanglements of those who place their stakes in the increasingly globalized conservation game.

Whatever the case, *Crocodile Hunter* makes little effort to account for the social implications of the conservation effort in Australia (competing environmental lobbies and management programs, rival landowners' claims, the ongoing dispute over indigenous entitlement), let alone elsewhere in the world where Irwin claims—however tongue-in-cheek—to be saving endangered wildlife. In this sense, up-to-the-minute programs like *Crocodile Hunter,* for all their postmodern knowingness and naked commercial opportunism, in some ways represent a throwback to an earlier, ideologically "innocent" National Geographic era whose time, if not yet fully acknowledged as past, may soon enough be gone. In assuming the transparency—the automatically shared goals—of the global conservation effort, such programs claim authority in the name of a carefully cultivated naïveté; and what better figure for that (false) naïveté than Steve Irwin, television's celebrated crocodile hunter, leading his spirited legion of Western middle-class viewers on the energetic chase to save the world's wildlife?

Conclusion

To some extent, eco-travel writing, insofar as it wishes to reflect upon pressing real-world problems, will always be likely to raise larger doubts about the social efficacy of travel writing as an interventionist genre. After all, it might well be asked, how can a genre traditionally known for

Eurocentric self-indulgence and nostalgic adventurism hope to address complex socioeconomic and ethical questions in anything other than a superficial, even an ideologically dubious, way? This chapter has suggested that, while travel writers' efforts to intervene in current environmental debates are well worth making, there remain formidable problems. The cost of popularizing environmental issues may be an impulse toward sensationalism or trivialization (an impulse by no means restricted to eco-travel writing, of course, and one that can be found in a great deal of media-conscious environmental debate). At times, as in other travel texts, popularization is also a form of disguised—in some cases involuntary—anachronism, thereby revealing one of the constitutive paradoxes of travel writing: that the more it attempts to be informatively cutting-edge, the more it is likely to appear out of date. The latest disaster scenarios thus give rise to perhaps the predominant form of contemporary eco-travel writing, the romantic jeremiad, with the result that well-intentioned, often well-informed, attempts to ward off a potentially disastrous ecological future are precipitated back into nostalgic laments for a fondly imagined communitarian past.

One of the problems attached to this form of romantic nostalgia is that it underestimates human agency, the continuing role played by human beings in shaping their environment to their needs; instead, travel writing's traditional dialectic of explanation ("science") and mystification ("religion") is transposed onto the natural environment, which then becomes a kind of living museum for the wildlife watcher, as well as a sanctum for the reverentially "untouched." Such nature mysticism is apt to produce licensed voyeurism even as it lays claim to ecological responsibility, often in the name of an "environmental ethic" (E.O. Wilson) paradoxically invoked to *substitute* for more direct forms of social action. An added problem for the type of eco-travel writer interested in broad ethical issues such as speciesism (Singer) or the putatively inherent value of nature (Devall and Sessions) is the degree of detachment built into the traditional adventure-writing genre. As several commentators have pointed out, travel writing not only covers distance, it also helps create it (Kerridge). In the context of environmentally oriented travel writing, this may lead to necessarily compromised attempts to create fictions of human-animal intimacy or ecological involvement that merely reinforce the gap that separates perceiver from perceived, the human-centered from the wider natural world. The phenomenological basis of nature writing is an attempt, of course, to address this essentially irresolvable dilemma. But as Richard Kerridge suggests, travel writers—however environmentally conscious—are perhaps too fundamentally egotistic, too historically fixed by their desire for an "encounter with the exciting Other" (165), to meet the greater ecological imperative to acknowledge the global interdependencies, as well as local connections, that might work toward dismantling the ingrained differences and traditional taboos that reinforce the common view of travel writing as an almost inherently conservative cultural form.

Kerridge is perhaps unduly pessimistic about the potential of eco-travel writing to engage with serious environmental issues, although he does acknowledge that the environmental crisis has already given rise to new, ecologically inflected modes of writing that question, if not dispense with, recognizable older forms (164–65). To some extent, these new modes, which remain less experimental than they might be, are reflections of structural changes in the global tourist industry: the attempt, for example, to move toward more environmentally responsible or socially participatory ways of traveling; the growing commitment to the role tourism plays in promoting conservation and sustainable development, both at home and abroad. As previously suggested, this newfound social and environmental awareness is often subsumed under the rubric of ecotourism. Ecotourism continues to divide those sympathizers who recognize the benefits of environmental sustainability (Fennell) from those skeptics who are more inclined to dismiss it as just another late-capitalist market trend (Gilbert). While eco-travel writing remains abreast of these concerns, it should not be seen as a direct consequence of the partial shift to ecotourism. Rather, like so many of their companions in the genre, eco-travel writers are often given to present themselves as embattled iconoclasts, and are much more likely to denounce tourism, in whatever form it might manifest itself, than to defend it.

A brief foray into two 1990s Lonely Planet books on Costa Rica, Rob Rachowiecki's guidebook *Costa Rica* (first published in 1991, reissued in 1997), and Stephen Benz's *Green Dreams: Travels in Central America* (1998), should suffice to demonstrate the ambivalence currently surrounding ecotourism. Both books concentrate, to some extent, on the ecotourism boom in Costa Rica. The boom, as is well known, has transformed the environmentally but also touristically minded Central American republic into a wildlife lover's paradise that indulges people's "dream . . . to see monkeys, sloths, caimans, sea turtles and exotic birds in their natural habitat" (Rachowiecki, n.p.); or, as Benz puts it more sardonically, into "ecotourism's wonderland, the place where green dreams come true" (105). At first sight, Benz's travel narrative, replete with (self-)deprecating insights, might be taken as an ironic counterpoint to the guidebook's familiar commercial myths. On closer inspection, however, a parallel skepticism can be detected toward Costa Rica's efforts to balance the competing demands of two kinds of tourism: small-scale ecotourism and mass tourism. As Rachowiecki summarizes it:

> From the top levels of government on down, the debate has been fierce. Local and international tour operators and travel agents, journalists, developers, airline operators, hotel owners, writers, environmentalists, and politicians have all been vocal in their support of either ecotourism or mass tourism. Many believe the country is too small to handle both forms of tourism properly. (25)

Benz's adventures in Costa Rica confirm these latter suspicions. Ecotourism, Benz discovers, often has less to do with sustainable development than with the various, frequently devious ways in which government agencies and tour operators can sustain themselves. Environmental awareness emerges as the latest marketing venture, as emblematized in the "disappearing" tree frog, which duly reappears in "promotional brochures, on T-shirts, postcards and gift mugs" (116). Tree frogs are not so rare that they cannot be spirited up by local guides for photo opportunities; for after all, as Benz acknowledges, "photographing rare and vanishing species is one of the biggest thrills for ecotourists, and much of ecotourism's popularity is due to the popular desire to see forests, animals and tribal cultures before they disappear for good" (117). Both Rachowiecki and, especially, Benz echo recent criticisms of ecotourism as the neocolonialist "product of a racialized justification for modernization" (Bandy, 541). Oddly, however, this negative aspect to ecotourism operates less as a deterrent than as a stimulus to the potential eco-traveler, who is merely encouraged to cast the net wider in the search for an environment that is less "touristic" and therefore, by definition, less "spoiled." The standard commodities of alternative, nature-based tourism can thus once again be mobilized, from the nostalgia for "disappearing" forests, animals, and tribal cultures to the "authenticity" such endangered species and cultures represent. Travel book and guidebook thus come together in advertising a highly marketable ironic self-consciousness that simultaneously demystifies and revitalizes the eco-traveler's utopian ambitions, at once frustrates and sustains his or her "green dreams."

In works like these, self-irony, in many respects the default mode of contemporary travel writing, signals the tactical awareness of an outdated romantic sensibility brought into unavoidable confrontation with incompatible modern trends. Certainly, the staged post-Enlightenment clash between a superseded, but still emotionally engaging, romantic idealism and a pragmatic imperative to keep pace with Western modernity goes some way toward accounting for the contradictions of eco-travel writing as both aspiring interventionist project and emergent literary genre. The utopian dimensions of much of the writing reflect these contradictions, illustrating eco-travel writers' awareness that nature cannot be "voiced" (or, for that matter, "saved") other than through human intervention; and that the sympathetic imagination cannot help but register the impossible necessity of crossing the species divide. This acknowledgment of the impossibility of its own ecocentric ambitions may sometimes plunge eco-travel writing into portentous lamentations about the inexorable fate of the "global commons" (Callicott), or into breast-beating pronouncements on the self-destructive human drive toward species extinction and environmental decline. At its best, however, eco-travel writing has been able to avoid the sentimental pieties that have proved so conducive to other forms of environmental discourse, and that have so often accompanied the (self-)redemptive mission of the Western conservation movement as it pontificates—often in defiance of the situated practices of other cultures—on how best to save the world. Eco-travel writing may well continue to share at least some of the colonialist attitudes that punctuate the history of Western travel writing. But it may also register a surprisingly clear and accessible understanding of the complex social, cultural, and economic issues at stake in negotiating the many locally situated environmental problems, as well as the larger structural environmental crises, that beset the world today. Accessibility remains eco-travel writing's strongest suit, even if the leap to activism has so far proved, perhaps by definition, to be problematic. By and

large, the genre appears better equipped to provide a modicum of passive—no doubt partial—understanding than to generate the active engagement that many of its practitioners encourage, and some of them
themselves energetically pursue. The jury is out on the immediate day-
to-day benefits of eco-travel writing. But despite their obvious limitations, eco-travel narratives, in reflecting on a variety of relevant issues,
provide a useful balance of entertainment and instruction, suggesting
that environmentalism, for all its own conspicuous faults, may yet prove
to be an effective mechanism for injecting greater social urgency into the
dangerously complacent modern travel-writing genre.

THREE

Un/Natural Disasters

Introduction

In their study *The Accelerated Sublime: Landscape, Tourism, and Identity* (2002), sociologists Claudia Bell and John Lyall pair ecotourism and adventure tourism as contemporary traveling practices that reactivate the sublime in such a way that their participants, "descendants of grand tourists viewing the 'sublime' landscape, no longer meander but [rather] accelerate through an increasingly compressed and hyperinscribed space. The passive viewing of nature has evolved to kinetic experience within this accelerated nature" (xii). Instances of the accelerated sublime can be seen in adrenaline-filled but still relatively safe leisure activities like alpine skiing, bungee jumping, and white-water rafting, while at the far end of the spectrum come base jumping, free diving, and other inherently dangerous activities that fall into the general, highly mediated category of "extreme sport." It goes without saying that even these more extreme pursuits have now become thoroughly commodified. The expanding leisure market controls, without ever fully domesticating, an ever-intensified search for experiential authenticity, inviting clients to be reckless by servicing their manufactured needs for the "more extreme, more dangerous, farther away, deeper, steeper, or faster," or by providing alternative outlets for a "retro-tourism" in which older, more endurance-based activities imply a "purer, less technologically mediated engagement with the site" (193).

The market's seemingly limitless capacity to reify the thrill of extreme sports and other related leisure/touristic activities in which privileged people competitively "put their lives in jeopardy for pleasure" (Ashcroft, xviii) might also help to explain the current vogue for *disaster tourism* in many parts of the First ("developed") and, particularly, the Third ("developing") Worlds. Disaster tourism embraces a wide variety of sometimes incompatible activities: from safely insulated, unashamedly voyeuristic appreciations of other people's extreme misfortunes, as in the commemorative disaster tour, to deliberately risky visits to current war-torn zones and dangerously unstable political sites. Disasters here, while usually man-made, may also be natural in their origins, although the category of the natural disaster nearly always involves some degree of human interference.[1] As disaster-relief experts generally agree, "Natural can be a misleading description for disasters such as the droughts, floods and cyclones which afflict much of the developing world. Recognizing these disasters as often un/natural, identifying the many human-made root causes and advocating structural and political changes to combat them, is long overdue" (Walter, 12).

This chapter aims to look at a selection of contemporary travelogs that are either responses to un/natural disasters or that appear to gravitate toward them, thriving on the awareness of danger and energetically courting extreme risk. These travelogs feature a number of what Kathleen Adams calls "danger-zone tourists." Danger-zone tourists, as defined by Adams, are "travelers who are drawn to areas of political turmoil. Their pilgrimages to strife-torn destinations are not for professional purposes but rather for leisure, although in some cases the professional identities of danger-zone tourists are related to their leisure pursuits" ("Danger-Zone Tourism," 266). Such tourists, who possess a wide range of motives and interests, run the gamut from worthy "humanitarian/activist travelers" to wildly irresponsible "adrenaline-rush pursuers," to discerning intelligence-gatherers "seeking first-hand journalistic experience" in turbulent sociopolitical sites. In this chapter, the definition of "danger-zone tourist" will be pushed still further to include extreme sportsmen, latter-day pioneer-explorers, and hardened professionals viewed as objects of tourism, and whose work, while not necessarily life-threatening, places them at dangerously high levels of risk. The stories in which these players feature encompass elements of the standard survival narrative (a staple, long since prone to parody, in the history of travel writing), while pushing it to the brink to visit new extremes of near-death experience and the fictionalized reconstruction of fatality. They are linked, loosely at best, by what Conrad's narrator Marlow famously describes in *Heart of Darkness* as "the fascination of the abomination" (10): by episodes of monstrous violence visited upon largely unsuspecting people; by heroic escapades gone horribly wrong; by apocalyptic scenarios of the world turned upside-down in which hugely destructive forces are, or are remembered as having been, unleashed.

Disaster writing of this kind is all too easy to dismiss as melodramatically fraught or crudely voyeuristic, merely taking to new and, some might argue, unacceptably morbid levels the opportunistic danger-mongering already inscribed within the travel-writing genre. A more nuanced response requires not only closer textual analysis but also a broadly historical understanding of the circumstances underlying the development of disaster writing as a distinct literary genre.[2] In the current context, three factors can be touched on that go some way toward explaining the enduring popularity of disaster tourism, its semantic correlates "thanatourism" (Seaton) and "dark tourism" (Lennon and Foley), and its contemporary narrative counterpart, the (post)modern disaster account.[3] These factors, to be treated briefly in turn here, are changes in the structure of leisure society under the conditions of postmodernity, the so-called crisis of masculinity, and the increasing normalization of disaster in "world risk society" (Beck).

As John Lennon and Malcolm Foley argue in their seminal study *Dark Tourism: The Attraction of Death and Disaster* (2000), so-called dark tourism points to "a fundamental shift in the way in which death, disaster and atrocity are being handled by those who offer associated tourism products" (3). This shift can be attributed to the changing circumstances of the (post)modern world under late capitalism, within whose relentlessly commercialistic ethos death and disaster have become further commodities "for consumption in a global communications market" (5). Dark tourism, in whose more extreme forms (e.g., thanatourism) acts or events that "might be deplorable or repugnant from a moral point of view [come to attain] considerable attraction as . . . spectator experience[s]" (Seaton, 234), stages narratives of suffering via media replication, offering a seemingly endless series of simulacral reenactments of often violent individual and collective death.[4] This theatricalization of death and the events surrounding it is paradoxical on several different fronts. On the one hand, it allows for the repackaging of an at best morally ambivalent touristic curiosity as socially responsible, mass-therapeutic compassion in the context of the "postemotional society" (Meštrović). On the other, it blurs the boundary between the private sphere of death, previously sanctioned by the respectful distance that Western bourgeois commemorative practices have traditionally observed toward it, and the public spaces of commerce and the media, thereby creating a signal tension between (mass) touristic mediations of hyperreal experience and the assertion of death itself as "the ultimate signifier of the real" (Phipps, 83).[5] These contradictions are well captured in the transformation of notorious "black spots"— mass grave sites, concentration camps, battlefields, grisly scenes ranging in scale from celebrity assassination to genocidal extermination— into fully serviced tourist attractions, and in the development of purportedly consciousness-raising "reality tours" that aim to give their clients firsthand experience of some of the world's most dangerous combat zones (Rojek, 170).[6]

The latter example points to the increasing visibility of the so-called leisure soldier (Diller and Scofidio), a virulent late-modern extension of Dean MacCannell's only part-ironic definition of tourists as "an expeditionary force without guns" (*Tourist,* xviii). "Leisure soldiers," simultaneously observers of war and war's would-be fringe participants, constitute a small but growing niche market in danger-zone tourism, well served by publications such as Robert Young Pelton's garishly sensationalist guidebook *The World's Most Dangerous Places* (1998). They represent an extreme version of the self-conferred view of "non-institutionalized travelers as 'risk-takers'" (Elsrud, 601): a view also supported by backpackers' all-too-familiar currency of hardship, which indicates that the dangers, both actual and fabricated, of budget travel function as a marker of value for that particular subgroup (607).

As Torun Elsrud suggests, the phenomenon of the risk-taking traveler rests solidly on "a historical foundation of colonial 'exploration' defined by *male* adventurers, in which adventure and risk are intertwined in a quest for progress" (601; emphasis added). While it is by no means the case, of course, that contemporary risk-takers are all men— Elsrud herself provides evidence to the contrary—a link can be posited between their exploits and what several social theorists currently refer to as a "crisis of masculinity" in late-modern Western society. As John MacInnes, for example, argues:

The public evaluation of masculinity has undergone a profound shift. What were once claimed to be manly virtues (heroism, independence, courage, strength, rationality, will, backbone, virility) have become masculine vices (abuse, destructive aggression, coldness, emotional inarticulacy, detachment, an inability to be flexible, to communicate, to empathize, to be soft, supportive or life-affirming). (47)

While the recent demographics of danger-zone tourism tend to suggest that the gender divide is not only being effectively challenged but is also quickly narrowing, signs of a male backlash can also be seen in the pursuit of reintensified ambitions: in high-risk endurance travel; in "participatory" combat tourism; in extreme sport. Action narratives are evolving, similarly, that either celebrate the exploits of the latest male adventurer-explorer or that, radically reinterpreting them as failures, attribute their shortcomings to anxieties over the changing role of manhood or to the perceived inadequacy of traditionally masculinist conceptions of determination, courage, and physical force.

Disaster writing takes on the mantle here of cautionary narrative, either by exhibiting the lethal recklessness of the individual risk-taker or by exposing the potentially devastating consequences of collective ideologies of risk. In this second context, a further connection emerges between the development of exacerbated forms of travel/writing in extremis and the evolution of a global "risk society" in which "the dark sides of progress [have] increasingly come to dominate social debate" (Beck, "World Risk Society," 2). As Ulrich Beck, usually credited with the coinage "risk society," suggests:

What no one saw and no one wanted—self-endangerment and the devastation of nature—is becoming the motor force of history. . . . Unlike the risks of early industrial society, contemporary nuclear, chemical, ecological, and biological threats are (1) not limitable, either socially or temporally; (2) not accountable according to the prevailing rules of causality, guilt and liability; and (3) neither compensable nor insurable . . . . [In the current dispensation,] the boundary between calculable risks and incalculable threats [is being increasingly] violated. To use an analogy, the regulating system for the "rational" control of industrial devastation is about as effective as a bicycle brake on a jetliner. (2)

While Beck's scenario of a "world contest between mega-risks for the title of most promising prospect of doom" (17) is unduly melodramatic, it gives a useful indication of the link between contemporary forms of high-risk tourism, the critical modes of travel writing and investigative journalism that accompany them, and more extreme apocalyptic visions of a terminally damaged world, inexorably impelled to self-destruct. In a global climate of potentially catastrophic self-endangerment—so this version of the argument might run—contemporary traveler-writers have responded by vigorously upping the ante. Displacing, but also extending, the genre's conventional "rhetoric of aggravation" (Holland and Huggan, 223, n. 28) onto current global conditions of social upheaval, political turmoil, and ecological devastation, increasing numbers of traveler-writers can be found enthusiastically intervening in the same violent imbroglios that "peace-loving" tourists are generally seen as going out of their way to avoid.

However, this is not necessarily to attribute to travel writing a newfound sense of social responsibility. The critical faculties of travel writing, after all, have historically proven to be limited. Traveler-writers' motives are nothing if not mixed: escapism, for many, is at least as likely to inspire as the opportunity for engagement; self-exonerating pleasure as likely to satisfy as self-reflexive concern. Perhaps it might be more appropriate in this context to see the realities of an endangered world as having begun to generate new and, in some cases, comparably self-destructive sources of touristic excitement. Alternative forms of enjoyment have sprung up in which endurance travel's conventional hardships are exchanged for the dysfunctional hedonisms of self-harm and suicidal self-deprivation; in which new levels of "visceral authenticity" (Adams) are sought that take one's own body past unimaginable pain-thresholds or conversely that seek, in the vicarious circumstances of witnessed disaster, to register an embodied appreciation for the full extent of other people's pain.[7]

These forms belong in part to a familiar postmodern cult of nostalgia in which what Bell and Lyall call the "retro-positioning" of the tourist indicates his or her attempt to recapture the authentic experience of extreme travel/exploration/adventure before modern technological advances made such potentially life-threatening activities and hazardous itineraries relatively secure (193, 88–89). But they are also at once responses to and symptoms of the routinization of disaster and widespread "compassion fatigue" induced, in large part, by the contemporary global media: simulacra of mass death; repeated news coverage of the latest ecological calamity or sociopolitical conflagration; rampant commodification of virtually all experiential modes of "the dangerous" and "the extreme" (Moeller). Notwithstanding, extreme travel, in both its "retro" and "accelerated" forms (Bell and Lyall), remains by definition dangerous; indeed, as Bell and Lyall predict at the end of their book, the boom in "participatory" disaster tourism is only likely to claim more casualties in the future, as sensation-seeking danger-zone tourists continue to outvie one another in their attempt, not just (passively) to witness but (actively) to experience the extreme. Travel writers, by and large, have been content to step back from, and in some cases to critique, these worst excesses, either by focusing—for obvious reasons—on autobiographical survival narratives, or by incorporating death and disaster into related subgenres such as the documentary reconstruction, the biographical portrait, and the eyewitness report. In exceptional cases, however, travel writers have been prepared to risk their lives in the pursuit of their literary livelihoods. One such case is that of the American adventurer-writer Jon Krakauer, and it is to Krakauer's vividly rendered account of a calamitous 1996 Everest expedition, *Into Thin Air* (1997), that the chapter turns next.

Death Zones

There is no more commodified site of extreme travel than Mount Everest, which has claimed well over a hundred deaths since it was opened up for commercial climbing in the second half of the twentieth century (Ortner). While Everest has always been "the paramount object of mountaineering desire in popular culture" (Slemon, 25), its very popularity has proved to be its downfall; so much so that the world's highest mountain, succumbing to the banality of extremity, now increasingly resembles—in Stephen Slemon's appropriately breathless mix of metaphors—"a mainstreet, a traffic-jam, a ship-of-fools party on the rooftop of the world" (25). Everest, for so long a rarefied object of colonial desire, has long since been transformed into a global site of mass consumption. As Slemon muses, "The old colonial question—[to] whom does Everest belong?—[has now become] postcolonial, reflective and brooding: 'who belongs on Everest?'" (25). A cynical version of the answer would be: anyone who can afford it. Climbers from all over the world, some with precious little mountaineering experience, now line up each year for the chance to "conquer" Everest, many of them shep-herded up the mountain by rival teams of expert guides whose com-pany names (e.g., Adventure Consultants) indicate the marriage of ex-treme sport and undisguised commercialism that characterizes the modern Everest experience. The sheer quantity of climbers on its slopes has hardly made the mountain less dangerous, however, and despite significant advances in technology, well-prepared trails to the top (e.g., the much-derided Yak Route), and no shortage of technical expertise and support, a combination of human error, physical exhaustion, and highly volatile weather conditions still claims more than its fair share of victims on Everest. Fatality has become normalized in the booming Everest business, with ascents arguably being measured less in terms of success than those of failure, and with "the risk of serious or fatal acci-dent," as the anthropologist Sherry Ortner provocatively puts it, "pro-duc[ing] the payoff of meaning," not least for mountaineers—both pro-fessional and amateur—themselves (139). Mountaineering literature, Ortner contends, revolves around the glorification of the victim, citing in support one writer who has gone so far as to suggest, tongue only half in cheek, that "unlike any other sport, mountaineering demands that its players die" (Barcott, quoted in Ortner, 139). Celebrity and death, as theorists as diverse as Ortner, Maurice Blanchot, and Elisa-beth Bronfen have argued, are the complementary ingredients most likely to produce mass-mediated success.[8] Certainly this is true—though not in all cases—for failed Everest expeditions, several of which have been memorably captured for the camera or sealed "immortally" in print.

The American journalist Jon Krakauer's contribution to Everest lore, *Into Thin Air: A Personal Account of the Mount Everest Disaster* (1997), is one of the best of a veritable assembly line of commercially successful disaster narratives that present eyewitness accounts of acci-dental fatality while also registering borderline experiences of personal survival. The story graphically recounts one of the worst Everest disas-ters in recent decades. During a violent storm high up on the mountain, the guided expedition in which Krakauer has been commissioned to take part loses four of its eight members, while several other climbers in parallel expeditions bring up the death toll to twelve in the space of only a couple of days. Krakauer, who survives the ordeal but has been understandably traumatized by it, sees his book as the "fruit of [his] compulsion" to relive the disaster and to purge himself of its memory (xii). This dual motive results in a suspense-filled but also morally anxious narrative, uneasily poised between alternative drives toward ghoulish fascination and dutifully mournful respect. Like many other such disaster narratives, *Into Thin Air* offers a part self-registered, part vicarious pleasure in affliction and a metaphysical counterpoint—some might call it an alibi—that helps translate catastrophic misadventure into transformative spiritual quest. In this context, climbing is seen, in contradistinction to other shamelessly egotistic extreme sports, as a self-chastening endurance trial driven by the quest not for momentary thrills but an achieved state of transcendence:

> Above the comforts of Base Camp, the expedition in fact became an almost Calvinistic undertaking. The ratio of misery to pleasure was greater by an order of magnitude than any other mountain I'd been on; I quickly came to understand that climbing Everest was primarily about enduring pain. And in subjecting ourselves to week after week of toil, tedium, and suffering, it struck me that most of us were probably seeking, above all else, something like a state of grace. (174)

This attainment of grace is likened to a stripping-down of life to the bare essentials, a "clear[ing] of the mind of trivialities" (92): a Zen-like exercise apparently confirmed by the insertion of the text into a genealogy of spiritually oriented mountaineering narratives that ally the rigors of physical exertion to those of metaphysical speculation, and that work, through a kind of willed congruence of the literal and the metaphorical, toward raising mountaineering history to the still giddier elevations of Western literary myth. Within this communal mythology, "climbing [becomes] a magnificent activity . . . not in spite of the inherent perils, but precisely because of them" (352). Krakauer recognizes, at the same time, that the noble life-philosophy that underpins the modern-day "culture of ascent" (23) sometimes amounts to little more than a clinical form of self-delusion. Everest, he admits, "has always been a magnet for kooks, publicity seekers, hopeless romantics, and others with a shaky hold on reality" (114). Such "Walter Mittys with Everest dreams" (358), as he calls them derisively elsewhere, are a menace both to themselves and to others; they are also a reminder that the mountain has become a factory for the production of celebrity, a socially differentiated site, as one embittered Sherpa puts it, for "those rich, arrogant outsiders who feel that they can conquer the world" (Krakauer, 370).

As Slemon suggests, Everest's still considerable symbolic capital is now invested in primarily neocolonial interests: "Climbing Everest still carries . . . the capacity to consecrate, but only for those benighted national administrators and . . . calculating corporate entities sufficiently distant from contemporary Everest realities to know what climbing Everest, now, really means" (26). If exploitation has become the norm, both for Everest ascents and Everest narratives, it seems almost "impossible for mountaineering literature . . . to frame a critique of classic [colonialist] Everest climbing practices without implicitly endorsing the neo-colonial discursive contract that underwrites the dominant idea of 'Everest' in the present" (26–27). Krakauer's narrative finds itself caught, accordingly, in a double bind. On the one hand, it is duty-bound to criticize the commercial opportunism that has rapidly overtaken the mountain, as captured for instance in the corporate triumphalism in which Everest expeditions are often framed, and for which they have increasingly become known. ("We've got the big E figured out, we've got it totally wired," drawls one high-profile guide, Scott Fischer, later ironically to lose his life on the mountain: "These days, I'm telling you, we've built a yellow brick road to the summit" [86].) On the other, it is forced to recognize its own complicity in the combination of tawdry circumstances—amateur ambition, corporate greed, media sensationalism, socioeconomic inequality—that have turned Third World attractions like Everest into notorious death zones, as well as expensive tourist traps. Krakauer himself is similarly torn between his distaste for the media frenzy that immediately followed the disaster and his awareness of his own later journalistic contribution to it; and while he vehemently contests the accusation—an occupational hazard of disaster writing—that he might have capitalized on other people's misery, he freely admits that he has probably angered friends and relatives of the disaster's victims by including speculative, at times critical, portraits of them in his account (349–55, 375).[9]

Alert to these controversies, the text, like the journey it reenacts, maintains a high degree of interpretive caution, even as the action unfolds amid a conjunction of sharply defined extremities: extreme elevation, extreme weather, extreme physical/mental strain and, in the end, extreme exhaustion. This combination of equivocation and excess is characteristic of a genre caught on the cusp between self-congratulatory survival tale and self-admonishing obituary; it can be attributed more closely here to Krakauer's ironic manipulation of the sacrificial rhetoric of mountaineering literature, a resolutely purist form of end-oriented travel writing in which, as Slemon puts it, "[the] narrative need for death . . . is grounded to the suturing of nostalgia for the mountain to nostalgia for the mountaineer" (21).

Into Thin Air is well aware of the self-defeating nature of its own nostalgia. On the surface, it wishes to invoke the glories of the pioneering conquests, feats that can only now be mimicked by defiantly tempting fate, by pushing the envelope of risk: "Prestige was earned [in the intensely competitive global mountaineering community] by tackling the most unforgiving routes with minimal equipment, in the boldest style imaginable. Nobody was admired more than the so-called free soloists: visionaries who ascended alone, without rope or hardware" (23). But such heroics, on present-day Everest, are just as likely to come across as self-indulgent antics. In a compensatory move, Krakauer turns his attention to the mountain's history of failures. Over time, these failures have turned the mountain's slopes into a staggered memorial of frozen corpses: the congealed remains of anonymous climbers whose disconcerting presence, however fleetingly it is recognized, is uneasily suppressed. But even here, death, robbed of its transfigurative power, appears strangely anticlimactic:

> At 21,000 feet . . . I came upon a large object wrapped in blue plastic sheeting beside the trail. It took my altitude-impaired gray matter a minute or two to comprehend that the object was a human body. Shocked and disturbed, I stared at it for several minutes. That night when I asked [the guide] Rob about it he said he wasn't certain, but he thought the victim was a Sherpa who'd died three years earlier. . . . At 21,300 feet . . . I came upon another body in the snow, or more accurately the lower half of a body. The style of the clothing and the vintage boots suggested that the victim was European and that the corpse had lain on the mountain for at least ten or fifteen years. . . . Few of the climbers trudging by had given either corpse more than a passing glance. It was as if there was an unspoken agreement on the mountain to pretend that these desiccated remains weren't real—as if none of us dared to acknowledge what was at stake here. (138–39)

Krakauer falls into line here with the thesis, itself nostalgic, that "death on Everest has [irretrievably] lost its suturing power. The bodies of dead climbers now litter the standard assault routes on Everest, and climbers take photos; but dead mountaineers now can never quite be-come the mountain—mourning is trivial, and the suture [between mountaineer and mountain] cannot take place" (Slemon, 26).

When death becomes banal, disaster writing can ill afford to pass it-self off as tragic; and yet this is precisely what Krakauer's narrative at-tempts to do. The opening epigraph, from the Spanish writer José Or-tega y Gasset, might hold a clue to unravelling the puzzle. The epigraph reads: "Men play at tragedy because they do not believe in the reality of the tragedy which is actually being staged in the civilised world." As with many of the epigraphs scattered throughout the text, there are sev-eral different ways to read this. A literal reading might imply that mountaineering, as an "activity that idealizes risk-taking" (358), is in-herently escapist; another equally valid reading, turning the first one around, would see such risks as last-ditch attempts to recover a sense of authenticity in a world increasingly difficult to experience as genuine or real. *Into Thin Air* maintains a balance between these equal and oppo-site readings. The text, framed as a tragedy complete with a full cast of dramatis personae and an epilogue (xix–xxvii, 367–74), proceeds to restage events that actually happened. Yet these real events, tragic though their consequences are for a number of individuals, may work to hide other realities (e.g., the larger connection between economic ex-ploitation and the devaluing of human life) that are more devastating still. Several different morals can be drawn here, each of which has wider implications for the disaster narrative/extreme travel writing nexus. One moral, even as it confirms the constitutive nature of repre-sentation, might point to the status of disaster writing as a paradoxi-cally *derealizing* genre. Another might stress the human causes of a tragedy brought on by a violent unleashing of the elements, and skill-fully dramatized as a variation on that clichéd form of divine punish-ment: "nature's revenge" (Buell). And a third, bringing the first two to-gether, might show the frequent emptiness of the genre's own moralizing:

> Walter Mittys with Everest Dreams need to bear in mind that when things go wrong up in the Death Zone—and sooner or later they al-ways do—the strongest guides in the world may be powerless to save a client's life; indeed, as the events of 1996 demonstrated, the strongest guides in the world are sometimes powerless to save even their own

lives. Four of my teammates died [including two guides] not so much because Rob Hall's [the expedition leader's] systems were faulty . . . but because on Everest it is the nature of systems to break down with a vengeance. (358)

That extreme travel writing is built, for all these dire moral injunctions, on perceived hierarchies of recklessness is reconfirmed in another, slightly earlier Krakauer best seller, *Into the Wild* (1996). *Into the Wild* recounts the story of Christopher McCandless, a young drifter from a well-to-do American family, who perished in the Alaskan wilderness in 1992. As in *Into Thin Air*, visionary quest narrative alternates with cautionary evolutionist parable, with McCandless's death by starvation being seen as a tragic example of "risk-taking [pushed] to its logical extreme" (182). McCandless's obsessions, Krakauer implies, are also partly his own, with narrator and protagonist trading places in a morality play exploring "the grip wilderness has on the American imagination, [as well as] the allure high-risk activities hold for young men of a certain mind" (Author's Note, n.p.). Thus, while McCandless's death might more easily be seen as the avoidable outcome of a combination of muddle-headed incompetence and adolescent arrogance, Krakauer insists on reading him as he appears to have read himself, as the heroic victim of an obsessive pursuit of individual freedom mutating into sacrificial creed. *Into the Wild*, in this last sense, is a work of sympathetic imagination in which Krakauer, who sees himself to some extent as a kindred spirit, attempts to get inside McCandless's character, to mimic the state of his psychological intensity and his eventual distress. Piecing together McCandless's story from interviews, letters, local-historical research, and snippets from McCandless's journal, Krakauer works toward assembling a vicarious travel narrative that combines elements of the inner biography, the survival-oriented adventure tale, and the metaphysically laden disaster account.

As in *Into Thin Air*, Krakauer makes good use of sometimes lengthy epigraphs from a number of disparate literary sources. Many of these epigraphs are drawn from books McCandless himself had been reading during his travels, which are discovered later in the bush along with his partly decomposing remains. With their help, Krakauer places McCandless within a tradition of mostly adolescent spiritual seekers, romantically "drawn . . . by nothing more than a hunger of the spirit, a yearning of such queer intensity that it beggars the modern imagination" (96–97). Meanwhile, the epigraphs function—again as in *Into Thin Air*—as a kind of alternative route-map, illustrating the twists and turns in McCandless's densely tangled psychological and emotional life. One such epigraph, from the American writer Theodore Roszak, refers to "the bad habit of creative talents to invest themselves in pathological extremes that yield remarkable insights but no durable way of life" (quoted in Krakauer, 70). But what evidence is there of McCandless's "creative talent"? And where are the "insights" yielded by his experiences? As Krakauer suggests, a convincing case can be made for McCandless as a fractious, psychologically confused narcissist, a "dreamy half-cocked greenhorn who went into the country expecting to find answers to all his problems and instead found only mosquitoes and a lonely death" (72).

Predictably enough, this view comes close to Krakauer's self-mocking reminiscence of some of his own near-fatal adolescent mountaineering escapades, which reveal a "youth who mistook passion for insight and acted according to an obscure, gap-ridden logic" in the pursuit of deliberately self-endangering goals (155). Krakauer identifies in himself, as he does in McCandless, a certain "psycho-neurotic tendency" (135), evidenced in the melodramatic tendency to turn the physical demands of extreme travel into a form of self-instantiated suffering, a displaced penance or pilgrimage that effects temporary release from "the accumulated clutter" of everyday life (143). This "action neurosis," as Frank McLynn in a related context calls it, is driven by sometimes wildly irrational impulses, but Krakauer falls short of calling it a mental illness or of mistaking "appalling innocence" and "hubris" for a death wish of the "agitated soul" (155).[10] Instead, he finds himself drawn to *defend* McCandless by seeing him as having attempted an "evolutionary" rite of passage, a fiercely uncompromising physical/mental trial in accordance with the "moral absolutism" of his beliefs (182):

> [McCandless] was fully aware when he entered the bush that he had given himself a perilously slim margin for error. He knew precisely what was at stake. . . . It is hardly unusual for a young man to be drawn to a pursuit considered reckless by his elders; engaging in risky behavior is a rite of passage in our culture no less than in most others.

. . . It can be argued that youthful derring-do is in fact evolutionarily adaptive, a behavior encoded in the genes. McCandless, in his fashion, merely took risk-taking to its logical extreme. (182)

For all his insistence that McCandless "didn't conform particularly well to the [dysfunctional] bush-casualty stereotype" (85), Krakauer portrays him as a young man singularly ill-adapted to the ways of the modern world. A classic "retro-traveler," to the point of self-parody, McCandless disdains even the more rudimentary forms of technological assistance that might have saved him. His are the inept survival fantasies of a self-described "aesthetic voyager" (165): a confused young man reared on the dated adventure novels of London and Kerouac; an out-of-touch romantic who, in determining to live his life according to the dictates of *Doctor Zhivago* and *Walden,* "wander[s] across North America in search of raw, transcendent experience" (Author's Note, n.p.); a would-be philosopher-writer who seeks to engage his overheated imagination by scribbling banalities in his journal about the "Insurpassable Joy of the Life Aesthetic" (168).

An epigraph, taken from an underlined passage in *Doctor Zhivago,* provides an insight into the "collective cliché" of an idealistic dreamer whose misguided wilderness doctrine, allied to his propensity for "contrived ascetism" and his "pseudo-literary" inclinations, eventually combine to put his own life at risk (72). In the passage, Pasternak's narrator describes "the two basic ideals of modern man . . . without [which] he is unthinkable . . . the idea of free personality and the idea of life as sacrifice" (quoted in Krakauer, 187). This sacrificial pact is later clinched in a breathless vision of McCandless's excruciating final moments: a time, Krakauer chooses to remember, when "the hunger vanishes, the terrible pain dissolves, and the suffering is replaced by a sublime euphoria, a sense of calm accompanied by transcendent mental clarity" (198). Accorded a mental clarity in death he rarely appears to have had in life, McCandless is sublimated into another of Krakauer's self-immolating counterculture heroes. This self-lionizing process is confirmed by a near-death, self-taken photograph of the woefully emaciated traveler, in which he strikes a defiant pose "under the high Alaska sky, one hand holding his final note toward the camera lens, the other raised in a brave, beatific farewell" (199). At the same time, the sheer *physicality* of Krakauer's description of McCandless's agonizing death indicates the price to be paid for substituting romantic idealism for practical knowledge, supporting the alternative view of McCandless as a foolishly self-destructive egotist, hooked on secondhand visions of "the wild" as a sanctified, countercivilizational space:[11] "Starvation is not a pleasant way to expire. In advanced stages of famine, as the body begins to consume itself, the victim suffers muscle pain, heart disturbances, loss of hair, dizziness, shortness of breath, extreme sensitivity to cold, physical and mental exhaustion" (198).

The rapt attention to physiological detail, here as elsewhere, registers a voyeuristic pleasure that exceeds the protocols of compassion. This pleasure is linked, in turn, to a sense of narrative fulfillment, with death finally achieved as the predetermined telos of a journey with no obvious geographical destination, no foreseeable end in sight. (Despite the sketchy information provided by the frontispiece map, McCandless's travels are directionless, inconsequential, nonreferential even; what interests Krakauer is the irreversible *narrative* process by which McCandless is driven, through an accumulated series of mostly avoidable errors and accidents, ever closer to his own destruction.) This narrative insistence is redoubled by the force of repetition: McCandless as mimic man, living out the myths of his literary heroes; Krakauer as secondary mimic, reenacting McCandless's fatal quest. Disaster narrative can be seen here as manipulating the "belatedness" of contemporary travel writing, using it to convey the illusion of an inevitable outcome, a pre-scripted version of unalterable events. Needless to say, there is nothing "natural" about the disaster being presented here; rather, what is naturalized is a vision of attenuated human agency, as the ever-weakening McCandless is rendered helpless by the disaster he had theoretically invited but has neither the practical intelligence nor the physical endurance to resist.

Maurice Blanchot, in an interesting passage in his correspondingly extreme philosophical reflections, *The Writing of the Disaster* (1995), also points to the temptations of passivity in the face of disaster. "The disaster," claims Blanchot, speaking in broadly phenomenological terms,

> is not of capital importance. Perhaps it renders death vain. It does not superimpose itself upon dying's scope for withdrawal, filling in the void. Dying sometimes gives us (wrongly, no doubt), not the feeling of

abandoning ourselves to the disaster, but the feeling that if we were to die, we would escape it. . . . The disaster . . . exposes us to a certain idea of passivity. (2–3)

Krakauer's factual account of McCandless's death is antithetical, in several respects, to Blanchot's deliberately abstruse theoretical speculations on disaster as a fundamentally indeterminate concept (116–17). Recognizing McCandless's romanticism for his own, Krakauer clearly wants to see him as having achieved the very release Blanchot would deny him. Disaster, for Blanchot, is precisely *not* about the attribution of significance to dying; on the contrary, it is a form of "limit-text" (28) that denies transcendence even as it gestures toward it. For both Krakauer and Blanchot, however—despite the apparent ludicrousness of the comparison—disaster writing is marked by the inevitable failure of its desire to make sense of other people's deaths, to wrest significance from their dying; and to attempt, impossibly, to make other people's yearning for the infinite one's own. Krakauer, ironically reflecting on his dreamy adolescence, ratchets up the high-romantic rhetoric with yet another implied analogy:

[In my youth] I didn't yet appreciate [death's] terrifying finality or the havoc it could wreak on those who'd entrusted the deceased with their hearts. I was stirred by the dark mystery of mortality. I couldn't resist stealing up to the edge of doom and peering over the brink. The hint of what was concealed in those shadows terrified me, but I caught sight of something in the glimpse, some forbidden elemental riddle that was no less compelling than the sweet, hidden petals of a woman's sex. . . . In my case—and, I believe in the case of Chris Mc-Candless—that was a very different thing from wanting to die. (155–56)

Krakauer's two best-known books are generally successful in upholding this distinction, even as they argue for the need to radically reinvent the survival-writing genre. Above all, books such as *Into Thin Air* and *Into the Wild* are vicarious meditations on death designed to test the experiential limits of travel writing. Disaster provides the link between the "too-far" (travel without return, the death of the traveler) and the "not-far-enough" (extreme travel that "plays at tragedy," that flirts with death by approximating or aspiring to the experiences of "martyred" travelers). Under the sign of the disaster, the survival ethos collapses on its own internally self-contradictory logic; thus it is, with death as their goal, that vicariously experienced travel narratives like Krakauer's are organized, in defiance of the conventions of the genre, around the necessary impossibility of return.

Into Thin Air and *Into the Wild* are critical accounts of a fatally misguided but still somehow cherishable "hunger of the spirit" (*Into the Wild*, 96), for which the most obvious objective correlative is a landscape of the *sublime*. In another 1990s best-selling disaster account, Sebastian Junger's *The Perfect Storm* (1997), a powerful dosage of popular—mostly medical and meteorological—science, added to the familar generic ingredients of adventure writing and semifictional biography, makes for a riveting incursion into what might provisionally be called the "scientific sublime."[12] Ostensibly, *The Perfect Storm* recounts the true, but self-admittedly embellished, story of a storm of epic proportions—claimed to be one of the most potent of the century (x)—that devastated America's North Atlantic seaboard in 1991, causing millions of dollars of terrestrial damage and claiming several maritime lives. Junger's focus is on the last days of an imperiled commercial fishing-boat, the *Andrea Gail,* which sank in huge seas off the coast of Nova Scotia in late October 1991, and whose six-man crew, presumably going under with it, have never been traced. Given the disappearance of the crew, Junger must rely on imaginative reconstruction, as performed in the culminating narrative sequence when he recounts, in vivid detail, the hypothetical experiences of the dying men (140–45). As elsewhere in the text, Junger proceeds by analogy, reconstructing the men's last panic-stricken moments by means of partial evidence drawn from existing nautical records, seamen's logs, and medical accounts of death by drowning. It is this last documentary source that catches the eye, not only for the chilling accuracy of its impersonal technical language but also for its approximation of the sublime, as registered in the vicarious experience of disaggregated bodies subjected to extreme conditions:

> The central nervous system does not know what has happened to the body; all it knows is that not enough oxygen is getting to the brain. Orders are still being issued—*Breathe! Pump! Circulate!*—that the body cannot obey. If the person were defibrillated at that moment, he might possibly survive. He could be given cardiopulmonary resuscitation, put on a respirator, and coaxed back to life. Still, the body is doing everything it can to delay the inevitable. When cold water touches

the face, an impulse travels along the trigeminal and vagus nerves to the central nervous system and lowers the metabolic rate. The pulse slows down and the blood pools where it's needed most, in the heart and skull. It's a sort of temporary hibernation that drastically reduces the body's need for oxygen. . . . The diving reflex, as this is called, is compounded by the general effect of cold temperature on tissue. . . . The crew of the *Andrea Gail* do not find themselves in particularly cold water, though; it may add five or ten minutes to their lives. And there is no one around to save them anyway. The electrical activity in their brain gets weaker and weaker until, after fifteen or twenty minutes, it ceases altogether. . . . The body could be likened to a crew that resorts to increasingly desperate measures to keep their vessel afloat. Eventually the last wire has shorted out, the last bit of decking has settled under the water. Tyne, Pierre, Sullivan, Moran, Murphy, and Shatford are dead. (145–46)

In extended passages like this one, sinking ship and dying body are brought together in a reciprocal allegory that matches the narrative's skilful blending of providential (metaphysical) and scientific (physiological/meteorological) accounts. The former register is supported, as in Krakauer's work, by the use of apocalyptic epigraphs, drawn in this case from a range of metaphysically oriented seafaring narratives (e.g., *Moby-Dick*), as well as from more direct eschatological sources (e.g., the Book of Revelation). Both registers are subsumed under the predictably unpredictable category of the "natural disaster." Repeated over time, this comes to assume ominously *super*natural proportions: "Men talked of strange dreams and visions they had [in the notoriously disaster-ridden north Atlantic fishing-grounds, Georges Bank], and the uneasy feeling that dire forces were assembling themselves" (45). Again as in Krakauer's work, the sublime near-death experience is accorded visionary status: "It's said that people in extreme situations perceive things in distorted, almost surreal ways, and when the wires start to crackle and burn, perhaps one of the crew thinks about fireworks—of the last Fourth of July, walking around Gloucester with his girlfriend and watching colors blossom over the inner harbor" (140). This sudden leap from the physical to the metaphysical is also legitimated by a stress on immeasurable proportions, suggesting that natural disasters exceed—defy—scientific calibration despite compulsive efforts to record them:

Scientists understand how waves work, but not exactly how *huge* ones work. There are rogue waves out there, in other words, that seem to exceed the forces generating them. For all practical purposes, though, heights of waves are a function of how hard the wind blows, how long it blows for, and how much sea room there is—"speed, duration, and fetch," as it's known. . . . A gale blowing across a thousand miles of ocean for sixty hours would generate significant wave heights of 97 feet; peak wave heights would be more than twice that. Waves that size have never been recorded, but they must be out there. It's possible that they would destroy anything in a position to measure them. (119)

Junger's account maintains a similar tension between its "scientific" desire to explain and rationalize disaster and its "providential" fear that disasters come unbidden and go unanswered, leaving only inevitable destruction in their wake. Meteorological prediction is at the center of this dilemma.[13] The storm that claimed the *Andrea Gail*, Junger suggests, can be seen as a spectacular collision of warring elemental forces that, in spite of highly advanced meteorological technology, eventually proved "beyond the powers of science to predict" (103). The weather forecast, for all its accuracy, comes too late to save the boat, which cannot escape the path of a full-blown hurricane, and as the navigational instruments and communications systems on which it relies are first incapacitated, then destroyed. The storm itself is represented as the pinnacle of an ascending inventory of dangers, confirming the inherent riskiness of a profession—commercial fishing—in which "everything seems to be extreme" (32):

Fishermen don't work in any normal sense of the word, they're at sea for a month and then home celebrating for a week straight. They don't earn the same kind of money most other people do, they come home either busted or with a quarter million dollars' worth of fish in their hold. And when they buy food for the month, it's not something any normal person would recognize as shopping; it's a retail catastrophe of Biblical proportions. (32)

Commercial fishermen's lives, Junger implies, are poised between calculable risk and uncontrollable catastrophe, the latter scenario no less real for being assimilated into a tradition of colorful sea-yarns and playfully competitive disaster accounts. Junger himself plays on this tradition, including an entertaining medley of historical and, in one or two cases, suspiciously apocryphal disaster narratives, culminating in the story of the "perfect storm," understood in the popular meteorological sense as one "that could not possibly have been worse" (x). Nearly all of these stories are told by men about other men, reconfirming not only the demographics of the modern fishing industry but also the at times self-ironic machismo built into the tradition of the seafaring disaster account. (The subtitle of *The Perfect Storm,* significantly enough, is *A True Story of Men Against the Sea.*) This machismo is redoubled in Junger's rendering of a complementary rescue narrative featuring the attempted recovery by Air National Guard (ANG) para-rescue jumpers of survivors from other boats that had capsized during the storm. Air National Guard jumpers (PJs for short) are militarily trained all-purpose rescue operatives whose peacetime mission extends to "sporty" civilian rescues in a variety of maritime crises (174–75). Junger makes it clear that he admires these professionals' extraordinary bravery and resilience: "There is, literally, nowhere on earth a PJ can't go. 'I could climb Everest with the equipment in my locker,' one of them said" (175). Yet in at least one case, the extreme weather conditions are too much even for these battle-hardened action men, and the rescuers themselves need to be rescued, with further fatalities sustained. Junger's approach, although it refuses to find fault with the ANG's aborted rescue mission, indicates that there is a fine line separating "heroic-survivor" from "tragic-fatality" disaster narratives while emphasizing the potential recklessness, and occasional futility, of the gestures of male bravado that underlie them both. Similarly, he demonstrates the slippage between the categories of the (reconstructed) fatal and the (documented) near-death experience, broadening out both to suggest that "anyone who has been through a severe storm at sea has, to one degree or another, almost died" (219). Junger's concern here is for the prolonged after-effects that such disasters can have on entire communities: "Like a war or a great fire, the effects of a storm go rippling outward through webs of people for years, even generations. It breaches lives like coastlines and nothing is ever again the same" (219–20).

This leveling-out of admittedly interconnected "human" and "natural" catastrophes might be considered characteristic of disaster narratives, which are often given to assume the unique importance or unparalleled ferocity of the specific events being reported, even as these are assimilated to a general symbolic economy in which one disaster can effectively be traded for another, and all disasters can be legitimately compared. This impression of an interchangeability of disasters is reinforced by their often explicit placement within a literary genealogy of disaster narratives whose generic boundaries are remarkably permeable, and in which respect for conventional fact/fiction distinctions is not always necessarily, or even desirably, observed. For these reasons, among others, significant areas of overlap exist between *disaster* narratives and *travel* narratives, even though the authors of the former may not necessarily be travelers themselves, or focus on the specificities of their own itineraries, or present reassembled/restaged versions of other people's travels in their own sympathetically rendered accounts. If disaster narratives, as previously suggested, tend to test the physical and cognitive limits of travel writing, then a conjunction of the two, however tentative, also requires a reassessment of conventional aesthetic categories like the sublime.

So much is clear in *Into Thin Air* and, especially, *Into the Wild,* both of which present variations on the catastrophic adventure narrative that are in accordance with Bell and Lyall's category of the "inverted sublime" (88–89). The inverted sublime, at its most extreme, implies a pathologically self-testing form of travel/writing that, situated at the far end of the endurance- or survival-travel spectrum, converts the experience of hardship into an amateur life-philosophy—what might best be described as the "hedonism of deprivation." Like other manifestations of the accelerated sublime, the inverted sublime is predicated on an intensification of experience that requires physical immersion in, rather than detached appreciation of, the landscape (59). In its inverted form, *slowing down* becomes a constitutive feature of this experience. The high risk involved in extreme travel may result, however, not so much in voluntary deceleration as in imposed immobilization. Under such potentially disastrous circumstances, the ultimate paralysis of death may beckon, as the already enfeebled body is reduced to a dangerously catatonic state. Death by freezing (*Into Thin Air*); death by starvation (*Into the Wild*); death by drowning (in a rather different, professional context, *The Perfect Storm*): each of these points quite literally to the end of travel, in which the annihilating power of the natural world—normally contained by the domesticating routines of the sublime (Soper, 228)[14]—is dramatically confirmed. In such instances, disaster/

travel writing enters the vortex of the "dark sublime" (Bell and Lyall, 198).[15] Here, one might easily expect, it is the capacity of nature to deal death that is awe-inspiring, cathartic, uplifting. Certainly, Krakauer and Junger are both concerned to present factually accurate accounts invested, along with their victimized protagonists, with the nobility of tragedy. Yet neither is able, in the end, to prevent death from featuring as an anti-climactic resolution in (self-)ironically derealizing disaster narratives that appear—perhaps against their authors' better instincts—to operate on the principle of simulacral repetition. In this sense, it might be argued, self-consciously "retro-positioned" accounts such as Krakauer's and Junger's are postmodern in spite of themselves; or, perhaps better, they are functions of the relentless commodification, and attendant trivialization, of death under the conditions of the late-modern/late-capitalist world. The next section of the chapter examines what happens when, under a similar set of conditions, one of the greatest unnatural causes of human death—war—becomes a further object of touristic curiosity; and when war is transformed, through the self-privileging tropes of Western disaster/travel writing, into that most dangerous of postmodern delusions, a self-invigorating game.

War Games

In the American journalist Philip Gourevitch's chilling account of the 1994 genocide in Rwanda, *We wish to inform you that tomorrow we will be killed with our families* (1998), one of his informants, survivor Theodore Nyilinkwaya, matter-of-factly describes the coercive methods used by the state to ritualize the practice of mass murder:[16]

> Everyone was called to hunt the enemy. . . . But let's say someone was reluctant . . . [and] runs along with the rest, but he doesn't kill. [The others] say, "Hey, he might denounce us later. He must kill. Everyone must help to kill at least one person." So this person who is not a killer is made to do it. And the next day it's become a game for him. You don't need to keep pushing him. (24)

The idea of killing as a game recurs later in the text when the makeshift Hutu militia responsible for commiting many of the murders, the *interahamwe*, is described as promoting genocide as little more than a joyous "carnival romp":

> Hutu Power youth leaders, jetting around on motorbikes and sporting
> pop hairstyles, dark glasses, and flamboyantly colored pajama suits
> and robes, preached ethnic solidarity and civil defense to increasingly
> packed rallies, where alcohol usually flowed freely, giant banners
> splashed with hagiographic portraits of [Hutu President] Habyari-
> mana flapped in the breeze, and paramilitary drills were conducted
> like the latest hot dance moves. (93)

Much of Gourevitch's text concerns itself with unpacking the conventional argument that scarcely imaginable atrocities such as genocidal
murder are implicitly derealizing, taking on the trappings of carniva-
lesque ritual or macabre spectacle even as the wider context behind the
carnage becomes increasingly mystified and unclear. Thus, while
Gourevitch grudgingly acknowledges the perverse excitement that
comes from perpetrating or, later, witnessing the consequences of mass
murder, he remains resolutely opposed to sensationalist views of genocide that either confirm a fashionable postmodern relativism—as in the
mass-mediated notion that "all massacres are created equal: the dead
are innocent, the killers monstrous, the surrounding politics insane or
nonexistent" (186)—or collapse extreme violence into routine apocalyptic visions of the absurd (259). Instead, he insists on a view of the
genocide in Rwanda as the politically motivated consequence of a series
of interlinked, historically verifiable factors: precolonial inequalities exacerbated by self-serving European colonial regimes; heightened fear
and insecurity in the postcolonial era as a result of political extremism,
ethnic absolutism, and near-total economic collapse; the toxic combination of arms and alcohol in the hands of a compliant, desperately impoverished rural populace; manufactured consent for war as a desirable, quasi-permanent civil state; and the indifference of an outside
world all too ready to see Africa as an undifferentiated hotbed of primordial tribal violence, in which repeated evidence of mass slaughter
merely reconfirms the unavoidable, perhaps fundamentally irremediable, chaos that is the "natural" accompaniment of Africa's sad array of
collapsed postcolonial states (95, 180).[17]

Such a view of Africa, as is well known, has been propagated by several generations of Western travel writers, many of whom have actively
contributed toward (re)installing the pernicious myth of an irre-
deemably tainted continent, repeatedly sucked back into the self-con-

suming Heart of Darkness it seems driven to recreate. Gourevitch is well aware of the historical variables that underlie this durable—and durably racist—vision of "African barbarity," seeing it reproduced even in well-meaning modern acccounts that seek to rescue Africa from itself by conscripting its accumulated history of human/ecological disasters into the service of a universal humanitarian cause. Part of the problem, for Gourevitch, consists precisely in what might be called the Western "biologization" of African social history: the continuing process by which specific social/political conflicts are likely to be reinterpreted in the West as typecast, essentially "incomprehensible," humanitarian crises—as variations on the periodic natural disasters that, taking particularly heavy toll on the world's developing countries, serve to confirm the misbegotten thesis that "Africans generate humanitarian catastrophes but don't really make meaningful politics" (226); or, in the more specific case of the genocide in Rwanda, to "prove" the trumped-up case that "Hutus and Tutsis [were] simply doing what their natures dictated, and killing each other" (168, 154).

As Gourevitch shows, "there was nothing inevitable about the horror" in Rwanda; nor could the mass murders of 1994 and after be simply attributed to some primordial "natural cause" (94). Genocide, after all, is not by any stretch of the imagination a natural disaster; yet it is often treated as if it were, and not only by the so-called international community, who take it upon themselves—often belatedly—to offer assistance in the context of such evolving global crises, but also by the local perpetrators themselves, who are keen to minimize their responsibility for the catastrophic chain of events they have set in motion, the wholesale human destruction they have either indirectly encouraged or immediately caused. (The governing idea behind genocide, argues Gourevitch, is the naturalization of the enemy; its main excuse the uncontrollability of the appalling violence it brings in its wake. Both ideas, turning the victim rhetoric of the natural disaster to their own advantage, belie the premeditated nature of genocide as a systematic program of planned destruction.)

For Gourevitch, attempts to see genocide in terms of (natural) disaster often amount to little more than an ideological smokescreen, designed to obscure human agency while distracting attention away from the violence's predominantly political root cause. He is equally critical of the role of the international media in capturing public sympathy for the humanitarian plight of the post-conflict Rwandan refugees, many of whom had previously perpetrated the murders, or in recasting the disease-ridden condition of the refugee camps as a form of divine retribution through which the "horror had been equalized" and the guilty punished for their crimes (164). International relief organizations are similarly taken to task for their failure to address the underlying causes of the events whose devastating consequences they later sought to alleviate, and for their apparent readiness to shelter, along with the innocent, a number of known criminals who, given time to regroup, then went on to commit further crimes. The world's (super)powers, finally, are held to account for their reluctance to intervene in the struggle, for offering to help the cleanup—"in the interests of public health"—but not to halt the killing (149, 154). In exposing the genocide in Rwanda as a scandalous "case-study in international negligence" (326), Gourevitch makes the larger point that the West's obsession with the reified figure of the suffering disaster victim reveals the blandishments of "international concern" to be, at worst, a form of sanctioned, perhaps politically strategic ignorance and, at best, a reprehensible decontextualization of the historical and political circumstances that make events like genocide possible, irrespective of the increasingly empty post-Holocaust credo that it must never be allowed to happen again. (This last point is reinforced by the phenomenon of selective commemoration, well brought out in the powerful scene when Gourevitch, waiting in line to visit the immensely popular United States Holocaust Memorial Museum in Washington, tellingly juxtaposes his reading of a newspaper featuring graphic images of the recent carnage in Rwanda with the arrival of museum staffers wearing lapel buttons with the slogans "Remember" and "Never Again" [152]. As he is moved to conclude a few pages later, "the West's post-Holocaust pledge that genocide would never again be tolerated proved to be hollow, and for all the fine sentiments inspired by the memory of Auschwitz, the problem remains that denouncing evil is a far cry from doing good" [170].)

Another problem that obtains is how to imagine a slaughter of genocidal intent and proportion, and how to do so *after* it actually happened—how to perform the necessary memory work of "[re]imagining what is, in fact, real" (7). Visiting the killing fields of Rwanda for the first time—his research for the book will involve further field trips over a three-year period between 1995 and 1998—Gourevitch freely admits to finding it difficult to imagine the horrific violence that had happened there just over a year before. At one of the killing sites in Nyarubuye, where cadavers have been allowed to remain where they lie in a kind of open memorial, Gourevitch confesses to looking without really seeing, and to being disturbed by the aestheticizing impulses of his own response:

> The dead at Nyarubuye were, I'm afraid, beautiful. There was no getting around it. The skeleton is a beautiful thing. The randomness of the fallen forms, the strange tranquillity of their rude exposure, the skull here, the arm bent in some uninterpretable gesture there—these things were beautiful, and their beauty only added to the affront of the place. I couldn't settle on any meaningful response: revulsion, alarm, sorrow, grief, shame, incomprehension, sure, but nothing truly meaningful. I just looked, and I took photographs, because I wondered whether I could really see what I was seeing while I saw it, and I wanted also an excuse to look a bit more closely. (19)

Gourevitch is torn, here as elsewhere, between the "natural" touristic curiosity that drives him not just to look at, but also to fetishize, the dead bodies of Rwandan genocide victims, and his investigative journalist's duty to inquire further into the possible reasons behind the carnage, to attempt to convert sight into understanding, and fleeting images into a (semi-)coherent picture of past events.[18] A threefold project—to *describe* what he sees, to *imagine* what has happened, and to try to *understand* why it happened—thus lies at the core of a text that combines the sensory alertness and surface inquisitiveness of the conventional travel book with the greater critical acuity and moral indignation of the war correspondent's investigative report.

Gourevitch's task is complicated by the removal of much of the prima facie evidence. Most of the corpses have long since been taken away, and many, though by no means all, of the killers have either fled or gone into temporary hiding. In some cases, such has been the efficiency of the killing that entire Tutsi-dominated villages have been wiped out, and all traces of the people who once lived there have effectively disappeared (19). Under such circumstances, *stories* must compensate for the enforced lack of visual evidence, as Gourevitch energetically scours the country, "collecting accounts of the killing" (23). The traveler-reporter emerges both as listener and as secondary raconteur, compiling survivors', and in a few cases perpetrators', accounts as a way of imagining what must have happened to the dead. These stories provide the raw material from which conflicting versions of the historical past are created; they also form a sequence of imaginative relays linking personal, emotionally resonant memories of the killings to "official," highly ideological accounts of recorded events. The stories operate, in other words, as a series of individual case histories, issuing a reminder of the metonymic function of ex post facto war reportage, which often seeks to move from the evidence provided by a number of specific witnesses, many of them previous victims of the violence, to a broader understanding of the enormity of the violence itself. Retold against the backdrop of an aestheticized Rwandan landscape, the stories create a deliberate dissonance between the beauty of nature and its function as both temporary refuge for the killers and illusory resting-place for the dead (20, 178).

Meanwhile, between stories, and sometimes by means of them, Gourevitch fills in snippets of historical detail, creating, in the best tradition of politically informed travel journalism, a kind of historico-political whistle-stop tour, a deliberately inconsistent, back-and-forth narrativization of epoch-making events. Many of these details are provided in an ostensibly "historical" chapter that, again as in the tradition of travel journalism, is informed but unashamedly imprecise, moving freely between history, legend, and myth. Repetition—in some respects, a structural property of travel writing—operates here as the guiding principle, as in the view of Rwanda's misguided Hutu revolutionaries as Naipaulian mimic men, reproducing "the abuses against which they [had previously] rebelled" (61). Gourevitch's insistence on the historical specificity of the Rwandan and, to some extent, the larger contemporary African crisis is thus undermined by his tendency to see recurring patterns in the violence that link it back to previous, even "originary" events.[19] This leads, as so often in writing of this kind, to the loose deployment of European analogy, as when Gourevitch compares modern-day Africa (straight out of the pages of a Naipaul, a Kapuściński, or a Kaplan) to medieval Europe, routinely plagued by feudal corruption, racked by war, and serially afflicted by epidemic bouts of population-threatening disease (325).

To see *We wish to inform you* as a politically oriented travel book, rather than an extended piece of morally concerned investigative journalism or retrospective war reportage, is no doubt to stretch the point a little; even so, Gourevitch uses many of the standard tropes and imaginative resources of travel writing, even if travel itself emerges as an incidental necessity, rather than a narrative focus or sustained object of reflexive inquiry, in the main body of his report. The question remains as to whether *We wish to inform you* can be seen, within the overarching context of this chapter, as a piece of *disaster writing.* Clearly, as suggested earlier, Gourevitch is wary of attributing the dialectical (coincidental/eschatological) properties of natural disasters to the genocide in Rwanda, even as he shows how both of these mystified aspects have been manipulated to create a self-exonerating version of "unavoidable" (in the first case) or "preordained" (in the second) events.[20] Gourevitch's primary concern, indeed, is to give the lie to genocide as a particularly extreme form of pathological human behavior, ideologically linked to either "innate" human aggressiveness or the "primordial" origins of ethnic violence. To write about an African genocide, at the same time, is to challenge those emptied-out, hypermediated visions of Third World disasters that, in creating the paradoxically reassuring impression of a "distant sense of random menace" (313), run the risk of anaesthetizing their complacent First World consumer public. (As Gourevitch remarks despairingly at one point, "perhaps even extinction has lost its shock" [201].) Within this context, Gourevitch's text is written in defiance of two, perhaps equally distasteful notions: that mass murder might become a *game* to those who perpetrate it; or that it might become a *bore* to those who, vicariously witnessing it from a distance, content themselves with assimilating it to quotidian media-disaster routines. Nonetheless, the text, for all its undoubted moral force and critical intelligence, arguably betrays some of the characteristics of much less considered forms of Western disaster writing: the sentimental concentration on victims rather than perpetrators; the aestheticization of the dead; and, perhaps above all, the persistent tendency to insert violence into "natural" cycles of destruction that, long after being acknowledged as politically motivated, are still paradoxically treated either as biological phenomena (viz. the "extinction" metaphor) or as functions of an originary violence, revisited on reconstituted "natural" enemies, that is made to seem simultaneously unforeseen and strangely preordained.

While roving investigative journalists like Gourevitch are always likely to hesitate to see themselves as tourists, other observers of war are more unashamedly touristic in their preoccupations, thriving on the manufactured excitement of some of the world's most dangerous combat zones. Such modern-day danger-zone tourists, Kathleen Adams suggests, usually have motives other than dignified commemoration, and their relationship to war sites is not necessarily, or even primarily, honorific, as other commentators on war tourism like somewhat defensively to suggest.[21] Rather, danger-zone tourists are more likely to be "fuelled by [contemporary] global politics, their itineraries [generally] inspired by the images of nightly news reports from the world's tumultuous zones" ("Global Cities," 37). Such places, highly mediated as they are, fall rapidly in and out of fashion. Some are active war sites, others fall more into the more speculative category of "camouflaged tinderboxes" ("Global Cities," 37). What matters to danger-zone tourists, in any case, is not so much the organized chance to pay their respects to historic, or even present-day, war victims, but rather the partly fantasized opportunity to involve themselves in a "site of ongoing political instability . . . where there is at least an imagined potential of violent eruptions" (Adams, "Danger-Zone Tourism," 268).[22]

Such extreme tourists, beguiling the line between survival and self-destruction, are well served by the market in what Adams calls "danger-zone entrepreneurialism." Danger-zone entrepreneurialism, Adams suggests, is a rapidly expanding fringe industry that looks to profit from manipulating the exchange value bound up in the putatively reconnective power of fear.[23] A conspicuous example of the industry in action is the spate of recent combat-zone travel guides that invite their clients to experience "life to the limit" in situations of maximum risk. The most notorious of these guidebooks is Robert Young Pelton et al.'s immodestly entitled *The World's Most Dangerous Places* (1998), already into its fifth edition, and described with uncharacteristic euphemism by the *New York Times* as "one of the oddest and most fascinating travel books to come out in a long time" (cover blurb). The book is framed by a series of disingenuous disclaimers. It is designed, for example, for "adventurers," not "thrill seekers" or "adrenaline junkies," these latter being vulgar tourists ill-equipped for the pressures and vocational challenges of extreme travel: "The people who practice sky surfing, bungee jumping and street luge can not truly claim to be adventurers but rather thrill seekers. Big wave surfers, mountain climbers and base jumpers seek a short jolt that affirms their need for thrills, but these sports are designed to create television commercials rather than meaningful accomplishments" (xv).

It is *not* designed, in any way, to encourage people to take life-threatening risks:

> This book is about places where you should not go (they *are* danger-ous). . . . Although we have an uncanny knack for predicting wars, massacres and kidnappings, Fielding [the publisher] and the authors cannot take responsibility for any misfortune, liability, or inconve-nience due to your interpretation, application or even understanding of the information in this book. . . . This book is intended for back-ground information only and may not be reliable after press time. (xvii)

The book advertises itself, rather, as a fashionably outrageous parody of the morbidity in which it gleefully traffics: DP (dangerous places) T-shirts are placed on sale ($18 a pop), together with a logo of a laugh-ing skull wearing sunglasses and an upturned DP baseball cap; and Mr. DP himself (said laughing skull) is adopted as an official club mascot, a "sort of Kilroy for the nineties" whose products sell so well "because people think they are so cool" (xviii). As Adams points out, the cartoon images of violence scattered throughout the book have a predomi-nantly domesticating function,

> seemingly "tam[ing]" the terrors of riots and warfare, [and] offering the subliminal message that dangerous travel can somehow be enter-taining. . . . [Thus,] while smiling gunmen and helicopters make fre-quent appearances in the pages of [the] book, there are no images of corpses or actual warfare. This and other similar books render danger-zone travel inviting yet thrilling. (Adams, "Global Cities," 48)

The rest of the book, meanwhile, contains tongue-in-cheek advice on how to incapacitate deadly attackers, how to avoid catching potentially fatal diseases, and how to survive in places—star-rated for risk value—where "tourists are considered the daily sustenance of bad people" (Pelton et al., 58).

Unsurprisingly, the book has thrived on the adverse publicity it has worked so hard to attract, with Pelton sneering on the very first page that "we have been accused of being tour packagers to war zones, a handbook for adrenaline junkies and even the precursor of bus tours to hell."[24] In fact, the book looks *back,* if anything, to the type of 1960s, Vietnam-inspired U.S. counterculture whose volatile mixture of post-adolescent defiance and premature cynicism had spawned such self-ironizing classics of war tourism as Michael Herr's *Dispatches* (1968). By the same token, the book is suffused with what Maxine Feifer has called a "post-touristic" sensibility: with the awareness that the moral dilemmas of tourism have been emptied of meaning, and that tourism—even war tourism—is, after all, a game.

Similarly tongue-in-cheek is Joshua Piven and David Borgenicht's *Worst-Case Scenario Survival Handbook* (1999), a runaway best seller later expanded into a cultish mini-series. (The market seems able to sustain any number of egregious spin-offs, e.g., Greg Emmanuel's almost entirely derivative 2002 anthology *Extreme Encounters: How It Feels to Be Drowned in Quicksand, Shredded by Piranhas, Swept up in a Tornado, and Dozens of Other Unpleasant Experiences.*) Also equipped with "don't-try-this-at-home-or-for-that-matter-away" disclaimers, the book is an arbitrary compilation of experts' advice on how best to confront life-threatening situations: how to get out of quicksand ("take the shortest route to firmer ground, moving slowly" [18]); how to "remove something (e.g., a limb)" from the jaws of an alligator ("tap it [gently] on the snout" [57]); how to jump from a building into a dumpster ("jump straight down, aiming for the center and landing flat on your back" [77]). Put together by two self-styled "inquisitive journalists," the book is based on the whimsical premise that "anything that can go wrong will" (14). The tone of the book implies, however, that even if it does, it doesn't really matter; and while ostensibly marketing their work as "an indispensable survival handbook," Piven and Borgenicht seem well aware of its occasional status as a curio for would-be-but-probably-won't daredevils, a mildly amusing stocking-filler that has surely enjoyed greater success than its authors might have dreamed. The importance of the book seems to lie precisely in the awareness of its unimportance—as if survival for the postmodern age had become a laughing matter; and as if the business of saving one's life were now good for a few throwaway remarks.

This postmodern insouciance toward the self-induced disasters of extreme travel is also much in evidence in the last example in this section, Alex Garland's influential novel *The Beach* (1996). *The Beach* is a good example of a subgenre that has come into prominence recently, the self-consuming travel novel, replete with seemingly statutory ironic references to the apocalyptic scenarios of *Lord of the Flies, Heart of Darkness,* and, above all, *Apocalypse Now.*[25] The novel, set in back-packer-besieged Thailand, wryly exposes the destructive underside of touristic yearning, the potential for violence in a "subculture born in opposition to mainstream tourism but [now] finding its [own] identity under threat" (Hatcher, 137). As John Hatcher suggests, reading the novel in the context of routine obituary announcements on travel/writing, "If [Waugh's] *When the Going Was Good* and [Fussell's] *Abroad* were elegies mourning the death of travel, *The Beach* is its apocalyptic wake" (137). Certainly, death and destruction are ever-present images throughout the novel, whose twenty-one-year-old narrator-protagonist, nurtured on the simulated horrors of a complacent post–Cold War generation, seeks to enliven his dully "paradisal" surroundings by concocting surrealistic scenarios of violent confrontation. Eventually, as might be surmised, this imaginary apocalypse turns real; but even when it does, the book is ironically distanced from—even cynically amused by—the violence its narrative logic so dutifully invites. As Hatcher correctly asserts, the novel, for all its up-to-the-minute feel and overnight cult status, takes its place within a long tradition of travel writing in which "travelers, from imperial adventurers to package tourists . . . destroy the very thing [they] seek" (142). What makes the book disturbing is the banality of its own self-consciousness, its playfully amoral "post-touristic" indifference to the violent destruction it unleashes. Thus, while Garland himself has made it clear that he intended the novel to be a critique of the "shallowness, pretentiousness and deception" (Gluckman interview, quoted in Hatcher, 143) of global backpacker culture, it is no surprise that it has inspired several real-life stories of—mostly male—fantasy-seeking backpackers, each vying with the others for press release of the latest adventure holiday gone wrong, the latest serpent in the latest paradise, the latest "beach."

In a sense, novels like *The Beach* are antithetical both to the moral concern of consciousness-raising investigative reports, like Gourevitch's, and to the action-hero theatrics of crossover survival/fatality narratives, like Junger's and Krakauer's, suggesting that the aesthetics of the sublime on which these latter rely is not only deeply flawed but deeply dull. In another sense, however, it is the connection—itself banalized—between middle-class boredom and the desire for violence that motivates Garland's, Junger's, and Krakauer's otherwise highly differentiated narratives, whether their mode is neodocumentary or fictional; whether the damage they describe is self-inflicted or vicariously explored. It remains to be seen if travel writing, along with the tourist industry on which it depends, can survive this latest onslaught on its own credibility. History suggests it will. But the contemporary obsession with disaster, as manifested in "new" forms of extreme travel and associated danger-zone tourism, suggests that the genre has come up against its latest moral impasse—one in which heartening accounts of heroic survival prove less newsworthy than voyeuristic spectacles of apocalyptic atrocity, and travel/writing appears increasingly incapable of distinguishing between the literal death of others and its own metaphorical dead end.

FOUR

Back to the Future

Introduction

Disaster narratives and itineraries belong to the vast machinery of present-day commemorative tourism, itself a notable by-product of the late-capitalist "cult of nostalgia" that is often seen as forming an alleviating counterpoint to destructive teleologies of modern progress (Rojek, 144). Modern rituals of remembrance, after all, often tend to point to "a paradox of institutionalized nostalgia: the stronger the loss, the more it is overcompensated with commemorations; the starker the distance from the past, and the more it is prone to idealizations" (Boym, 17). This nostalgia finds an outlet in different, at first sight incompatible, modes of touristic activity. One mode—overtly public and commercial—moves in the direction of escapist entertainment. A good example is the heritage theme park, in which the "authentic" and "inauthentic" promiscuously mingle, and visitors are given a variety of prepackaged opportunities for fantasized excursions into a fondly reimagined past (Rojek, 151). Another mode—more obviously private, less conspicuously consumer-oriented—tends rather toward elegiac consecration. A counterexample here is the war memorial site, in which visitors are enjoined to pay their respects to the dead and, in so doing, to consolidate their own most cherished values, thereby attesting to the process of commemoration itself as a "register of sacred history" (Schwartz, quoted in Smith, 254).

These two touristic modes appear in several respects to be incommensurable. The one is geared primarily toward the indulgence of the living, the other orients itself rather toward the appeasement of the dead. These modes are linked, however, insofar as both offer alternative symbolic investments into a recollected past that is always liable to merge with the present and the future. Memory, of course, always involves an accommodation of the events of the past to the interests of the present.[1] But as Chris Rojek rather floridly suggests, "Under post-modernity . . . everyone is a permanent *émigré* from the present. For the present is acknowledged to be a sign system in which images and stereotypes from the past and the future, from the locale and the globe, are implacably intermingled, admitting no principle of determinacy" (168). Within this overarching system, private memories compete with public displays of historically unsubstantiated nostalgia, blurring the lines between remembered and reinvented histories, imagined recollections of the present and future-oriented perceptions of the past.

Such temporal indeterminacy is always likely to cause as much anxiety as pleasure. Certainly, anxiety is a feature of what several historians now refer to, often less than generously, as the global "memory industry." As the American historian Sherwin Lee Klein declares sardonically at the beginning of a 2000 essay: "Welcome to the memory industry"; for who can now dispute that "memory has become the leading term in our new cultural history?" (128). Why the memory boom? And why the ambivalent response to it? Several factors can be cited here: the recent revival of attempts—many of them within the framework of the Holocaust—to come to terms with personal and collective trauma, releasing deep-seated anxieties not just over the past, but over the specific forms in which it should be recalled; the further anxiety that with the much-vaunted "acceleration of history" (Nora, 7) in contemporary postmodern culture, the art of remembrance itself might run the risk of being lost; the centrality of memory to contemporary discourses of personal and cultural identity, and the linkage of these discourses to emancipatory social movements, victimized individuals, and embattled ethnic groups; the quasi-religious belief in the power of collective memory to act as an antidote to the worst excesses of history, and to counteract baleful "postmodern reckonings of history as the marching black boot and of historical consciousness as an oppressive fiction" (Klein, 145); and, not least, the increasing commodification of memory as the function of a consumer-driven late-capitalist society in which historical consciousness has been eroded by nostalgia—a society of the souvenir as much as the spectacle, in which an ever-growing number of pseudo-historical reconstructions and commercially viable memorabilia has granted the illusion of access to, while effectively substituting for, the lived experiences of the past.

Contemporary travel narratives are an integral part of this thriving global memory industry. The reasons for this are hardly difficult to fathom. First and foremost, travel literature is usually classified as a subset of *memoir*, freely mixing personal reminiscence and self-exploratory recollection with often extravagantly imaginative forays into other countries' and people's collective histories and individual pasts. Travel writing, in this sense, is more than just a vehicle for the exercise of the author's personal memories; it is also a significant repository of *cultural* memory, which can be loosely defined here as "a collective activity occurring in the present in which the past is continuously modified and described even as it continues to shape the future" (Bal, Crewe, and Spitzer, 1). Implicit in this view is that cultural memory—memory at large—is mediated through a wide range of *representations*.[2] These representations are at once a powerful vehicle for the transformation of the past in the present, and a reminder of the large number of positions we may inhabit toward to our own, as well as other people's, histories (Huyssen). Second, travel writing, down through the ages, has frequently been motivated by *nostalgia*: by the search for "other" times, as well as places, and by the inevitably unsuccessful attempt to "obliterate history and turn it into private or collective mythology, to revisit time like space" (Boym, xv). This search has intensified in the (post)modern era, evolving into what Svetlana Boym calls a full-fledged "global epidemic of nostalgia"—one in which nostalgia, "reappear[ing] as a defense mechanism in a time of accelerated rhythms of life and historical upheavals," looks to mobilize "affective yearning for a community with a collective memory, a longing for continuity in a fragmented world" (xiv). Third, travel writing is well positioned to capitalize on the symbiotic link between memory and *spatiality*: a link explored in Frances Yates's seminal work on the architectonics of memory in classical, medieval, and Renaissance philosophy, and, more recently, in Simon Schama's historical reflections on the sedimentation of memory in landscape and Pierre Nora's exhaustive study of modern-day *lieux de mémoire*.

Nora's work, in particular, seems worthy of closer scrutiny here, not least because it emphasizes the geographical situatedness, as well as the historical selectivity, of memory. Memory, for Nora, is perhaps best seen as a form of spatialized remembrance, generally attaching itself to different sites, whereas its dialectical counterpart, history, tends to associate itself with particular events. In the justly famous introduction to his encyclopedic study, *Les Lieux de mémoire* (1989), Nora distinguishes between these sites' material aspects (e.g., their relative size or topographical location) and their functional import (e.g., their shared significance or pedagogical effect). He then differentiates between sites that symbolize a dominant culture or view of culture (triumphal architecture, solemn official ceremonies) and those that symbolize a dominated culture or view of culture (places of refuge, unofficial pilgrimage sites). Two main conclusions can be drawn from Nora's richly suggestive introduction: first, that a typology of memory sites is potentially endless (although one might well imagine that the number of sites contained in seven volumes of *Les Lieux de mémoire* is more than sufficient); and, second, that these sites constitute a scattered bulwark against the fear—itself nostalgic—that the cultural milieux that previously sustained collective memory are now increasingly diminished, and that memory itself has fallen into an irremediable state of atrophy: in Nora's plaintive terms, "we speak so much of memory because there is so little of it left" (7).

Modern travel writing neatly captures the double bind of Nora's romantic-nostalgic view of memory. It articulates the fear of losing attachment to an often imagined homeland; but it also generates momentum from its often equally imagined interventions into other places and time zones, interventions that belie a coherent narrative of the past. In this last sense, travel writing mediates the dialectical relationship between memory and geography, as well as that between memory and history, suggesting that while our memories are tied up with particular places, place itself is codified by memory and filtered through selected, at times competing, narratives of the past. Travel writing also explores the multiple processes by which particular sites or places are invested with symbolic significance, indicating that an "imaginative geography" (Said, *Orientalism*) coexists, often uneasily, alongside actual (historically verifiable) places, and that it can become difficult to distinguish between real and imagined places, partly because the places we remember change, but also partly because we recreate them in our memories.

Finally, travel writing is particularly evocative in suggesting that memory belongs to a *geography of desire,* in which places are not just described as they are, or were, but as their perceivers would like or would have liked them to be. This chapter aims, accordingly, to track the geography of desire across a range of contemporary travel writing and traveling practices, with emphasis being given to narratives and practices that engage with traumatic modes of memory, modes that are often seen as obstructing rather than opening access to the hidden spaces of the past.

Hauntings

Cultural criticism, it has been suggested, is currently going through a Gothic period, characterized by an outpouring of often densely theoretical work on trauma, mourning, and various aspects of contemporary late-capitalist "wound culture" (Seltzer). "Spectrality," particularly in connection with Jacques Derrida's radically revisionist study *Specters of Marx: The State of the Debt, the Work of Mourning, and the New International* (1994), has become a key term within this Gothicized cultural-critical vocabulary. As Derrida speculates in *Specters of Marx:* "If there is something like spectrality, there are reasons to doubt . . . the border between the present, the actual or present reality of the present, and everything that can be opposed to it: absence, non-presence, non-effectivity, inactuality, virtuality, or even the simulacrum in general" (39). Spectrality posits a challenge to an entire metaphysical tradition, belonging to what Derrida punningly calls a surreptitious counterphilosophy of "hauntology." As Bill Spanos, glossing Derrida, puts it: "Haunting is fundamentally an ontological condition. Haunting derives from the forgetting of a domain of being . . . which the thinking and the language of the Western tradition, as it is developed in the present technological moment, has obliterated by way of reifying the unsayable" (1).

At a less rarefied level, spectrality may be more immediately associated with the ubiquitous figure of the *ghost* or *specter.* Ghosts, argues Derrida, are characterized above all by their *untimeliness.* The anxiety they cause is a function, not just of their general capacity to unsettle us, but also of the temporal uncertainty surrounding their appearance; for if they probably belong to the past, who is to say that they do not belong to the future? As "figures of a lost past" (Derrida), ghosts can easily become vehicles for cute nostalgia; but they are also disconcerting manifestations of the in-between. Neither quite dead nor fully alive, they straddle worlds, simultaneously occupying nominally separate time zones, or inhabiting ontologically indeterminate shadow spaces. Ghosts continue to haunt us despite the reparative work of mourning. In this last sense, they can be seen as anti-commemorative; for whereas mourning domesticates the past with a view toward eventually exorcising it, ghosts move freely between the past and the present, confronting us against our will.

This section of the chapter asks what role ghosts might have to play in contemporary travel writing. More specifically, it looks at the work of one of the best, and surely one of the strangest, of late twentieth-century travel writers: the (late) German expatriate, W.G. Sebald. Sebald's work, combining elements of fiction, biography, memoir, real and imaginary travel, photography, and history, makes a virtue of its own unclassifiability. Whether it is travel writing or not is moot, but—rather like the work of Sebald's contemporary, Bruce Chatwin—it certainly counts as a contemplative exploration of the *poetics* of travel: a sustained inquiry into the "metaphysics of restlessness" (Ignatieff) and its motivating influences, as well an experiment in linked digression and the synchronic dimensions of "spatial form" (Frank).[3] This poetics is underpinned by a debilitating nostalgia, an at times almost unbearable apprehension of the weight of the past upon the present; and by a hypersensitivity, as well, to the ethical responsibilities attached to a freewheeling textual/intellectual practice marked by fluid movement across a large number of seemingly parallel ontological spaces. Sebald's writing is haunted in several senses, not just in the most obvious sense that it restlessly shuttles between the realms of the dead and the living, but also insofar as it articulates the anxieties of a traumatic aftermath that contains within it the memory of not one, but multiple disintegrated worlds. The Shoah looms large here, particularly in the expansive fictional biography *Austerlitz* (2001) and the intricately structured post-Holocaust requiem *The Emigrants* (1992); but for Sebald, "aftermath" is not so much a reckoning with the specific legacies of historical catastrophe as part of his general vision of a world poised between the calamities of the past and the apocalypse to come. This vision involves the negotiation of a double residue: one through which catastrophe survivors, in recollecting their own painful experiences, also bear witness to friends and family long gone, but whose haunting presence still powerfully remains. In negotiating between these two residues, Sebald takes upon himself, in an elaborate transferential process, both the differentiated traumas of the living and the accumulated burden of the dead. Sebald's entire oeuvre can be seen, in fact, as a deeply poignant, and highly unusual, ghost story: a story in which past and present coalesce, each intruding on the other's consciousness, and in which the writing process may be likened at once to an agonized rehearsal of the memories of the living and to an imaginary communion—at times deliberate, at others involuntary—with the massed ranks of the dead. Sebald's work constitutes, in thus sense, a variation on *uncanny travel writing,* in which the narrating consciousness—who both is and is not the author—roams, with tormented uncertainty, through a half-lit Gothic landscape of ephemeral images, macabre dream-visions, eerily duplicated resemblances, and disquieting shadow selves.[4]

Travel, in this context, is perhaps best seen as an unfulfillable penance, in which the traveler-writer, suffering from an incurable condition of "originary displacement" (Porter), joins himself to a confraternity of lost and restless souls (*Emigrants,* 67).[5] Travel-as-penance, needless to say, provides rich opportunity for melancholic self-reflection, triggering memories that, together, constitute a vast litany of suffering and loss. Physical travel, under these oppressive conditions, is often excruciatingly slow-moving, and runs the risk at times of turning into its own opposite, almost total immobility or paralysis (*Saturn,* 3; *Emigrants,* 115). But it also provides the impetus for astonishing feats of imaginative divagation, so that the boundaries between actual, remembered, and imagined journeys are continually blurred.

Probably the best illustration of this is in Sebald's third book, *The Rings of Saturn* (1998, originally published in German in 1995), a characteristically heady blend of fiction, travel, and history, loosely based on the author's convalescent wanderings through Suffolk in the late summer of 1992. Two epigraphs to the text, an excerpt from a letter by Conrad and a dictionary definition of the rings of Saturn, place the book within the context of a latter-day pilgrimage circling around its melancholic subject. Melancholia, indeed, provides the theme and tone for the mental and physical circumnavigations that follow, which involve, as to some extent in Sebald's other books, the unremittingly lugubrious traveler's concerted efforts to surround himself with the places, objects, and people that most resemble himself.[6]

Melancholia, like nostalgia, on which it often draws, is perhaps best seen as as a "disease of the afflicted imagination" (Boym, 4), in which memory becomes, overpoweringly, "a source of unhappiness and perturbed consciousness" and a "burden of remorse" (Chambers, 31). Melancholia is always incomplete and unfulfilled; it is a kind of "eternalization of pensiveness" (Chambers, 169) that feeds incessantly on its own accumulated sorrows. The work of the melancholic text, similarly, is never finished, embodying a strand of "exiled modern thought which, having no [other] option, is continually propelled forward, never ceasing its mulling over of things" (Chambers, 173). According to the literary theorist Ross Chambers, the melancholy condition is almost always physically debilitating; but it may also be imaginatively stimulating, since melancholy points *both* to the capacity of memory to hang heavy on the conscience, inducing physical torpor, *and* to the fertility of associative memory, its uncanny ability to create an imaginary kinship between seemingly disparate things (166–69). This ability points to the protean character of melancholy, captured in Julia Kristeva's felicitous phrase "melancholic jouissance." Max Pensky, likewise, in his book on the German philosopher-critic Walter Benjamin—one of several literary ghosts to appear in Sebald's pages—sketches out the lineaments of Benjamin's "melancholy dialectics," its availability as a "source of critical reflection that . . . empowers the subject with a mode of insight into the structure of the real at the same time as it consigns the subject to mournfulness, misery, and despair" (19). Melancholic reflection thus becomes, as Pensky claims for his exemplary subject Benjamin, both a potential route to secret knowledge and a perpetual reminder of "the impossibility of recovering what was lost" (19).

The Rings of Saturn serves as an excellent example of the workings of melancholy dialectics. The narrator's wanderings are underpinned by a dark, distinctly Borgesian, premonition that the "real" world is dying, to be replaced inexorably by the secondary and tertiary worlds of the imagination (68–71). Similarly, the present is receding, revealing beneath its fading colors the much more extravagant—often extravagantly violent—narratives and images of the past. These competing narratives and images merge with dreams and elaborate flights of fancy, attesting to melancholic writing's combination of physical lassitude and imaginative excess. Both qualities are projected in the text onto a succession of forlorn, if hardly empty, East Anglian land- and seascapes, creating a marked contrast between the "waning splendour[s]" (37) of modern England and its hyperanimated past. As in other Sebald works, an atmosphere of gloominess and "encroaching misery" (42) is created through linked images of dereliction, and by the author's spectrally indistinctive photographs, which back up the apocalyptic foreboding— again taken from Borges—that "life is no more than the fading reflection of an event beyond recall," and that "time [itself] has run its course" (154). The narrator's feeling of alienation is only increased by the affinities he nurtures with his past and present interlocutors. These belong to a wider pattern of Baudelairean *correspondances* in Sebald's fiction, which often creates disconcerting parallels between the life of the narrator and his imagined precursors (182, 187). In particular, the narrator's ventriloquistic "conversations" with his eclectic band of literary forebears—Sir Thomas Browne, Conrad, Chateaubriand, Swinburne, and several others—create the unnerving impression that, in willingly absorbing his own experience into the lives of others, he is performing a "colloquy with the dead" (200).

The phantom presences of others, allied to a series of uncanny experiences of "ghostly repetition" (187), contribute to a feeling of bewilderment and insubstantiality: as if the narrator himself belonged to a different time and space; as if he himself were a ghost speaking from somewhere beyond the grave (255). This pattern is repeated, with the insistence of an idée fixe, in Sebald's other fictions, particularly in the early travelog-cum-psychoanalytic case study-cum-metaphysical detective story *Vertigo* (1999, first published in German in 1990). *Vertigo*, like *The Rings of Saturn*, plays skillfully between memory and imagination, making it clear that each serves the other, but sometimes in ways that produce "a vertiginous sense of confusion" by which the traveler-writer risks becoming "undone" (17, 15). Also as in *The Rings of Saturn*, memory mediates between real and imaginary worlds to create a crosshatched narrative of suffering—a martyrology of sorts, in which the traveler-writer allows or, perhaps better, invites himself to be haunted by the various places he has visited, the people he has encountered, and the books he has read. Many of these people appear alarmingly to share his own afflictions: melancholia, depression, pathological nostalgia, and a creeping anxiety that sometimes escalates into full-blown paranoia and panic attack.

Travel, in this context, becomes an outlet for the mass projections of neurosis, as even revelling holidaymakers in Italy, absurdly likened to zombies, are made to appear inconsolably morose (93). Uncanny travel writing, meanwhile, is taken to its own preposterous limits, with multiply duplicated journeys, a succession of ominous doppelgängers and impostors, and a wide range of other Gothic motifs supporting the narrator's (and the world's) imagined path to "gradual destruction" (63). All roads appear to lead to death, and the traveler imagines his whole life to have been predestined, his every journey to be cursed. In this manner, the text establishes a semiosis of the haunted imagination, suffused with conspiratorial portents of impending disaster, in which travel becomes but the interregnum between one calamity and another, and the traveler-writer is propelled toward the apocalyptic conclusion that "history is now nearing its close" (133). Religious (leit)motifs freely scattered throughout the text—exterminating angels, martyred saints, devil figures, all taken from a grotesquely overexercised Catholic imaginary—provide further warnings of this rapidly approaching apocalypse, convincing the fearful traveler-writer of the catastrophe that awaits him, and of "the torments and travails that await us all" (224). A hallucinatory vocabulary thus builds up, culminating in a vivid dream-vision, brought on by reading Pepys's diary, of the Great Fire of London: a calamity to end all calamities, and a foreshadowing, perhaps, of "the end of time" itself (262).

To a greater extent than *The Rings of Saturn*, *Vertigo* parodies the conventions of the Gothic, producing an operatic vision of the past that is frequently appalling but just as frequently absurd (212). Childhood fears and phobias, magnified over time, conjure up a rogue's gallery of dangerous assassins and vaguely threatening spectral figures, while places—Vienna, Venice, Padua, Verona, Sebald's own home village in southern Germany—take on the aura of almost interchangeable ghost towns, inflected and infected by the narrator's all-consuming fantasies and fears. The narrator is haunted, likewise, by the specters of European literature, who operate throughout as "ghostly shadow[s] of his own restlessness" (152). In one way or another, these literary figures—Stendhal, Flaubert, Grillparzer, Kafka—all come across as being afflicted, either by a degenerative condition of extreme melancholy and depression, or by a hyperactive imagination acutely given over to representations of suffering and distress. The portrayal of Kafka ("Dr. K"), in particular, gives credence to Svetlana Boym's wry historical observation that nostalgia, at least in the minds of many of those who believed they suffered it, often "shared some symptoms with melancholia and hypochondria" (5). This neuralgic combination, while it sometimes provided a stimulus to artistic creativity, often proved to be incurable (Boym, 5–6). Certainly, Dr. K, like several other doctor-figures, real and imaginary, in Sebald's work, proves ineptly unable to heal himself; while in a further recurring pattern, the place of convalescence metamorphoses into a place of death, another of Sebald's ubiquitous mortuary sites.

The deeper structure embedded in the text, and within the greater body of Sebald's work, belongs to the topography of elegy. *Lieux de mémoire* (Nora)—churchyards, battlefields, dilapidated houses and hotels, ghost towns—double as *lieux de mort,* offering plangent reminders of the inevitability not just of death, but of prolonged earthly suffering. This pattern is at its most apparent in what is probably Sebald's best-known work, *The Emigrants* (1997, first published in German in 1992). In *The Emigrants,* the narrator imaginatively retraces the journeys of four German Jews in exile. These journeys create a densely cross-referenced emigrants' trail that winds its way across Europe, the Middle East, and North America, with touchstone locations in the decayed cities of Manchester and Jerusalem, the one presented as a now hollow "miracle [industrial] city" (151), the other as a crumbling sacred site. These places, and others like them, create a haunting atmosphere of semi-ruin that corresponds to, while always threatening to unravel, the narrator's affectionate reassemblage of the fragments of his subjects' largely forgotten lives. These subjects—a doctor, a teacher, a painter, and the narrator's own great uncle—are all, like the narrator himself, highly gifted but inconsolably melancholic misfits, whose lives are touched with sadness and over whom the shadow of death is described as hovering "like a bird in flight" (63). These figures function, to some extent, as the narrator's intimately imagined travel companions; they are also his physical/spiritual guides, conducting him through a variety of uncannily familiar landscapes, allowing him to reinhabit and be reinhabited by the haunting spirit of place.

Travel, in this context, becomes both a reminder of the condition of originary displacement and a desire for death as an entry point into other, partly or wholly imaginary, spaces (46). In both cases, memory is the vehicle through which the dead are brought into concert with the living, and through which an imaginative geography that combines the intersecting worlds of the past, present, and future can be explored. Memory, however, as elsewhere in Sebald's work, is as likely to prove debilitating as enabling. As the narrator muses at one point, "Memory . . . often strikes me as a kind of dumbness. It makes one's head heavy and giddy, as if one were not looking back down the receding perspective of time but rather down on the earth from a great height, from one of those towers whose tops are lost to view in the clouds" (145). At times like these, memory provides a source of momentary disorientation. At others, it is a source of lasting pain, as when the narrator, in rehearsing the recollected thoughts and writings of others, creates the pathological conditions under which the pain of separation, intensifying over time, conveys an impression of repeated or multiplied loss.

Sebald's (partly) Proustian deliberation into the uncanny effect of time on place and the transpositional effects of involuntary memory is informed by two main conceptions of temporality. The first of these is *open-ended* time, in which there is no clear dividing line between past, present, and future (207); the second is *apocalyptic* time, in which an accretion of past and present experience apparently confirms a process of inexorable decline (137).[7] Both of these conceptions underscore a general apprehension of untimeliness, further reinforced by shared nostalgia and by the distinctly anachronistic language of the narrator, whose contemplations and dream-visions are expressed in elegantly circuitous, archaically gentlemanly prose.[8] Illustrations and photographs, meanwhile, establish a visual counterpart to untimeliness, either by creating an uncanny geography in which topographical images, dispersed across time, carry the burden of resemblance, or by accumulating images of decay (disused factories, semi-derelict hotels, abandoned gardens, etc.) in what amounts to an iconography of desolation and despair. The individual memories these images evoke overpower and paralyze the senses, confirming the painter Max Ferber's darkly melodramatic view of time itself as "nothing but a disquiet of the soul" (181). Collective memories, similarly, contribute to a mood of paralyzing anguish, in which the active desire to remember is overshadowed by the countervailing need to extinguish the pain of memory—to forget (114).⁹

By verbal/visual means such as these, Sebald's book works toward establishing an open-ended genealogy of representations that creates the impression of a merging of different consciousnesses, of voices drifting over time. The operating principle, as elsewhere in his work, is one of cumulative haunting. The "spectrality" of the text is an effect of a superimposition of ghostly representations: its pictorial equivalent is Ferber's palimpsestic portraits that, obsessively reworked, contain within them the memories of previous creations, each portrait in itself a gallery of "ancestral faces" (161). Ferber himself is something of a ghost: an indeterminate presence hidden in the shadows of his gloomy studio or, "walk[ing] about amidst [Manchester's] immense and time-blackened nineteenth-century buildings," a shadowy descendant of Benjamin's quintessentially melancholic flâneur (156).

Meanwhile, Ferber is haunted, in turn, by his memories of Germany, a country "frozen in the past, destroyed, a curiously extraterritorial place, inhabited by people whose faces are both lovely and dreadful" (181). As one might expect from an expatriate with an at best ambivalent relation to the country from which he fled, and to which he returns with obvious trepidation, the unquiet ghosts of the German past are everywhere in Sebald's fiction: in translated Holocaust testimony (*Austerlitz*); in grisly photographic histories of war and transferred visual/verbal metaphors of the concentration camps (*The Rings of Saturn*); in neglected memorial sites such as the overgrown Jewish cemetery in Kissingen (*The Emigrants*); in abundant family archives— letters, diaries, journals, photo albums—that recall better days, but always carry within them the hint of future destruction (*The Emigrants*); and in Sebald's sleepy home village of W., in which childhood memories become entangled with hallucinatory visions of apocalypse, producing a surreal "chronicle of calamities" (240) in which history merges imperceptibly with myth and legend, and the narrator's obsessive cataloguing of death and human suffering hovers somewhere between the unbearably poignant and the patently absurd (*Vertigo*).

These oppressive recollections, far from demonstrating the allegedly healing power of mourning, contribute to a melancholic's heightened awareness of his own entrapment within a self-perpetuating cycle of sorrow, pain, and failure. As Ross Chambers suggests, referring to the

"melancholic writing" of the French Symbolist poet Charles Baudelaire, "Memory is . . . a double or even triple source of painful self-consciousness, since the remembrance of lack and loss is accompanied by
the burden of an obsessive sense of irreparable failure, as well as by a
lightness of being, a sense of fragmentation and dispersion of identity,
that makes one feel like a living residue" (32). Chambers's diagnosis of
Baudelaire's writing also fits Sebald's very well: from its identification
of the repeated suffering caused by memory, to the melancholic's paralyzing sense of failure, to the dizzyingly fractured identity of the narrating consciousness, scattered and split between a host of real/imaginary
surrogate selves. Above all, Sebald's writing is characterized by its intense, though at times also playful, contemplation of a series of linked
residual states operating under the sign of the spectral. The writing
"travels" between these already volatile states, moving back and forth
not so much between as among the multiply intersecting worlds of the
present and the past, the living and the dead.

Travel can be considered, in this last sense, as an exploration of extreme states of ontological confusion; it creates an irresolvable uncertainty about who one is, where one belongs, or even whether one is "in
the land of the living or already in another place" (*Vertigo*, 115). At the
same time, travel expresses the desire for a release from the eternal rep-
etitions (what Derrida might call the "frequentations") of the spectral.[10] This desire is perhaps best captured in a characteristically cryptic
Kafka parable that appears as a leitmotif in *Vertigo*. In the tale, Gracchus the huntsman falls one day to his death but is subsequently unable
to complete the "journey beyond" that might lay his soul to rest. As a
consequence, he turns into a ghost who "has been voyaging the seas . . .
ever since, without respite, . . . attempting now here and now there to
make land" (165). According to the narrator, "the meaning of Gracchus
the huntsman's ceaseless journey lies in a penitence for a longing for
love . . . precisely at the point where there is seemingly, and in the natural and lawful order of things, nothing to be enjoyed" (165). This unsubstantiated longing—call it nostalgia—appears to be the greatest impulse behind the narrator's own tormented travels in *Vertigo*; and
perhaps, by a risky corollary, we might conclude that it is the main impulse behind Sebald's melancholic travel texts. Nostalgia is the afflictive
condition of the restless soul, "possessed by a mania of longing"
(Boym, 4). Travel, Sebald suggests, merely confirms the shared pain of

worldly entrapment; while nostalgia, signalling the desire for travel to "other" worlds, ultimately registers a longing for the journey to end all journeys, the "journey beyond." A strange kind of travel writing, this, that is always looking to eradicate the conditions of its own existence. But such is the geography of desire in Sebald's haunted fictions. If haunting can be seen as an iterative function of the unfinished work of mourning (Derrida), Sebald's travel writing articulates a desire to have that process end, to find a time—out of time—and a place—beyond place—where the haunting might cease. Yet this desire is acknowledged, at the same time, as being essentially unfulfillable. Hence the narrator's melancholia, his contrary desire for *further* haunting;[11] and hence his aching, inevitably unanswered, question: "And how are we to fend off the fate of being unable to depart this life?" (167).

Travel Writing, Postmemory, and the Holocaust

Sebald's work can be seen in part as articulating the constitutive dilemmas of contemporary post-Holocaust writing. The primary dilemma binds the ethical necessity of remembering the past to the seeming impossibility of representing it. Its offshoots can be phrased here as a series of part-rhetorical questions: Can contemporary Holocaust narratives bear witness to the past without simultaneously trivializing it? Can they do justice to the individual responses of the living as well as the collective experiences of the dead? Can they avoid the temptation to turn private grief into a public commodity? And if so, *whose* Holocaust is it that is being represented, and for which, not necessarily stated, aesthetic purposes and political ends?

These problems are arguably aggravated rather than allayed by the sheer number of available representations. These together make up what Norman G. Finkelstein has provocatively called a late twentieth-century "Holocaust Industry," one connected in turn to the (post)modern memory industry at large. There are at least two different ways of looking at this industry. As Andreas Huyssen suggests in his 1995 book *Twilight Memories,* "the problem for Holocaust memory [today] is not forgetting, but rather the ubiquitousness, even the excess of Holocaust imagery in our culture, from the fascination with fascism in film and fiction . . . to the proliferation of an often facile Holocaust victimology in a variety of political discourses that have nothing to do with the

Shoah" (215). Huyssen, among others, sees evidence here of a "melancholic fixation [that,] reach[ing] far beyond victims and perpetrators," reveals an intimate connection between the "unchecked proliferation" and the "traumatic ossification" of the master Holocaust trope (216). On the other hand, says Huyssen, such "multiple fracturing of the memory of the Holocaust" can be considered paradoxically enabling insofar as the "multi-layered sedimentation of images and discourses" that arises from it offers a "potential antidote to the freezing of memory into [a single] traumatic image or the mind-numbing focus on numbers" (257).

To what exent can these images and discourses be assimilated to the narrative conventions of travel writing? After all, it could be said, the entire history of European Jewry is contained within narratives of dislocation and displacement, of which Holocaust transportation and its devastating consequences represent only the most extreme form (Hilberg). The *literary* representation of the Holocaust, however, raises several specific problems that suggest that Holocaust narratives are only partly categorizable as examples of a particular, pedagogically oriented mode of extreme travel writing. The first of these problems relates to the moral intensity of Holocaust writing, the ethical parameters of which are remarkably consistent given its high degree of variability as both literary expression and broader cultural form. The second relates to reliability, hardly a quality that more conventional kinds of travel narrative are known for, but one to which most Holocaust narratives aspire, and on which their imaginative power of recall depends, in spite of the selectivity and embellishment that are intrinsic to memory itself. A third, finally, relates to the issue of interpretability. Here, as James E. Young argues, Holocaust narratives, whatever their degree of factuality, set up a particular, often complexly encoded relationship between writer, text, and reader in which "narrative strategy, structure, and style all become forms of commentary on the writing act itself" (420). The evidential status of the text is by no means guaranteed; instead, the reader is enjoined to search, less for direct evidence of lived experience than, via "the conceptual presuppositions through which the narrator has *apprehended* experience," for mediated knowledge of recorded events (420; emphasis added).

What all of this suggests is that Holocaust narratives need to be analyzed, precisely, as *narratives,* but that the particular conventions they deploy are atypical of Western travel writing as a whole. Nonetheless, the trope of travel—almost always coerced—is a frequent feature of these narratives, as are the particular, dialectical forms of interplay between memory and history that their traumatic journeys, with their generally even more traumatic outcome, perform. (The history-memory dialectic continues to be a key issue for Holocaust scholarship, particularly though not exclusively in late twentieth-century Germany, where what the historians Martin Broszat and Saul Friedländer call "the moral sensitivization of history" has involved a renewed coming-to-terms with the atrocities of the Nazi past [87]. Broszat's view is that "respect for the victims of Nazi crimes demands that [their own forms of] mythical memory be granted a place" in the annals of German history—a view taken still further by other historians such as Christian Meier, who contends that "the mythical quality that [Broszat] attributed to the memory of the victims is [also] inherent in the event itself" [37].)

Perhaps a more convincing case can be made for second- or third-generation Holocaust narratives as travel writing insofar as these narratives, in recording the journeys of earlier Holocaust victims, are also likely to make commemorative journeys, both historical and geographical, of their own. These range in form from relatively straightforward, fact-based journeys of (self-)discovery to elaborately fictionalized inter-generational quest narratives, and in what follows, I will look at prominent examples—Martin Gilbert's *Holocaust Journey* (1997) and Anne Michaels's *Fugitive Pieces* (1996)—of each. A common link, however, between these otherwise highly disparate post-Holocaust narratives is their exploration of what the American scholar Marianne Hirsch has called the condition of "postmemory." Postmemory is characterized by a condition of belatedness that finds literary expression in the subgenre of the post-Holocaust elegy (Zipes and Morris). In literary works of this kind—and I will argue that both Gilbert's and Michaels's texts are examples of post-Holocaust elegy—postmemory signals the impossibility of access to the original experience, which is in turn likened to the impossible task of the translator to capture the original meaning of the text. Instead, the later text is left to sift the multiple intergenerational layers of post-Holocaust memory, incomplete access to which is provided through the part-translation of a wide array of earlier, more or less foundational Holocaust texts. The post-Holocaust elegy, in other words, is a study in *intertextuality* that looks at the ways in which memories are encoded and decoded across the generations, but also at the ways in which these memories are explicitly textualized in a loosely connected body of writings that travel across both time and space. Post-Holocaust elegies—like postmemory itself—are potentially therapeutic and recuperative, but their capacity to perform an imaginative refashioning of the past is balanced against their agonized awareness of what, in some cases, can only be acknowledged as irrecoverable loss. In the name of an "unmasterable past" (Maier), they probe—like several other narratives in this book—the conceptual limits of morally educative travel by implicitly challenging the self-privileging claims to discovery and knowledge made in more conventional travel texts.

Despite its title, Martin Gilbert's *Holocaust Journey* (1997), an acclaimed historian's tortured account of a two-week trip to European sites associated primarily with Jewish experience during World War II, is probably best seen not as a variant on the post-Holocaust memoir, but rather as a broader imaginative reconstruction of several centuries of European Jewish life. Its itinerary is determined by the Holocaust but not necessarily dominated by it; and its primary motivation is an interest—one shared by Gilbert's university students, who accompany him on his meticulously preplanned journey—in learning more about the history of Jewish communities in Europe, some of them stretching back over at least a thousand years (249). This history is recounted via a plethora of different texts—diaries, journals, chronicles, memoirs, letters—that become the composite means by which a "lost world" of European Jewry is imaginatively brought back to life (309). Gilbert's own chronological narrative, presented in diary form, binds these various texts together while also reflecting on their significance for the modern post-Holocaust pilgrim, whose painful journey of discovery is conducted across a series of mostly well-documented tourist sites. Touring these sites, as well as reading about them, provides imaginative access to the experiences of generations of European Jews: experiences, all too often sucked into the annihilating vortex of the Holocaust, that connect the considerable social and cultural achievements of the contemporary Jewish diaspora to those of the more distant European past.

While Gilbert insists that he, along with the other, mostly much younger members of his party, should not "allow ourselves to become depressed by the past," his is largely a depressive's account, "collectively savaged by the burden of [historical] knowledge" (103) it shoulders, and seemingly fixated by the appalling stories of suffering and death it narrates. The unbroken chronology that accompanies Gilbert's epistolary style merely reinforces this impression of relentlessness, creating a sensation of numbness in both writer and reader that is the end result of the individual stories' overpoweringly cumulative effect (76). As a consequence, *Holocaust Journey* comes across as a curiously undramatic reconstruction despite the obvious sensationalism of its material, reading at times almost like a funeral oration in commemoration of an only partly retrievable past. To some extent, the flatness of the narrative is the result of an unresolved tension between its warring desires to reconstruct European Jewish life and to elegize its passing. At their most extreme, the two desires cancel each other out, leaving Gilbert to confess to being suffocated by the sheer weightiness of his material, and to acknowledge his greatest fear: that his painstaking historical work may end up offering illusory protection from the past it is attempting to preserve:

> The survivor, the historian, the teacher and the student, each from their own perspective can try to invest streets, individual buildings, wall plaques, with meaning. The historian, the teacher and the student can retell, through readings and through the written word, the recorded atmosphere of the time, the detail, the poignant moment, the end of hope; but even the recorded atmosphere, as set down by eyewitnesses in letters and diaries, or by survivors in their memoirs, comes close to defying the most vivid imagination. If one really could "imagine" what one reads and studies, would one not go mad? (75)

Further difficulties are encountered, meanwhile, in Gilbert's attempt to view Holocaust experience through the less than accurate lens of travel narrative. One obvious difficulty is that of reconciling the blandishments of everyday tour-guide language to the histories that language often serves to conceal or euphemize (39, 42, 249). Another is that of accommodating the highly visual language of travel writing to a narrative of disappearance. (A combination of spectrality and irony seems to be the best way of doing this, as in Gilbert's half solemn, half tongue-in-cheek descriptions of Zamość as one in a succession of Central European ghost towns, or his unglossed citation of his fellow traveler, Polish Holocaust survivor Ben Helfgott, who melancholically describes the

Warsaw ghetto as the ruin of a ruin, in which "there are almost no buildings left of a world that is itself no longer," and "what we see to-day—block after block of identical, dull apartment buildings—obliter-ates the memory of a vibrant life" [309].) Still another difficulty consists in the circumstances surrounding what Gilbert calls, citing an extract from Korczak's diary, "the marketing of spiritual commodities"—a global market well provisioned by the tourism of acute conscience that Holocaust pilgrimage represents (324). *Holocaust Journey* is not partic-ularly reflexive in this regard about its own motivations, although some pertinent thoughts are offered in the Epilogue, which makes it clear that Gilbert sees the book as emerging out of a concatenation of recorded journeys—recycled touristic itineraries, written accounts of fateful journeys to the death camps, almost miraculous tales of escape and sur-vival—that link the present to the past through a tracery of textualized memories, and that confirm the status of his own tour party as a com-mitted band of "fellow-adventurers, fellow-searchers after knowledge, and fellow-journeymen" (399).

In this way, *Holocaust Journey* demonstrates tourism's profitable but not always comfortable relationship with the history of pilgrimage, a relationship linked to the courtly coming-of-age narrative, in which pilgrimage provided the opportunity for eligible young knights to "ac-complish the social transition from youth to adulthood through terri-torial mobility," while attaining a certain recognition along the way that might be useful for their future career (Leed, 184–85). The kind of pilgrimage that Gilbert's students undergo is a good deal less self-serv-ing than this, but it is still suitably educative for its participants, while the journey itself enacts a repeat performance of the one Gilbert had made a year earlier with his own son. Gilbert clearly sees himself in a mentor's role, but he also relies himself on other, earlier mentors, as in the readings he studiously prepares and solemnly delivers, which offer up moral guidance within the invented tradition of Holocaust narrative as modern sacred text. In this sense, the book is as much a work of morally sanctioned literary tourism as the written record of a testing physical journey; and, as such, it is unsurprisingly suspicious of the physical presence of other spiritual tourists, like the coachloads of mostly Jewish students who converge on Majdanek and Auschwitz from all corners of the world (280). Auschwitz, in particular, is described with scarcely disguised distaste as a global tourist attraction, bustling with visitors—over half a million of them a year—and with plans afoot to open a supermarket just outside the Main Camp gate (174). Birkenau, by contrast, is presented as a contemplative site for mourning and pilgrimage, a morally revitalizing counterpoint to Auschwitz Main Camp as a consumer-oriented tourist site (175).

Such problems of authenticity are compounded in the text by the conventional forms of mass tourism its party almost inevitably uses, with the centerpiece of an already accelerated journey being the brief consecutive visits to the four "iconic" death camps (291). Seen in this light, the readings Gilbert offers can be seen as part of his attempt to slow things down, to explore the possibility of alternative temporalities that are unsympathetic to the breathless ideology of modern consumer capitalism, and unreduced by the tinseled superficiality of the standard (Western) travel text. What these readings require, the text suggests, is a capacity for durability and patience: qualities amply exhibited in the stories themselves, many of which illustrate astonishing powers of resilience against seemingly impossible odds. It is through literature, rather than geography, that the journey acquires its sense of place as well as its awareness of the epic scale of dislocation; compare this to the Holocaust Museum at Wannsee, which tries and fails to tell "the story of the Holocaust in fifteen rooms" (49). At the same time, literature itself, used in low gear, risks putting a halt to movement altogether, achieving paradoxically what modern museums themselves cannot quite capture—the crystallization of the recent past. *Holocaust Journey* thus becomes the slow-pulse account of a journey undertaken at great speed, as if in ironic imitation of the very state of emotional anaesthetization and paralysis it is so desperate to forestall.

Many of the problems Gilbert's narrative confronts are related to the condition of postmemory: the lingering suspicion that its imaginative attempt to link "a Jewish world that no longer exists . . . to Jewish existence today" (405–6) may founder on the increasing loss of collective memory; on the tortured awareness of the difficulties involved in demarcating a post-Holocaust "topography of terror" when many of its primary landmarks are no longer visible, and when many of the signs and sites that struck fear into previous generations have now been converted into something else (28). In this context, the question of what triggers memory—a monument? a plaque? a building?—is underscored by the anxiety that such commemorative markers may actually represent memory's loss:

> Belzec . . . Sobibor, Majdanek, Treblinka and Chelmno . . . these death camps, the ultimate in human suffering, are now graveyards, museums, or monumental parklands. They should be there for posterity, although as monuments they can never measure up to the scale of human misery which prevailed in them over fifty years ago. And then there is this gnawing, worrying thought: what would it be like for visitors, thirty or fifty years from now? With the absence of survivors and eye-witnesses, who will see to it that the Shoah does remain in our collective memory? (405)

Similar dilemmas of postmemory are set out in the Prologue to the Canadian writer Anne Michaels's award-winning poetic novel *Fugitive Pieces* (1996). During World War II, the Prologue recounts,

> countless manuscripts—diaries, memoirs, eyewitness accounts—were lost or destroyed. Some of these narratives were deliberately hidden— buried in back gardens, tucked into walls and under floors—by those who did not live to retrieve them. . . . Other stories are concealed in memory, neither written nor spoken. Still others are recovered, by circumstance alone. (1)

The novel duly tasks itself with bringing some of these hidden stories to light, and attempting to interpret them, against a dual post-Holocaust background of restorative translation and irretrievable loss. This dual background is underscored by the insistent redoubling of the narrative, whose second section involves a part-mirroring—a necessarily incomplete translation—of the first. In the first part, a young boy, Jakob Beer, is rescued from the Nazis by a Greek scientist, Athos Roussos. Roussos then takes the boy to live with him on the island of Zakynthos. After the end of the war, Athos takes up a position in the geography department at the University of Toronto; Jakob accompanies him and, in Toronto, meets his first wife Alex, while also embarking on his career as a poet and translator. In the second part, a young professor of meteorology, Ben, meets the now sixty-year-old Jakob and his second wife Michaela at the home of a mutual friend. Fascinated with Jakob, Ben becomes his unofficial biographer and, eventually, his mourner when

Jakob is killed not long afterward in a car accident in Athens, to be survived by only two days by his wife.

Such, for what it's worth, is the novel's plot, but *Fugitive Pieces* is anything but a conventional plot-driven novel; it makes more sense to read it in terms of the layering of its elemental images, from the first, startling image of the boy Jakob being lifted from the mud of an excavated Polish city, Biskupin. This defining moment gives rise to an image repertoire of burial and reemergence that runs throughout the novel, and that corresponds to its countervailing desires to hide and reveal oneself; to make oneself invisible, but also to make visible that which was previously concealed. On the one hand, burial and other modes of self-confinement are literal means of survival for Jews relentlessly hounded by the Nazis; on the other, "burial" becomes a metaphor for the repression of traumatic memories (Jakob is in hiding when the Nazis come and gun down his family, and this and other associated memories haunt him throughout his life).

Through these linked images of burial and reemergence, the novel seeks to address some of the crucial questions surrounding post-Holocaust narrative. How is it possible to express one's memories without being overcome by them? How is it possible to deliver oneself from the past, to "cleanse [one's] mouth of memory" (22)? And how is it possible—*is* it possible—to inhabit other people's memories; to bear witness to events one has not seen, but that nonetheless give fundamental shape and meaning to one's life? These questions are never really answered, nor—the text suggests—are they ever likely to be. Instead, the novel directs its energy toward placing the history of Jakob Beer and other Jewish fugitives in the context of what might best be called a geographical metanarrative, one that repeatedly circles around territorial images of sedimentation and excavation, death and rebirth. One version of this narrative is *archaeological,* as exemplified in Athos's partial excavation of Biskupin (the "Polish Pompeii," which Himmler ordered destroyed because it provided evidence of an advanced culture that wasn't German; the novel counteracts this originary violence by showing that it is impossible to conquer history simply by erasing the traces of the past [104]). Another version is *geological,* and is captured in the novel in the interplay—encapsulated in the paradoxical notion of the "gradual instant" (77)—between inexorable processes of slow change and sudden, cataclysmic shifts. A third version is *meteorological,* and is primarily associated with the second narrator (Ben), whose work involves the charting of human biorhythms through a series of often subtle climatic variations. Last but not least is a version linked to the history of *exploration.* The geography department at the University of Toronto is fronted up by a member of Scott's Antarctic expedition, allowing for further ruminations on the dialectics of confinement and exposure: the contrast, for example, between the wide open spaces of the Antarctic and the stifling confinement of the explorers' tent (37).

Taken together, these different versions, and the metanarrative under which they are gathered, establish the text as a multiply displaced post-Holocaust travel vehicle in which it is words, as much as people, that do the traveling, and where the luxuries and necessities of movement are intimately related to the ways in which words, and the people who fashion them, are translated over (historical) time and across (geographical) space.[12] Translation, the first narrator tells us, is

> a kind of transubstantiation [in which] one poem becomes another. You can choose your philosophy of translation just as you choose how to live: the free adaptation that sacrifices detail to meaning, the strict crib that sacrifices meaning to exactitude. The poet moves from life to language, the translator moves from language to life; both, like the immigrant, try to identify the invisible, what's between the lines, the mysterious implications. (109)

Translation, it is suggested, is also an act of memory. It registers the passage, not just from one text but from one time-frame to another in an affect-laden process that is as much spiritual as it is material, and that implies the ethical imperative of the translator to retrieve and, in retrieving, to consecrate the past. Passages such as these involve both travel and its opposite, the momentary abolition of travel: "Every moment is two moments. . . . History and memory share events; that is, they share time and space" (138). This philosophy of convergence is demonstrated spatially, as well as temporally, through the creation of a series of mirror geographies. The sunken city of Biskupin morphs into the ravine-crossed city of Toronto (built in the bowl of a prehistoric lake), while the windswept expanses of Antarctica provide a reverse-image of the sun-soaked archipelagic islands of Greece. Above all, however, the doubleness of the text reveals itself through the (un)conscious linkages of *writing,* as in Jakob's first collection *Groundwork,* dedicated to his savior and mentor Athos; or in Ben's later, part-curatorial part-transformative translations of Jakob's work.

Through spectral connections like these, the novel traces shadow lines between Holocaust survivor testimony (in the Old World) and a postcolonial migrant aesthetics (in the New). As the Australian theorist Paul Carter has provocatively argued, collage is "the normal mode of constructing meaning" in postcolonial migrant societies (186). Postcolonial collage, Carter suggests, maps the gaps and "interzones" in language where discontinuities have been previously suppressed:

> Far from making a fetish of the word, post-colonial collage aims to recover the spaces between words. . . . [I]t lets languages cross-fertilize, deform and reform each other, [but] not with the object of imposing a new language . . . but in order to focus interest on the [specific] occasions of speech. Within the ritualized performances of language, where it is supposed only outer states are communicated, there is latent a deeper poetics, a suppressed logic of association mediated through sound, cadence, rhythm, pitch and stress. To become aware of this bird-like dimension of language is to become the subject of language, not its object, the actor not the acted upon, the singer not the silence. (198)

The dense metaphorics of *Fugitive Pieces* represent the working through of a similar logic of hidden association. The traditional Holocaust poetics of loss and silence are brought into concert with a modern postcolonial poetics of the fragment; each translates the other and, through this process, is creatively transformed. *Fugitive Pieces,* in this sense, explores the interstitial spaces occupied by survivor/migrant memory, in which all languages read double. For the immigrant poet-translator Jakob Beer, English is the language of renewal, "an alphabet without memory" (101); but it is equally clear that English also functions as a language of mourning: his translations are simultaneously effusive transformations of the original and elegiac lamentations of its loss.

This brings us back to the ambivalent status of the text as a post-Holocaust elegy that, even as it helps unearth the hidden connections between different Holocaust representations, casts doubt on the recuperative/transformative capacities of elegy itself (Zipes and Morris).

Like *Holocaust Journey, Fugitive Pieces* shows both the impossibility of gaining access to the original Holocaust experience and the extreme difficulty of translating the testimony that experience provided into later, commemorative forms. At one level, Michaels's novel certainly performs the work of elegy: constituting one of its own hidden memoirs, it mourns the lives of Jakob, Athos, and countless unnamed others in the ravaged European-Jewish past. But, at the same time, it simultaneously confirms the insufficiency, even the impossibility, of elegy; the forms of remembrance it enacts unconsciously conceal as much as they consciously disclose. Perhaps, in the end, the novel suggests that it is folly, through the act of controlled remembrance, to attempt to "complete" the lives of others. Those lives, and the work produced from them, continue uncontrollably, with an afterlife that is always in motion, and forever incomplete.

Fragmented narratives both, *Holocaust Journey* and *Fugitive Pieces* gesture toward what Huyssen calls "the fundamental ambiguity of [a] postmodern, post-Auschwitz culture [which is] obsessed with remembering and the past [but is also] caught in a destructive dynamics of forgetting" (260). Intertextuality, as I have been suggesting, is the technical means by which this ambiguity is examined in both narratives. Hidden connections between texts are established through a selective process, conscious or not, of "quotational memory" (Plett). Taken together, these connections constitute what Walter Benjamin might call the "afterlife" of the original (71); but this translated afterlife registers both the desire for continuity and the awareness of irrecoverable loss. Intertextuality, in other words, is an attempt to come to terms with the *spectrality* of post-Holocaust experience—an attempt that, by its very nature, can only ever be partially successful or complete. In this context, Gilbert's and Michaels's texts—like Sebald's—can be seen as gesturing toward the unfinished process of remembrance that is integral not only to post-Holocaust narrative, but to the mechanism of intertextuality itself.[13]

Said, Khouri, and the Split Subject of Travel Memoir

Like *Holocaust Journey* and, in a different context, *Fugitive Pieces*, the Palestinian American cultural critic Edward Said's memoir *Out of Place* (1999) counteracts the repressive tendencies of traumatic memoir by effecting the imaginative reconstruction of a "lost world," a forgotten way of life (xiii). *Out of Place,* as Said explains in the preface, is motivated by the desire, quickened by the awareness of terminal illness, to leave behind a "subjective account of the life I lived in the Arab world" (xi).[14] This imaginative reclamation sets up a Palestinian counterpoint to Jewish experiences of expulsion and dislocation, examining the process by which the Palestinian people have not only suffered a fate similar to that of many of their European Jewish counterparts but have done so, primarily if by no means exclusively, at the Jews' expense (113). The geography the text traces is thus one of *disruption,* chronicled in the Said family's multiple relocations and displacements; but also one of *affect,* in which the different countries between which the family moves—Palestine, Egypt, the United States, Lebanon—carry both an emotional charge and a historical burden, underscored by Said's fear that all places are the wrong place, and that he is destined, for all the force of his commitment, never to belong.

Travel memoir is Said's chosen vehicle for the emergence of an exilic sensibility in which the dawning sense that "home was something I was excluded from" (222) is partly redressed by the cultivation of a sophisticated inner life. As he says of his secondary schooling in Egypt:

> It was while I was at VC [Victoria College] in Cairo that I began to notice the almost absolute separation between my surface life at school and the complicated but mostly inarticulate inner life I cherished through the emotions and sensations I derived from music, books, and memories intertwined with fantasies. It was as if the integration and liberty I needed between my [different] selves would have to be endlessly postponed, although I subliminally retained the belief that one day they would somehow be integrated. (202)

Memory emerges here as a conscious act of imaginative recall aimed at unearthing a "second self" buried beneath the public, gentlemanly persona that has been carefully constructed for him by his affluent family, partly as a means of protecting him from the destructive enmities and entanglements that are seen as characterizing the region's social and political life (217). This "second self," the product of multiple displacements from "countries, cities, abodes, languages, environments," is a self in transit, continually "fabricat[ing] occasions for departure" amid the growing fear that each journey might be the last one, and that travel

itself might merely reconfirm abandonment, effecting a kind of voluntary self-banishment from the comforts of home (217–18). Travel,
whether voluntary or not, thus contributes to the gradual accrual of
disorientation, the existential premonition of a permanently alienated
sensibility that memoir proves only capable of reliving, even as its author "feel[s] the pressure of time hastening and running out" (222).

What Said repeatedly calls the "provisionality" of his own existence
is reinforced by his recognition of a fractured subjectivity, in which the
"split between 'Edward' (or, as I was soon to become, 'Said'), my public, outer self, and the loose, irresponsible fantasy-ridden churning
metamorphoses of my private, inner life was [increasingly] marked"
(137). This fractured subject conforms to the generic requirements of
travel memoir, in which identity, usually posited as multiple and discontinuous, reveals the conflicted patterns of belonging and allegiance
that are by-products of an irrepressibly kinetic sense of self. Yet the effect is exaggerated, in Said's case, by an ontological confusion surrounding split identities—Edward/Said, Arab/American, Christian/
Palestinian, and so on—that emerge out of a particular set of historical
circumstances, and through which the mirroring of divided selves and
places reflects Said's own ambivalence toward Palestine, in particular,
as an "admirable country for *them* [the Palestinian people] (but of
course not for *us*)" (142; emphasis in original).

By *us,* Said is referring to the members of his cosmopolitan family,
who are at once protected by their privilege and effectively partitioned
by it from the collective experiences of a people whose "raw suffering"
is a helpless response to the loss of virtually everything they had (121).
Said knows better than to compare his own imaginative self-construc-
tion as an exile to the material plight of the Palestinian refugees he reg-
ularly encounters, even if he remains acutely conscious of, and inevitably touched by, the recent history of the region: "the broken
trajectory imposed on so many of us by the events of 1948" (113). In
fact, Said's identity crisis is aggravated, rather than alleviated, by the secure knowledge of his own privilege, which implicates him in a waning
colonial authority represented by his English-medium schooling and
which contributes to his mounting feeling that as a "non-Arab" in the
Arab world, a "non-American" in America, he seems destined to "remain the outsider, no matter what I did" (236, 248).

Examples are not lacking in the text to illustrate this status. In

Egypt, Said experiences the "fundamental dissonance" of the privileged foreigner, with access to the best schools and social circles, but "without recourse to [a] real point of origin"—a separation intuitively linked to "the collapse [and] disappearance" of Palestine itself (127–28, 116). In Lebanon, his shifting attitude to Dhour—the family's luxurious holiday retreat—is similarly symptomatic of what he fatalistically calls his "unrequited attempt to belong to and somehow retain a place that, in the end, will set its course as part of a country more volatile, more fragmented, more bitterly divided than any of us [had] suspected [before]" (270). America, meanwhile, merely "accentuates the disorientation that has accrued to me," despite the obvious material advantages that living and working in one of the world's wealthiest countries affords (222). But it is in Palestine that he experiences his own sense of existential self-division most keenly, registered through the displaced form of the "departures, arrivals, farewells, exile, nostalgia, homesickness, belonging, and travel itself . . . that [are] at the core of my memories of those early years" (xiv). Most of this travel is hardly forced; much of it relates to his father's business interests. But mobility, in *Out of Place,* still manages to generate considerable anxiety, for all Said's best efforts to recuperate the existential freedom and fluid subjectivity of the privileged traveler, whose volatile identity, distilled into a "cluster of flowing currents," is to be preferred to the reassuring fiction of a "solid self" (295).

In his best-known work, *Orientalism* (1978), Said had already shown ironic awareness of his own construction as an "Oriental," albeit one who, "traversing the imperial East-West divide," has self-consciously "entered [into] the life of the West" (336). "My study of Orientalism," he says a touch archly, "has been the attempt to inventory the traces upon me, the Oriental subject, of the culture whose domination has been so powerful a factor in the life of all Orientals" (25). *Out of Place* extends this inventory by critically exploring the idea of an "imaginative geography" in which "all kinds of suppositions, associations, and fictions appear to crowd the unfamiliar space outside one's own" (*Orientalism,* 54). As *travel writing,* the text is split between an imaginative geography whose naturalized distinctions are at the heart of the self-sustaining project of Orientalism, and a concerted attempt to undo the ideological workings of this geography, in which the right to travel is linked, implicitly if not explicitly, with the imagined freedoms of the West. As *memoir,* the text is similarly torn between the willed autonomy of memory and the recognition that memory may serve as an ideological conduit through which certain, sometimes willfully distorted, versions of the past are represented, while others are systematically repressed. In this double context, it might be fair to say that Said's memoir, while explicitly anti- or counter-Orientalist, still manages to perform some Orientalizing maneuvers of its own.

Said's Freudian distinction between manifest and latent varieties of Orientalism may be helpful in explaining this. A good example of manifest Orientalism in the text is Said's experience at Victoria College. The would-be "Eton of the Middle East" (180), the college provides an exercise in colonial subject formation that, under the guise of maintaining Western standards, Orientalizes its majority Arabic-speaking students, who are regarded as incurable delinquents hopelessly ill-equipped for the school's mission to reinvigorate a moribund colonial elite:

> There was a great distortion underlying the Victoria College life, which I was unaware of at the time. The students were seen as paying members of some putative colonial elite that was being schooled in the ways of a British imperialism that had already expired, though we did not fully know it. We learned about English life and letters, the monarchy and Parliament, India and Africa, habits and idioms that we could never use in Egypt or, for that matter, anywhere else. Being and speaking Arabic were delinquent activities at VC, and accordingly we were never given proper instruction in our own language, history, culture, and geography. . . . [W]e all felt that we were inferiors pitted against a wounded colonial power that was dangerous and capable of inflicting harm on us, even as we seemed compelled to study its language and its culture as the dominant one in Egypt. (185–86)

If Orientalism, as Said claims, "Orientalizes the Orient" in the interests of upholding Western imperial authority, then Victoria College (as its name suggests) is a classic case. More interesting, perhaps, is the *latent* Orientalism that accrues to the text as a displaced travel narrative organized around a series of readily identifiable "Oriental" tropes. It is the ambivalent position of Said as the text's primary speaking subject that is crucial here. In classically Orientalist travel narratives, the narrator operates as an enabling interlocutor, usually for the purpose of peddling stereotypes under the guise of supplying cultural information that might prove useful to the West. A variant on this is the type of account produced by what Rob Nixon calls a "semi-insider," such as someone born and bred in the Orient, but reporting back on it from and for the West (28). *Out of Place,* as might be expected, resists these facile binary categories; indeed, the whole of Said's work can be seen as a cumulative attempt to contradict, or at least complicate, the inevitably reductive generalizations and provocatively instant formulations that have tended—with renewed vigor after 9/11—to govern the relationship between the "Arab world" and the "West." Said's position, however, remains torn between that of an articulate, self-critical Western commentator and that of a privileged spokesperson for the Palestinian people—both compromised roles, as the text indicates, but still ones that the text, despite the apprehension of dissonance that attends it, never quite manages to reject. Travel memoir is the literary device by which these different roles are precariously held together, but also the unreliable vehicle through which they are always at risk of falling apart. Another way of saying this is that the text's "out-of-placeness" is the effect of an inevitably unsuccessful attempt on Said's part to reconcile his public, conspicuously Westernized persona with his private, residually but ambivalently Palestinian self. What results is a text that struggles against its own latent Orientalist impulses, even as it displays the internal differentiations that disqualify any easy understanding, or specious application, of the manufactured categories of the "Arab world" and the "West."

Out of Place, I have been suggesting, inhabits its own contradictions; not that this has prevented Said's adversaries from triumphantly bringing these to light. The reception of the text indicates what Leigh Gilmore calls the "crisis of legitimacy" that often surrounds the truth claims made by memoir as a testimonial form. An extreme example of this is Justus Reid Weiner's bitter accusation, in a piece published in the partisan Jewish cultural-historical journal *Commentary,* that *Out of Place* offers only a partial, significantly belated corrective to the "tissue of falsehoods" that surrounds Said's autobiographical work (25). Weiner's article, it quickly emerged, was not without its own ideologically motivated inaccuracies. What interests me here, though, is the process by which memoir, oscillating as it does between reality and fantasy, is nonetheless held accountable to a "moral grammar" (Gilmore) that insists on incontrovertible facts. Perhaps we should distinguish here between two apparently incompatible types of memoirs: those that work toward confirming the authenticity of recovered memory, and then those that tend to challenge it. The first type always risks being seized upon as an object of censure (e.g., through its exposure as "fraudulent" narrative); the second recognizes the inevitable entanglement of identification with fantasy and desire (Gilmore). In reality, however, the two types are frequently commingled—a blurring that is particularly problematic in the case of memoirs that seek to account for experiences of individual or collective suffering, and more problematic still when that suffering takes the form of buried memories of sexual abuse. In this latter case, Gilmore suggests, we shouldn't leap to accusations of "false memory" but rather try to contextualize the process by which memories are deployed in a "therapeutic narrative about sexuality"—including memories, not necessarily our own, that are co-opted as a means of making "a kind of symbolic sense that what really happened failed to provide" (26, 47). In what follows, I propose to read Norma Khouri's controversial memoir *Forbidden Love* (2003), accordingly, as an example of a displaced trauma fantasy that simultaneously manipulates the conventions, and reader expectations, of subaltern testimony and Orientalist romance.

Forbidden Love tells the "true" story of a young Jordanian woman (Dalia), who enters into an illicit romance with an officer (Michael) from the Royal Jordanian Army. She is Muslim, he Christian—an impossible affair that, when found out, results in an appalling "honor killing" that interpellates her as a sacrificial victim of the indomitable "Arab way of life" (24). The story is narrated by the autobiographical figure of Norma, a self-styled "dissident émigré" (*sic*), who, looking back six years from the beginning of the fateful adventure, now seizes the opportunity to reach out to progressive non-Arab women readers across the world (207). Generically, the text is armchair travel disguised as humanitarian treatise, with its stock romance plot unfurling against a background of Jordanian geography and history—touristic snippets of cultural information intended primarily to support the authenticity of the text. The text itself, however, has taken second place to the scandal surrounding its exposure as "tainted testimony" (Whitlock)—as the largely fabricated story of an author who, capitalizing on global post 9/11 insecurities, has fashioned a shoddy parable aimed at reasserting the moral authority of the West. Certainly, the text is full of dire pronouncements on the intrinsic violence of Islam, categorically denounced as a "totalitarian regime operating under the guise of a religion," and as a social pretext for the "total submission of women" to unchanging Muslim law (60, 68).

The emphasis here is on the "barbaric practice" of honor killing, seen as a "cultural hangover of tribal life that pre-dates both Islam and Christianity," and likened bizarrely to headhunting as a "primitive . . . anthropological" rite (195–96). Dedicated to the memory of Dalia, Norma's close friend, the text thus looks to mobilize Western feminist-humanitarian sympathies, metaphorically lifting the veil of the Oriental woman in the name of "liberating" her, only to reveal the ideological obsessions of the "liberated" West (Yeğenoğlu, 12). Gillian Whitlock, whose detailed account of the "Khouri affair" is particularly illuminating, summarizes it as follows:

> *Forbidden Love* suggests how "rights discourse" can be used in bad faith in these times. . . . [The text's labeling] as non-fiction, its claims as testimony to the truth of honour killings in Jordan, courted a connection to authenticity and made claims on the reader's empathic response which are quite different to the appeal and logic of romance. Khouri aspired to the status of an authoritative interpreter of Arab culture, launching her book as a vehicle of activism through the human rights campaigns [orchestrated by] non-government organizations. [And] for a short time, she became an "expert witness," representing Arab culture (both Islamic and Christian) in terms of a binary logic that privileges the west as the representative of universal values of human rights, democracy and free speech. (175–76)

I would agree with all of this, except for the fact that the text retains its status as a romance, very much of the Orientalist variety, and that it displays its generic hybridity as authentic testimony/exotic fantasy from the start. As Maggie Nolan and Carrie Dawson usefully suggest in their introduction to the volume in which Whitlock's essay appears, more attention needs to be paid to *genre* in ascertaining degrees of autobiographical reliability. A genre-based approach, the authors contend, might help counteract the polarized view of "false" literary testimonies that either castigates them as self-serving appropriations that pander to cultural stereotypes, or celebrates them for their thought-provoking analyses of the fluid subjectivities they explore (xvii).

Bearing this caveat in mind, my contention here is that *Forbidden*

Love is a fantasized "real-life" story, an outsider's inside report that self-consciously combines, but also shamelessly manipulates, the generic conventions of traumatic testimony and exotic romance. As in *Out of Place,* the position of the autobiographical narrator is crucial. Ostensibly, Norma represents the figure of the "semi-insider," semi-liberated Arab woman, covetous of the modern freedoms of the West and star witness for the prosecution of a residually archaic Arab world. Speaking from and for the West, this figure invokes "the metonymic association between the Orient and its women," which serves to turn the Oriental/Arab woman into an overdetermined symbol of the oppressive, unfree nature of the entire Arab world itself (Yeğenoğlu, 99). It is important to note, though, that there are *two* women in the text. Taken together, these women (Norma and Dalia) represent the twin components of a split Oriental female subject; this dyad functions through the linking of the figure of the Westernized interlocutor (Norma) to the sacrificial discourse (the murder of Dalia) that then allows the fully emancipated figure of the Western female subject (Norma as "dissident émigré") to emerge. As Elisabeth Bronfen (1992) might put it, Norma's freedom is pronounced over Dalia's dead body, and all within the context of an Orientalist trauma fantasy that "speaks through" the subaltern woman in the name of a liberated West (Bronfen, *Over*).

This split subject stands at the center of a dialectic of revelation and concealment that is integral not only to the romance plotline, but to the cultural and political circumstances that surround the production of the text. One way of looking at this is through what Whitlock sardonically calls the genre of the "veiled best-seller" (neither Norma nor Dalia wear the veil, but that doesn't stop a veiled woman from featuring lavishly on the front cover of Khouri's book). As Whitlock points out, the paratextual elements of the book—front-cover image, back-cover blurb, and so forth—trade on a consolidated genre of mainly American feminist writing about the region (169). In this genre, the veil features largely as a symbol of oppression, thereby confirming the post-Orientalist transition of the Oriental woman from figure of sexual allure to object of sexual abuse. Exotic romance thus forms a cover (a veil?) for human rights abuses, self-evidently attached to Islam, that demand the active intervention of the West. This contemporary version of the Orientalization of the Orient endorses humanitarian imperialism in the shape of sensationalized life narratives by Arab women that offer privileged Western readers "the pleasures of empathic identification" (Whitlock, 170) while providing the moral bonus of their own "self-affirmation as empowered agents of social change" (Schaffer and Smith, 12). The dialectic of revelation and concealment, in this context, revolves around the journalistic, deliberately romanticized exposure of oppressive sexual practices that modernized Arab countries like Jordan are keen to shield from the public eye. At the same time, the duplicities of a social system that tacitly upholds honor killing are reproduced in Khouri's false true narrative: one that, apparently inviting its own exposure, melodramatically conceals the shameful secret at its heart. The truth claims of the text thus correspond to what Meyda Yeğenoğlu calls the Orientalist logic of veiling, whereby the veil "represents simultaneously the truth and [its] concealment"; "the truth of the Orient," she suggests, "is an effect of the veil" insofar as it emerges in "the traumatic encounter with its [own] untruth" (48).

This admittedly generous view of the text implies that it is using romantic license to cover its own deceptions, and to set up a compact in which the reader is jointly co-opted as moral agent and cultural voyeur. It also suggests that loaded terms like *hoax* and *fraud,* while neither inappropriate nor unjustified, fail to do justice to the tangled motivations of Khouri's text. If, as I have been arguing so far, it is the split nature of the book as *memoir/romance* that is at the center of the puzzle, then that split is partly negotiated by its intermediary status as *travel text.* This status is far from obvious. Most commentators on the text have understandably preferred to see it as playing on the conventions of subaltern testimony—that morally satisfying genre that usually consists in "the subaltern giving witness to oppression, to a less oppressed other" (Spivak, "Three Women's Texts," 7). Traumatic testimony of this kind draws moral authority from what Gilmore calls "the cultural power of truth telling" but also from the authenticity of shared experience, the affective bond that links up the writer with the reader of the text (3). Seen in these terms, *Forbidden Love* cannot help but be seen as violating the trust of the readers whose help it enlists and whose sympathy it fosters—a legitimate reaction, but one still tied to a particular set of generic expectations of the text. Another possibility, however, would be to see the text as being indirectly related to *travel memoir,* a form that tends to undermine the authority of the witness by emphasizing the distance—in both time and space—that separates the teller from the tale. While travel memoir is generically split, it also produces a split narrating subject; its imaginative recall can only ever be partial, such that it often creates the uncanny effect (*Out of Place* is a good example here) of a continual, or at least continually repeated, estrangement from place. More to the point, travel memoir sets up a contract between writer and reader that is qualitatively different from that of either testimony (where trust is invoked) or romance (where disbelief is suspended), although its distinctiveness as a genre derives, precisely, from its capacity to forge a working relationship between these two apparently incompatible genres. What kind of contract is this? At the risk of oversimplifying, I would say that it is a contract based on (1) the expectation of embellishment, (2) the possibility of shared voyeurism, and (3) the mutual recognition of a split perspective, both at the level of narration and, more occasionally, reception of the text. What I am suggesting here—without wishing to defend Khouri, or to claim that the problems of the text are solved by it being seen as travel memoir—is that travel memoir is constitutively ambivalent, and that it draws the reader into complicity with the uncertainly remembered events it relates. The moral complexities of travel memoir are still greater when, as is the case with *Out of Place* (a travel memoir by design) and *Forbidden Love* (a travel memoir by default), the story told is also a record of acute suffering, however much that suffering is unconsciously transferred (Khouri) or deliberately displaced (Said).

It is a truism that traumatic memories are hazardous to handle; another that their representations of abuse and suffering convert the reader into an accomplice or voyeur. Whatever the case, as Gilmore rightly asserts, memoirs and other testimonial forms court attention for their intimate secrets; they provide a popular medium for the introjection of the private into the public realm (49). And when their veracity is contested, there is the strong likelihood that, tapping the ideological pulse of the moment, they will become more public still (49). That defining moment, certainly for *Forbidden Love,* is 9/11. Both *Forbidden Love* and, prophetically perhaps, *Out of Place* are 9/11 narratives connected to what Said calls the "imaginative demonology" of the Orient—to paranoid fantasies of a simultaneously threatened and threatening Arab world (*Orientalism,* 26). The two writers' responses, of course, could hardly be more different. Said's text is dedicated to the undoing of Orientalist binaries; Khouri's is largely concerned with reinstating them. But both, in their very different ways, explore the distinctive entanglement of identities—exile/refugee, Christian/Muslim, foreigner/local—that, emerging from current conditions of globalization, also contributes, like globalization itself, to a violently divided world.

Postscript: After Bali

In the notes to his essay "Tourists, Terrorists, Death and Value" (1999), Peter Phipps cites an "ongoing litany of violence" directed against tourists and tourist destinations:

> [Achille] Lauro: hijacking . . . Beirut: "playground of the rich" to civil war . . . Tokyo: subway gassing . . . TWA: mysterious explosion and crash . . . Lockerbie: bombing . . . Manchester: bombing . . . Cambodia: hostages . . . London Docklands: bombing . . . Irian Jaya (West Papua): hostages . . . Egypt: random attacks on foreign nationals . . . Gulf War: travel angst . . . Uffizi Gallery Florence: bombing . . . Dubrovnic, World Heritage listed city: destruction by shelling in Balkan war . . . Balangalow State Forest, New South Wales: backpacker serial murders . . . Port Arthur, Tasmania: mass murder . . . World Trade Building, New York: bombing . . . Jerusalem tunnel: riots/civil war . . . Sri Lanka: repeated hotel bombings and Temple of the Tooth bombing . . . Miami: tourist serial murders . . . Empire State Building: mass murder . . . Kashmir: Al-Faran hostages . . . Luxor, Egypt: massacre of tourists. (90)

Another addition to this depressing list is what has loosely come to be known as the "Bali bombings": the Jemaah Islamiah–instigated bombs that ripped apart the Sari Club at Kuta Beach, a popular tourist nightspot, and that resulted in over two hundred civilian deaths, nearly half of them Australian holidaymakers. The Bali bombings reconfirmed the vulnerability of tourists, particularly Western tourists, in a globalized environment of extreme political instability: a post-9/11 world described as being in a collective state of emergency, where global space has come increasingly to assume the character of a lawless frontierland, and in which "the bluff of local solutions to planetary problems has been called [and] the sham of territorial isolation has been exposed" (Bauman, 84). It is not difficult to see why tourists have become such an easy terrorist target: they are readily available "marked bodies" (Diller and Scofidio); their behavior and appearance are often conspicuous; and their relative affluence and perceived sexual license always run the risk of attracting local resentment. Tourists tend to flaunt the freedoms that other people covet, or to exhibit unrestrained forms of behavior that, if not directly disrespectful, can easily be taken as a badge of Western materialist excess. Above all, tourists are, as Phipps bluntly puts it, nothing less than "value in motion, both in their regular operation as consumers, and in their more rarefied symbolic value as exchange objects embodying another nationalism, for example as 'normalizers of relations' (US visitors to China post-Nixon), or as hostages, such as in the Kashmir situation" (79).

Although, in a globalized world, specific tourist identities have arguably become blurred to the point of being interchangeable, the ambassadorial function of tourists as *national* representatives, possibly "indirect representatives of hostile or unsympathetic governments" (Richter and Waugh, 235), can be seen paradoxically to have gained in strength in present times.[1] To some extent, this is an effect of the shaping role of national as well as international media. International publicity, of course, is one of the primary objectives behind acts of terrorism, which can itself be generally defined as both "a symbolic event and a performance that is staged for the benefit of media attention" (Sönmez, 439). But at the same time, the media representation of terrorist victims, frequently framed within a martyrology of "slaughtered innocents," is often explicitly nationalist in sentiment. This was certainly the case with the Bali bombings, where Australian media coverage repeatedly sought out analogies, both with the destruction of New York's Twin Towers ("October 12" as Australia's very own, equally nightmarish version of "September 11"), and with the elegiac nationalist iconography of repatriated Australian bodies being flown back in the aftermath of the Vietnam War.

In the months following the Bali bombings, it emerged more clearly that the bombings were connected with the work of Jemaah Islamiah, a highly organized Southeast Asian Islamic militant network with links to al Qaeda; and that their main motive was a revenge killing for perceived acts of anti-Islamic state terrorism: "I carry out jihad," said one of the bombers, Imam Samudra, "because it is the duty of a Muslim to avenge, so [that] the American terrorists and their allies understand that the blood of the Muslim community is not shed for nothing" (quoted in Elegant, 3). Bali was selected, added Samudra, because "it is the meeting place of international terrorists like the U.S., Britain, France, Germany, Belgium, Australia, Israel, [and] Communist China. Bali is a sinful place located in a country where Muslims are the majority" (quoted in Elegant, 5).

The garbled testimony given by Samudra and his main ally in the bombings, Ali Ghufron (alias Mukhlas), emphasizes terrorism expert Walter Laqueur's point that the "new terrorism" tends to be inspired by a jumble of ill-defined, often seemingly irrational, motives. Terrorism, argues Laqueur, "has proceeded from limited to total and indiscriminate warfare; certainly as far as the targets are concerned, quite often the aim is simply to kill or maim as many people as possible" (281). Tourists may be targeted, in this last sense, not just because they carry symbolic capital as agents of Western imperialism/affluence/decadence but for no other good reason than that they are simply there in force. They are quite literally moving targets, whose individual freedoms may provide just cause for resentment, but whose collective behavior makes it fairly easy to identify them with, and in, particular places. In addition, Samudra's designation of international tourists as "terrorists," for all its indiscriminate rage, is not quite as counterintuitive as it seems. As the sociologist Sevil Sönmez among others has suggested, tourism and terrorism are inextricably entangled. Thus, while it is obvious that terrorism—or any other calculated act of violence—will have a negative effect on tourism, it is also true that "international terrorism and tourism share certain characteristics. They both cross national borders, involve citizens of different countries, and utilize travel and communications technologies" (421).[2] More surprising, perhaps, is that terrorism spawns—as has been argued throughout this book—new forms of participatory tourism: the type of "combat" or "danger-zone" tourism that takes pleasure in the "thrill of political violence" (Pitts, 224); or various kinds of more or less interventionist post-conflict tourism that are either motivated by the desire to bear witness to catastrophe, or to commemorate it, or to report back from the site.

A brief excursus on Bali, and the variety of touristic responses it has elicited, may help to shed light, not only on the 2002 bombings, but also on several of the tourism-related themes—globalization, the self-induced perils of "world risk society" (Beck), the lure of disaster, the memory industry—that have provided the main subject for this book. Bali, after all, in the several decades since it first opened up to international mass tourism, has become one of the world's foremost tourist icons. For many travelers, it is both the epitome of the nostalgic tropical paradise and the symbol of what happens when tourism, taking over a fragile island ecology, transforms but also irreparably damages it—with tourism featuring here in its familiar, but not entirely mythological, guise as the creator of the beauty it then destroys. A good example of this double script can be found in Lonely Planet's 2001 guide to Bali. The opening paragraphs of the guidebook read as follows:

> Say Bali, and most Westerners think of paradise and tourism. Bali offers plenty of both and much more. The image of Bali as a tropical paradise dates back to Western visitors in the 1920s, and this image has been cultivated by the international tourist industry rather than by the Balinese, who do not even have a word for paradise in their language. Nevertheless, Bali is a good candidate for paradise—so picturesque it could be a painted backdrop . . . [its landscape,] imbued with spiritual significance, forms a part of rich cultural life of the Balinese, whose natural grace fits the image of how people should live in paradise.
>
> There's no denying that Bali has become a mass tourism destination, and perhaps this is a disappointment to some visitors who not only expect a paradise, but expect it to be untouched by the rest of the world. It's still a great place for a tropical island holiday if that's what you want—and many people do. (Lyon, Greenway, and Wheeler, 11)

The bathos that accompanies the transition from the first paragraph to the second is characteristic of Lonely Planet's ironic pragmatism in the face of rapid touristic expansion: an expansion that its own spectacularly successful commercial enterprise has of course done much to assist. In fact, the stages through which Bali has gone since its evolution into a mass tourist destination in the 1960s and 1970s are almost uncannily mirrored by equivalent developments in Lonely Planet's marketing strategies and ideological approach. Two stages are predominant, the first associated with the allegedly countercultural aspects of international backpacker travel, the second bound up with an increasing recognition of the limitations, and likely self-deceptions, of the free-wheeling backpacker approach. These stages will be treated briefly in turn here before being linked up more immediately with Bali; the postscript will then consider the implications of both sets of developments as a means of bringing the themes of the book together and of ushering it to its close.

The initial Lonely Planet ethos is spelled out in some of the early volumes of its tellingly named "Travel Survival Kit" series. This ethos is characterized by, among other things, a tendency to reify the now thoroughly clichéd distinction between the discerning traveler and the vulgar tourist. In the first edition of *South-East Asia on a Shoestring* (1975), for instance, Tony Wheeler—founder and self-styled guru figure of the Lonely Planet enterprise—explicitly distinguishes between the roles of the traveler and the tourist: "Certain places in the region attract the tourist crowds but once you have escaped the byways there are perfect places . . . that only the people who are willing to put in a little effort and withstand some discomfort will really appreciate" (4). This particular, by now all-too-familiar form of "anti-tourist tourism" (Holland and Huggan) is backed up by appeals to peripheral destinations and alternative, low-impact styles of cultural tourism, even though the term *backpacker* by which such styles would probably now (ironically?) be recognized did not appear in the guides themselves until the publication of the Papua New Guinea "travel survival kit" in 1981.

In fact, as Gillian Kenny points out in an article on Lonely Planet, the company has always been ambivalent about the "alternative" claims of backpacker culture, mischievously inclined to poke fun at the comforts, and comforting myths, of Western bourgeois orthodoxy but, at the same time, not averse to warning readers of the likely fallout of exaggeratedly anti-establishment behavior, for example, in conformist Asian cultures (115). The early guides, according to Kenny, were equally ambiguous in their attitude toward the touristic search for authenticity, neither subscribing wholeheartedly to the existential gains to be derived from, say, the cultivation of adversity and physical hardship, nor choosing to embrace the "comfort-zone" alternatives of touristic insulation and guaranteed institutional support (116). Despite obvious inconsistencies and contradictions in the early guidebooks, not all of whose writers shared the same views or ideology, a pattern began to emerge that helped to articulate a distinctive identity for Lonely Planet's readers/travelers, to describe a new type of independent-minded budget travel, and to define the parameters of an emerging backpacker culture (118). Summing up, Kenny usefully identifies seven defining characteristics: "an assertion of the identity of the traveler as opposed to that of the tourist; peripheral destinations; the hard work of travel; an ambivalent attitude to western counter-culture; independence; the search for experience; and a dynamic identity which revealed a shift toward catering for an increasing number of mainstream tourists in addition to its traditional backpacking readers" (118–19).

As Kenny asserts, "the modern 'backpacking' phenomenon has arguably itself become a mainstream form of travel in its permeation of the international travel scene; it is becoming less distinguishable from the tourism the series distanced itself from in the early guides" (119). Certainly, Lonely Planet's extraordinary rags-to-riches success—the company currently employs more than four hundred staff in four different countries; some six hundred products bear its logo; and, from self-dramatized "humble origins," it now controls a sizable percentage of the lucrative guidebook and associated products market[3]—owes much to its skill in anticipating, as well as servicing, the latest global touristic developments. Two of these developments, which serve to some extent as mutual correctives, are the fanning out of current options within the "responsible tourism" sector—ecotourism, educative tourism, enlightened cultural alternatives—and the diversification of mainstream tourism itself, which now takes in and effectively recycles a variety of previously marginal activities and "lifestyle" choices.

Sensibly, Wheeler now makes little attempt to stake a claim for his company as a purveyor of alternative or peripheral travel, even though he bullishly stands by his view that the Lonely Planet empire supports environmentally and culturally sensitive travel in an age of unparalleled ecological destruction and recrudescent racist/xenophobic beliefs.[4] However, it is difficult to be supportive of this view given the relentlessness of Lonely Planet's commercial opportunism (the company wasted no time, for example, in "moving in" to war-torn Afghanistan after media coverage had helped establish it as a fashionable danger zone, and it continues to milk profits by sending tourists to places where greater cultural sensitivity would undoubtedly be demonstrated by staying at home). For all its considerable marketing skills, Lonely Planet is neither saved by its trademark self-irony nor exonerated by its strategic admission of responsibility. There is something disingenuous, distasteful even, about Wheeler's admission that the ubiquitous back-packing culture he helped to spawn has had a negative, as well as a dy-namically transformative, effect on many local societies and cultures. "The place I always look at is Kuta Beach on Bali," he says in a 2001 in-terview, published in the magazine *Time International*: "It was really quite a wonderful place, and I go back now and think, 'What a hell-hole'" (Roderick et al., 8).[5]

Wheeler adheres to the common view here of Bali as a ruined par-adise, a view that has not stopped more than a million tourists visiting the island every year. Unsurprisingly, these figures tailed off sharply af-ter the bombings, with some hotel occupancy rates dropping below 10 percent (*Bali Travel News,* February 2003). The Indonesian govern-ment's response, meanwhile, was to strengthen security on the island while attempting to improve damaged public relations by announcing 2003 as the Year of Peace and Anti-Violence. More recent figures sug-gest a recovery. The Balinese tourist industry—like its vassal, Lonely Planet—has been creative enough to adapt to new conditions; it ap-pears less likely in the future to fall victim to crime than to its own suc-cess. Even so, the familiar trope of the "turning point," already much in evidence since 9/11, made regular appearances in the media, particu-larly in Australia. Consider, for example, the cliché-laden opening sen-tences of the Australian journalist Alan Atkinson's "instant book" on the Bali bombings, *Three Weeks in Bali* (2002):

> The Bali bombings have been a turning point. Carefree tourists and honeymooners have long flown to Bali from Australia and many other countries. They have been looking for a holiday with a difference and a brief taste of Asia in what has been a safe haven away from violence in other parts of the region.
>
> Now that has changed. Kuta Beach, its nightclubs, bars and cheap shopping are no longer an attractive lure for many young people and probably won't be for some time to come. And it may be a long time

before other tourists return to sample the island's rich Hindu traditions, temples, breathtaking scenery and the legendary friendliness of its people. (5)

Atkinson's book is characteristic of on-site responses to the bombings that claimed a common sympathy with stricken Balinese hosts, as well as distraught foreign victims, and that shied away from political readings in favor of providing a "personal touch." The book is an example, in other words, of a liberal strand of humanitarian travel journalism that trades on public interest in disasters while generally avoiding introspection into their larger, structural cause. Not that politics is left out of the picture altogether; for Atkinson, in considering who might have perpetrated the bombings, does at least speculate briefly on the potential of both U.S. and Indonesian governments to use the opportunity, in the first case, to call for further action against Iraq and/or al Qaeda, and, in the second, to "blame terrorists, controlled from outside, rather than have the fingers of suspicion pointed at myriad groups within the country with political axes to grind, or at a notorious rabble of military rebels" (67). Mostly, however, he avoids inquiring into the obvious relevance of international *tourism* to the bombings, preferring to see the host-guest encounter as a paragon of intercultural harmony whose reciprocal generosity has only been temporarily disturbed (107–11). Nor does he comment on the alternative touristic forms that sprang up in the wake of the bombings, despite evidence that the crime scene was "trampled by sightseers" (74), and that a major concern for the Balinese police in the wake of the tragedy was to prevent crowds of eager onlookers from restricting access to relief workers at the site (58).

In several respects, Atkinson's book, as well as the events it relates, are illustrative of tourists' "dialectic of innocence" (Phipps): the tangled process by which "their very innocence as consumers propels them into being guilty participants, even agents, of global exploitation and corruption" (Phipps, 86). This anxiety is expressed, in turn, in a great deal of modern travel writing, attuned as it is to the shifting parameters of international tourist culture, and torn as it remains between the countervailing desires to *engage* in the world—the perceived obligation to "make a difference"—and to *retreat* from the world into a manufactured environment of often imagined contentment—the felt need to "make an escape." While nostalgia, in its many guises, still provides one of the mainstays of contemporary travel/writing, its primarily escapist sensibility is insufficient to account for the several new—perhaps better, revitalized—travel practices that seek a more kinetically charged connection with the world(s) in which travelers act and through which they move, often at great speed and with considerable risk. (These practices also indicate that the thrill of speed and risk often substitutes for more direct forms of social action.) The Bali/Lonely Planet nexus helps bring out this "new," increasingly frenetic spirit of touristic interventionism: a spirit in which the older-style authenticities of *endurance* that used to epitomize and valorize "the hard work of travel" (Kenny, 119) are now making way for an unprecedently accelerated, potentially self-consuming authenticity of *endangerment.* By no means all contemporary travel practices carry a warning sign, of course; while an increased blurring of the distinction between "actual" and simulated practices is often suggestive, less of a newfound desire to bridge the gap between "passive" consumption and "active" experience, than of a fashionable post-touristic disdain for any attempt to make a meaningful distinction between the two (Ritzer and Liska). Nonetheless, it is an undeniably endangered world that competes for the attention of modern tourists: one in which global attractions like Bali can be potentially repackaged, not as paradisal sanctuaries from a world in conflict but as the world's latest disaster/memorial sites.

The twenty-first century has so far shown every sign of prolonging the "age of extremes," the British historian Eric Hobsbawm's vivid designation of the century that preceded it. These extremes are evidenced in the routine occurrence of disaster and atrocity; in the mounting risk of environmental apocalypse; and in an active memory industry that helps to further reify suffering as spectacle and to confirm the formidable symbolic power of death. Tourism is a product, but also a symptom, of this increasingly endangered global environment; its ideologies, as Phipps observes, are thoroughly "implicated in the structuring of the violent times in which we dwell" (75). As Dean MacCannell first suggested more than thirty years ago, tourism is a barometer registering the fluctuations and seismic shifts of modernity. The current conjuncture is arguably marked by a global state of emergency in which tourists can be seen both as potential victims of other people's violence and as unwilling/unwitting violators in their own right. Agents of global capital, tourists embody some of the worst excesses of modernity, not least its apparent propensity for self-destruction. In this radically unstable context, the confusion of tourists with soldiers, or the counter-image of the tourist as terrorist, are by no means as preposterous as they might first appear. In such extreme conditions, travel writers—as many of them are only too well aware—carry considerable responsibilities: in their capacity to critique the tourist industry they serve, but also in their ability to offer alternative ways of looking at, engaging with, and imaginatively transforming the worlds through which they travel, and the world in which we all live. For travel writing—tourism itself—is far from just another consumer-oriented entertainment vehicle; it has the potential to offer a powerful response to global processes of social and cultural transformation. Meanwhile, it remains profoundly implicated in those transformation processes—which calls to mind another, equally powerful counter-image of the tourist: that emblematic figure for globalized modernity's violent disruptions and displacements, the refugee.[6]

Notes

Chapter One

1. For further thoughts on this homology, see Goldstone, especially chap. 3, "The Biggest Business in the World." Goldstone shows the different ways in which tourism, which generates over 10 percent of the world's gross domestic product, drives especially smaller economies within the context of an American-dominated world order in which tourism is considered essential both to "the evolutionary scale of development" and to the promotion of international trade and goodwill (61).

2. See, for example, McMaster: "Refugees . . . encapsulate the contemporary [global] political identity crisis. In their homelessness and statelessness refugees are the unwilling representatives of a cosmopolitan alternative to the idea of a homeland. The ideal homeland can be seen as unrealisable, or alternatively recognised as the site of struggle against the reductionism of national identity" (21). For an analysis of the relationship between refugees and globalization, see Richmond; on the cosmopolitan-refugee relationship, see the discussions in this chapter.

3. Critical cosmopolitanism, for Mignolo, is a form of dissenting cosmopolitanism that, while self-consciously internationalist in its outlook, remains "attentive to the dangers and excesses of [grand] global designs" (723). It seeks alternatives to dominant "center-periphery" understandings of global modernity while recognizing that cosmopolitanism can only be critical from inside modernity itself (724). For alternative versions of critical cosmopolitanism, see the essays in Breckenridge et al., one of which is Mignolo's; for a succinct summary of the implications of critical cosmopolitanism, see also Walkowitz. Just how critical Iyer's cosmopolitanism is is a moot point; a much clearer case, at least prima facie, would be the work of Suketu Mehta and, particularly, Amitava Kumar, whose self-consciously cosmopolitan travel narratives are analyzed later in this chapter.

4. *Glocalization,* a term originally taken from business discourse, refers to

the cultural mutuality of the local and the global in any globalization process; in Tomlinson's gloss on Robertson, the term insists "that the local and the global do not exist as cultural polarities but as mutually 'interpenetrating' principles" (Tomlinson, 196; see also Robertson, 30). Glocalization works both ways, implying, for example, that while globalization is necessarily shaped by local interests, it also plays an active role in how the local is *produced*. For an extended discussion of glocalization, in both theory and practice, see Appadurai, *Modernity*.

5. *Conviviality* has become a key term in recent cultural studies discussions of alternatives to narrow conceptions of cultural affiliation in both the national and transnational contexts; see, for example, Mignolo and, especially, Gilroy. Much like Mignolo, Gilroy posits the notion of a "planetary conviviality" based on "radical openness," and the capacity to cohabit and interact peacefully and productively in multicultural contexts, against the implicit or explicit triumphalism of a globalism often based on "imperial universals" and the desire to develop and consolidate "supranational systems of control" (xii, 9, 66). See also Gilroy for a discussion of the links between conviviality and cosmopolitanism, particularly in its demotic or vernacular variants; for further thoughts on the implications of vernacular cosmopolitanism, see the discussion of Mehta's and Kumar's work that follows in this chapter.

Chapter Two

1. Apocalypse, claims Larry Buell in chap. 9 of *The Environmental Imagination,* is "the single most powerful master metaphor that the contemporary environmental imagination has at its disposal" (285). While Buell is referring specifically to modalities of environmental *writing,* several of the apocalyptic topoi he mentions—irreversible degradation, the loss of escape routes, "nature's revenge," etc.—permeate the discourse of environmentalism as a whole.

2. The anthropocentric versus biocentric dichotomy is central to the different versions of what is generally known as "deep ecology," one version of which is presented as follows by John Porritt: "The belief that we are 'apart from' the rest of creation is an intrinsic feature of the dominant world-order, a man-centred or anthropocentric philosophy. Ecologists argue that this ultimately destructive belief must be rooted out and replaced with a life-centred or biocentric philosophy" (206). Deep ecologists, or "Dark Greens," generally like to distinguish themselves from environmentalists ("Light Greens"), whom they usually see as being less radical, and as seeking a primarily "managerial approach to environmental problems" (Dobson, 13). (See also Cheryll Glotfelty, who argues that the prefix "enviro-" is "anthropocentric and dualistic, implying that we humans are at the center, surrounded by everything that is not us, the environment" [Glotfelty and Fromm, xx].) But as Andrew Dobson among others has pointed out, there is a tension between the radical aims of deep ecology and "the reliance on traditional liberal-democratic means of bringing [change] about" (23). See Pepper for a useful, if overstated, Marxist critique of deep ecology's "bogus radicalism," and of the misguided—even misanthropic—tendencies of "one-world" eco- or biocen-

tric philosophies that "ignore the importance of struggle to change the social order" (141). For a more balanced view of deep ecology that acknowledges its continuing commitment to social transformation, see Merchant. Finally, see Curtin, who endorses "weak anthropocentrism" as a means of combining agendas for ecological freedom and human justice, and who sees the traditional binaries of evironmental philosophy (including that between anthropocentrism and biocentrism) as outdated.

3. *Ecological imperialism,* according to the historian Alfred Crosby, refers to the deliberate, as well as adventitious, means by which environmental (mis)management historically contributed to systems of European imperial rule. For a fuller exploration of the term, as well as a number of historical case studies, see Crosby's book of the same name. Crosby's focus, almost exclusively, is on the destructive impact of imported European practices on indigenous habitats subjected to imperial expansionism. For a partial corrective to Crosby, which also suggests the ecological *benefits* brought about by imperial systems of governance, see Grove. For the relevance of the term to contemporary postcolonial studies, see also Ashcroft, Griffiths, and Tiffin.

4. For a detailed study of nature writing in the European Romantic tradition, see Bate. Subsequent works, such as Buell's, which have attempted to correct what they see as Bate's implicit ethnocentrism, might however be accused of an (in Buell's case, American) ethnocentrism of their own. Self-designated "ecocentric" critics like Bate and Buell, while more sophisticated than most, are still sometimes tempted by the somewhat naïve universalism arguably inherent within ecocentrism as a "one-world" philosophy (see also note 2, this chap.). For alternative critiques of the alleged culture-blindness of ecocentrism, see Curtin and Pepper; for sustained examinations of the ethnocentric tendencies of Euro-American travel/nature writing, see Holland and Huggan and, especially, Pratt, *Imperial.*

5. On the status of the factual in travel writing, see Holland and Huggan (esp. chap. 1); for an attempt to define the poetics of environmental nonfiction, see also Buell (esp. chap. 3). As Buell suggests, environmental writing is never merely referential; rather, its sometimes complex attempts to represent the relation between the "givenness" and the "constructedness" of the natural environment require a radical rethinking of assumptions about the nature of reference and representation themselves (2).

6. As Kane explains early on in the narrative, the Oriente, particularly the cluster of finely differentiated microsystems to be found in the hilly borderlands where the Amazon meets the Andes, constitutes one of the richest biotic environments on the planet, boasting more than 10,000 species of plants and nearly 500 species of birds, "or about two-thirds as many as are found in the entire continental United States" (26). The richest section of this region is the traditional Huaorani homeland (26–27).

7. Travel writing has historically been associated with the mixing of genres: see, for example, Campbell and Pratt, *Imperial.* For evidence of genre blurring in contemporary travel narratives, see Holland and Huggan; for the view that the

borders of travel writing are more porous than ever, and that distinctions between travel writing and putatively "nonfictional" forms such as ethnography have become if anything increasingly tenuous, see also Holland and Huggan.

8. "Environmental imperialism" is associated first and foremost in the text with top-down models of environmental "assistance," at least some of which are little more than corporate buy-offs or expedient agreements between high-level officials with little or no knowledge of the local conditions over which their purportedly magnanimous decisions hold sway. In some cases, the decisions arrived at are bizarrely ironic, as in the Ecuadorian government's ex post facto decision to allow the Huaorani to "monitor" the environmental operations of the very oil company (Maxus) that had already cut a swath through their and other Indian nations' traditional territories, carving up sovereign land for resource extraction while zoning off other areas of previously protected National Park for industrial use (Kane, 232–33).

9. For a discussion of the characteristics of this subgenre, with particular reference to works by O'Hanlon and Matthiessen, see Holland and Huggan, esp. chap. 2, sec. 1 and chap. 4, sec. 2. For an analysis of the role of ecological romance in upholding the "myth of the Amazon," see also Slater.

10. On the strategic uses of amateurism in travel writing, see Holland and Huggan, esp. intro. and chap. 1, sec. 1. The amateurism of Kane's text is clearly displayed in its use of substandard snapshot photography, a common ploy in travel narratives keen to accentuate the "authenticity" of the traveler's experience and to narrow the gap between the lived realities of intercultural contact and the partly mythologized memories of eyewitness travel report.

11. For the view of foreign aid as the "smooth face of imperialism," see Hayter (1971); for a more evenly balanced view, brought more up to date with contemporary global realities, see also Browne.

12. "Touristic shame," says the American sociologist Dean MacCannell, "is not based on being a tourist but on not being tourist enough, on a failure to see everything the way it ought to be seen. The touristic critique of tourism is based on a desire to get beyond the other 'mere' tourists to a more profound appreciation of society and culture" (*Tourist,* 10). While the disaffiliation from "other" tourists is a standard feature of touristic behavior—and also of modern travel writing (Holland and Huggan)—it is given an extra twist by the ecologist Pye-Smith insofar as touristic irresponsibility and arrogance have profound environmental implications. Mass tourism, predictably, is seen as throwing up the worst culprits (e.g., 61–62), thereby allowing Pye-Smith to reinstate the tired traveler-tourist distinction (Buzard; MacCannell, *Tourist*) by rationalizing it in ecological terms.

13. Belatedness is a feature of much modern travel writing, bolstered in some cases by the—inevitably part-ironic—imperial nostalgia with which the latter-day traveler-writer affects to remember the days of pretouristic travel when men were men, the masses were firmly in their place, and the prizes of adventure could still be won. For a sophisticated analysis of belatedness in European travel writing, see Behdad; also Porter.

14. For a critical review of the ethnocentric and, in some more extreme cases,

misanthropic tendencies of radical schools such as deep ecology, see Curtin; see also Dobson for a more nuanced differentiation between the conflicting radical positions within contemporary Green thought.

15. On the crossover between travel writing and ethnography, see Holland and Huggan; Nixon; Pratt, "Fieldwork." Recent evidence suggests that the boundaries between travel writing and ethnography may be becoming more blurred than ever. For a discussion of the implications of this convergence, see Holland and Huggan.

16. As Richard Kerridge, among others, has pointed out, the environmental movement, as well as travel writing, should be seen as "historically interwoven with colonial relations" (164). Kerridge cites the usefulness, for example, of ecological management techniques for early colonial administrators (see also Bonyhady and Grove, both designed in part as historically contextualized rejoinders to Crosby's overstated view of the incommensurability of global ecological sensibility and European colonial practice). Kerridge's provocative but viable conclusion is that "both environmentalism and travel writing can be read, in many cases, as continuations, in a post-colonial world, of types of sensibility formed in colonial conditions" (164; see also the conclusion of this chapter).

17. For a discussion of the relevance of imperialist nostalgia to contemporary travel writing, see Holland and Huggan, esp. intro. and chap. 1, sec. 1.

18. This is, of course, a somewhat caricatured view of the split within contemporary ecology; for an informed study of the history of the discipline that attempts to account for its implicitly individualistic, as well as overtly communitarian, dimensions, and which investigates its paradoxical status as an inclusive specialization—a profession more than usually welcome to amateur enthusiasts—and as an "anti-scientific" science, see Worster.

19. See, for example, Hertsgaard's mission statement in the introductory chapter: "Scientists had long since studied whether elephants in the wild and dolphins in the deep were heading for extinction. I wanted to shift the gaze and turn the binoculars on my fellow humans. Just as scientists compare a given animal's behavior with the dynamics of its habitat to determine whether it is endangered, I planned to analyze human behavior in relation to the earth's ecosystems to gauge the environmental prospects of *Homo sapiens*" (7). Note the focus, here as throughout the text, on the effects of *human* impact. As Hertsgaard observes while traveling in China, studying the environment without simultaneously confronting the evidence of human settlement is next to impossible in many parts of the world: "In all the thousand miles of scenery I observed during my travels, there was not a single place that did not betray the signs of intense human settlement" (230). Eco-travel writing can be seen here as deliberately distancing itself from the *promeneur solitaire* fantasies of certain strands of romantic nature writing, engaging instead the pragmatic recognition that travel is rarely solitary and almost never a source of innocent pleasure, and that the spectacle of nature it often likes to invoke is a product both of human sense-perceptions and of changing social concerns.

20. The American anthropologist Clifford Geertz has memorably described this kind of travel writing as "one damn thing after another"; for an analysis of

the rhetoric of aggravation that informs it, see also Holland and Huggan, esp. their discussion of the "bad trip."

21. Spivak is referring not so much to the literal silencing of socially/culturally subaltern peoples as to the preassignment of a subject position where they are effectively spoken for, hence the title of her famous essay "Can the Subaltern Speak?" Many of Hertsgaard's informants—especially those to whom he attributes Third World status—occupy this subaltern subject position, their words being drawn upon to confirm what he already knows or his knowledge had led him to suspect.

22. As Hertsgaard informs us in his first chapter, "I financed my wanderings by traveling light, living low on the food chain, and writing occasional magazine articles from the road" (7). While this low-impact tourism (of the backpack-and-bicycle variety) is certainly worthy, it has more than a tinge of romantic anti-technologism about it that contradicts Hertsgaard's considered view that "Third World travel . . . cautions one against romanticizing the nontechnological life" (334).

23. Mimetic excess, for Taussig, involves a surfeit of images of the other, to the extent that it may become unclear which is self, which is other, and who is imitating whom. For a more detailed description of the workings of mimetic excess, see *Mimesis and Alterity,* esp. the introductory chapter and the concluding section.

24. For an illuminating—also entertaining—essay on the various tricks used throughout the history of Western ethnographic film to convey the illusion of unmediated reality, see Weinberger.

25. Probably the most obvious recent example here is the eccentric English naturalist Redmond O'Hanlon; for a critical discussion of O'Hanlon's work, in which buffoonery is paradoxically used to bolster scientific authority, see Holland and Huggan.

26. "Steve's Most Dangerous Adventures," Discovery Channel (Animal Planet), 1999.

27. For a fine essay that locates Crocodile Dundee both within and, to some extent, against the tradition of the laconic Australian "bush hero," see Morris. While the perennially wide-eyed Irwin is a much more effusive—self-consciously hyperbolical—figure than the understated Mick Dundee, it seems clear that *Crocodile Hunter* is capitalizing, in "real-life" terms, on the international success of Faiman's playfully self-ironizing movie, to the extent of reproducing not only its crocodile-wrestling Australian hero but also its independent-minded American female lead.

28. "Steve's Story," Discovery Channel (Animal Planet), 1999.

29. On the classic "drug-and-tag-movie," a derisive moniker for the type of conservation-minded nature documentary (e.g., *Wild Kingdom,* underwritten by a U.S. insurance company) where wild animals are rounded up and captured in order that they might be saved, see Alexander Wilson, 132–36. As Wilson sardonically observes, such movies, whose popularity in the 1960s coincided with the development of the global conservation movement, emphasized that "human expertise—which turned out to be a tangle of medical technology—would be necessary for the survival of wildlife" (133). *Crocodile Hunter,* with its populist dis-

dain for modern technology, implicitly seeks to reverse the process, exemplified in the "drug-and-tag" movie whereby the camera focus shifts "from the face of the animal . . . onto the technics that intervene in rescuing it on our behalf" (136). Instead, it tries to turn the clock back to a version—admittedly parodied—of hillbilly heroics, with the American Hill Country/Wild West (in another winning television formula) being mapped onto Australia's Deep North.

30. As part of its rags-to-riches scenario, the series makes much of the fact that Australia Zoo, a highly successful commercial enterprise with over 500 animals on 20 acres of prime northern Queensland real estate, began modestly as the small family-run Queensland Reptile and Fauna Park, with most of its specimens rustically lassoed by Irwin and his father, a self-designated pioneer of snake and crocodile capture techniques. The zoo, like the television program, aims to create an educational family adventure that trades off the publicity of sensational crocodile-capture in order to promulgate its serious conservationist message about the need to preserve animals in the wild. This is, as Bryan Norton would say, "strategic conservationism" of the kind that educates primarily by stimulating the senses, and in which instances of daredevil attention-seeking and force-fed media excitement are legitimately expected to net a wider audience and, perhaps, a lasting conservationist reward.

31. For an interesting, if somewhat untheorized, essay on the relevance of the "comic mode" to contemporary biological/conservationist practice, see Meeker (in Glotfelty and Fromm). As Meeker argues, "comedy is concerned with muddling through, not with progress or perfection" (160). Conservation-minded vehicles like *Crocodile Hunter* or the travel narratives of Redmond O'Hanlon (see also note 25, this chap.), even while they turn what Meeker calls "the comedy of [biological] survival" into farcical human-centered amateur theatrics, arguably provide a viable alternative to the self-regarding pathos of "tragic" nature writing and/or programming that prefers elegiac or apocalyptic modes. For a further discussion of the implications of the comic mode for ecological thinking and environmentalist practice, see also O'Brien.

Chapter Three

1. Disasters may be technically defined as "situation[s] or event[s] which overwhelm local capacity, necessitating a request to national or international level for external assistance" (Walter et al., 171). This chapter, expanding the meaning of disaster to include the category of the personal catastrophe, comes closer to following the all-purpose definition of disasters as "distinct event[s] that interrupt the accustomed flow of everyday life" (Erikson, 18). Erikson's conventional distinction between natural and man-made (e.g., technological) disasters is as follows: "Natural disasters are almost always experienced as acts of God or caprices of nature. They happen to us. Technological disasters, however, being of human manufacture, are at least in principle always preventable, so there is always a story to be told about them, always a moral to be drawn from them, always a share of blame to be assigned" (13–14). For further, useful commentary on disasters, see the essays in Couch and Kroll-Smith, and the first chapter of Davis.

2. That the genre is alive and well can be attested to in a random rundown of millennial titles: Frances Ashcroft, *Life at the Extremes* (2000); Bernie Chowdhury, *The Last Dive: A Father and Son's Fatal Descent into the Ocean's Depths* (2000); Martin Dugard, *Knockdown: The Harrowing True Account of a Yacht Race Turned Deadly* (1999); Greg Emmanuel, *Extreme Encounters* (2002); McKay Jenkins, *The White Death: Tragedy and Heroism in an Avalanche Zone* (2000); John Keay, ed., *The Mammoth Book of Travel in Dangerous Places* (2002); Nick Middleton, *Going to Extremes* (2001); James O'Reilly et al., eds., *Danger! True Stories of Trouble and Survival* (2000); Joshua Piven and David Borgenicht, *The Worst-Case Scenario Survival Handbook* (1999); Tony Wheeler et al., eds., *Unpacked: Travel Disaster Stories* (1999); Clint Willis, ed., *Wild: Stories of Survival from the World's Most Dangerous Places* (1999). More recently in vogue, matching extremes of geography, physical endurance/adventure, and climate, have been accounts of failed Everest expeditions (see also next section) and biographical renditions of the lives of Shackleton and other fated polar explorers.

3. *Thanatourism* may be defined as "travel to a location wholly, or partly, motivated by the desire for actual or symbolic encounters with death" (Seaton, 240). *Dark tourism,* the more inclusive term, refers to the network of interlinked social processes by which disaster zones, of both past and present, are turned into tourist attractions and "late-modern pilgrimage sites" (Lennon and Foley, 3).

4. Bronfen's and Dixon's studies trace "the links between public consumerism of images of violent death and scandal and the needs of the . . . entertainment marketplace" (Dixon, 19), paying particular attention to the phenomenon of "celebrity martyrdom" within the context of late-modern/late-capitalist societies in which death has become a "desired object, to be courted and pursued" (Dixon, 39).

5. See here Chris Rojek's important argument that the collapsing of the boundaries between sacred and profane realms, private and public spaces that is in evidence in so many contemporary touristic practices (e.g., related forms of disaster and heritage tourism) can be attributed in large part to postmodernist processes of "'de-differentiation,'" in which "the private sphere can no longer be analytically or symbolically separated from the public sphere. . . . The division between work and leisure is no longer clear-cut, [and] in short, the divisions which gave stability to the Modernist order of things seem to be untenable—they do not correspond with people's actual experience of things" (5). Under these conditions, death zones (celebrity cemeteries, state memorials, killing fields and other officially sanctioned atrocity sites, etc.) are treated less as ritual arenas for the solemn observation of respects and reverential contemplation than as legitimate touristic "sights" that satisfy curiosity as well as affording an opportunity for the therapeutic display of casual grief (Rojek, 170; on the casualization of grief as an epiphenomenon of "dark tourism," see also Lennon and Foley, 155).

6. "Reality tours" provide a reminder of the entrepreneurial spirit of disaster tourism, selling packaged action holidays, often in the name of humanitarian conscience or social responsibility, to well-heeled tourists for whom the direct experience of danger, and the symbolic capital likely to be accumulated from that experience, are at least as significant an objective as the opportunity to learn first-

hand from visiting the troubled site. For a variety of perspectives on reality tours, see Adams, "Danger-Zone Tourism"; Diller and Scofidio; and Phipps; see also the discussion later in this chapter.

7. As Adams argues, the increasingly common, postmodernism-inspired view of knowing "post-tourists" as guilt-free revelers in the inauthentic does not necessarily discount the continued search for authenticity in a variety of contemporary touristic pursuits. Adams mentions three forms of authenticity, each of which is served by the modern tourist industry. The first of these is grounded in a desire for social solidarity, while the second implies a "quest for privileged insider knowledge of [current] political hot-spots" ("Danger-Zone Tourism," 275). The third, meanwhile, "refers to a kind of visceral authenticity which includes the sense of heightened awareness (on a very physical level) experienced during endangerment" (275; also 279, n. 10). What I am referring to in this chapter (and throughout this book) as "extreme travel" may combine all of these nominally separate quests for authenticity; alternatively, extreme travelers—and, by extension, extreme travel writers—may well be moved to pursue one form or other of "the authentic" *in spite of* their knowledge of authenticity as a manufactured category designed to mediate their experiences of "the real." For further commentary on the play of authenticity and simulation in modern travel/writing, see Holland and Huggan, esp. chap. 4; see also the by now classic discussions of touristic authenticity in the work of MacCannell (*Tourist*) and Ross.

8. See, for example, Blanchot; Bronfen, "Faultlines"; and Ortner. On the intimate relation between death and celebrity culture in the context of Hollywood film, see also Dixon.

9. The extent of this awareness can be seen in Krakauer's establishment of a foundation designed to help the victims' families, a move also made by Sebastian Junger in the wake of the huge international success of his disaster account *The Perfect Storm* (treated later in this chapter).

10. See McLynn for an in-depth discussion of different forms of "action neurosis" among nineteenth- and early twentieth-century European explorers of Africa: these include, according to McLynn, the death drive, sublimated sexuality, and the desire for martyrdom. See also the discussion of McLynn's work in Bell and Lyall, 148–49.

11. On the tropology of "the wild," see Taussig (*Shamanism*), and, particularly, Nash. Nash begins his comprehensive study by stressing the difficulty of defining *wilderness;* by arguing the need for historicization; and by summarizing modern dictionary definitions of wilderness as "uncultivated and otherwise undeveloped land in which people are usually absent, wild animals generally present, and—not necessarily place-specific—experiences of loss and confusion ('bewilderment') are induced" (1–3). For Nash, wilderness is alternately threatening and reassuring; in this latter sense it functions as "a sanctuary in which those in need of consolation can find respite from the pressures of civilization" (4). Krakauer's narrative, like Nash's study, makes it clear that wilderness is largely subjective; that its definition and interpretation will depend on what different people at different times *think* and *feel* it to be (Nash, 6). Christopher McCandless's interpretation of wilderness turns out to be self-indulgently romantic, and

also appropriately double-edged insofar as the Alaskan wilderness features both as proposed sanctuary/life-restorer and eventual prison/sacrificial site. See also Soper for a discussion of the temporal, as well as spatial, dimensions of wilderness.

12. The "scientific sublime" may be defined here as the attempt to account for, while also celebrating, the extraordinariness of certain natural phenomena by scientific means. A good, if obviously anthropocentric, example of the scientific sublime is Ashcroft. A physiologist by training, Ashcroft focuses from a popular medical perspective on "the physiological response of the body to extreme environments and explores the limits of human survival" (xviii).

13. For an interesting discussion of the ideological function of weather interpretation, particularly in the context of mass-mediated representations of environmental crisis, see Ross. For Ross, climatic prediction—like other interpretations of natural phenomena—is never simply a question of "empirical verifiability" (219); rather, it is an exercise of cultural power that demonstrates the link between the language of scientific expertise and specific forms of cultural elitism and entitlement. Meteorology, as Junger also suggests in his own way, should not be understood as an exact, universally applicable science but as a historically fluctuating, culturally variable, and politically manipulable amalgam of traditional "weather folklore" and modern "systematic [technological] prediction" (Ross, 229).

14. The sublime, says Soper tellingly, is less about the experience of fear or awe in the face of nature than, paradoxically, "about [the human] ability to feel secure in the midst of danger" (228). Awe of nature does not imply surrender to it but, on the contrary, human mastery and/or transcendence of it, supporting Soper's more general thesis that the Western "aesthetic of nature has to be thought in relation to the history of human domination" (245). See also Freeman's admirably concise definition of the sublime as "a more or less explicit mode of domination . . . a struggle for mastery between opposite powers, as the self's attempt to appropriate and contain whatever would exceed and, thereby, undermine it" (2).

15. See, particularly, the concluding chapter of Bell and Lyall, which, closely following Lennon and Foley, draws an explicit parallel between modern "disaster tourism"—also called, with obvious irony, "tourism noir"—and the "dark sublime."

16. Genocide is defined in the text, in accordance with the dictates of the 1948 Genocide Convention, as an act or acts "committed with intent to destroy, in whole or in part, a national, ethnic, racial or religious group" (quoted in Gourevitch, 149). Few would now dispute that the 1994 killings in Rwanda, which left over 800,000 people dead in the space of 100 days, constituted an act of genocide, although Gourevitch recounts—with obvious disgust—initial attempts by the "international community," particularly the United States, to avoid using such a highly charged, and of course morally binding, term. For an overview of current definitions of genocide, see Hinton; for more details on the genocide in Rwanda, see—for example—Destexhe; Lemarchand; Malkki; Pruner. Of further note is that genocide, though often coexisting with civil war, is not necessarily driven by

it or dependent on it. Gourevitch rightly makes this distinction in the context of Rwanda: "Although the genocide coincided with the war, its organization and implementation were quite distinct from the war effort" (98).

17. For a critique of the so-called primordialist thesis of interethnic/tribal violence, see Appadurai, *Modernity;* also Appadurai, "Dead Certainty," for a study of the ritual dimensions of large-scale ethnic violence.

18. On the fetishization of the dead body in the context of (post-)Holocaust catastrophe, see Buettner; see also Bronfen, *Over,* and, particularly, Goodwin and Bronfen, esp. intro., for a discussion of the symbolic power, and political instrumentality, of the corpse.

19. Gourevitch gives particular play to the biblical legend of Abel and Cain, and to the (ab)uses to which it has been put, both by the European colonial powers in Rwanda, who inserted naturalized distinctions between "Hutu cultivators" and "Tutsi herdsmen" into their own, self-serving versions of race thinking; and, later, by Hutu Power ideologues, who turned the Hamitic myth of Tutsi "superiority" to their own advantage, using it to assert their own victimhood in the face of an oppressive elitist minority, and to justify mass violence in the name of "postcolonial emancipation" and "popular democracy" (47, 62).

20. On the dialectics of disaster, see particularly the work of the American cultural theorist and historian Mike Davis, whose work constitutes an ongoing record of changing attitudes to, and functionalizations of, disaster and catastrophe, especially in the volatile context of the modern American West. For a critical view of natural disasters as existing in dialectical tension between chance and fate or, to use Davis's own terms, "coincidence" and "eschatology," see more specifically Davis, chap. 1. Both terms, as Davis makes clear, have a potentially obscuring function, drawing attention away from human responsibilities for disaster and political manipulations of both disaster's actual effect and imagined cause.

21. For Valene Smith, for example, "tourism to war-related sites is [predominantly] honorific. . . . Wars are the time-markers of society, and the effects of war covertly invade our cultural beliefs and human behavior" (263). Smith is aware, however, of other potential motives for war tourism, pointing out that "despite the horrors of death and destruction (*and also because of them*), the memorabilia of warfare and allied products . . . probably constitutes the largest single category of tourist attractions in the world" (248; emphasis added).

22. That the experience, as well as the remembrance, of war can be a source of touristic pleasure is acknowledged by Diller and Scofidio, whose 1994 collection of essays still represents the most sustained attempt to explore the intersections between war and tourism to date. As Diller and Scofidio point out in their introduction, "Tourism and war appear to be polar extremes of cultural activity—the paradigm of international accord at one end and discord at the other. The two practices, however, often intersect: tourism of war, war on tourism, tourism as war, war targeting tourism, tourism under war, war as tourism are but a few of their intersecting couplings" (19). On the connections between war and tourism, see also Lisle, "Consuming Danger."

23. As Phipps suggests, "[the] threat of death and danger is something that

tourism relishes so as to retain its imaginative power as a space for reconnection with the 'real' which remains so elusive . . . in the order of highly stratified, regulated and abstracted capitalist postmodern society" (83; also quoted in Adams, "Danger-Zone Tourism," 268).

24. A related phenomenon is Fielding's Black Flag Cafe, an "advisory" Web site catering to travelers about to go to, or having just returned from, dangerous places. As might be expected, a currency of competitive machismo dominates the entries, suggesting that many "danger-zone travelers" are looking—or are persuaded by their peers—to graduate from medium-risk off-the-beaten-track travel to an acquaintance with, or even involvement in, high-risk combat zones and politically volatile sites (Adams, "Global Cities"). A typical entry, compiled by Adams, reads as follows: "A traveler in many 'soft' DP [dangerous place] countries over the past ten years, I have decided it is time to go for my first war zone. Armed with my clippings, letters of intro and mass bullsh**, where should I go for my first ringside view of armed conflict? Should I dive right into the thick of it—'Chechnya?'—or should I find a good 'intro' hotspot?" (quoted in Adams, "Global Cities").

25. *The World's Dangerous Places* is similarly studded (pun intended) with references to Hollywood action-hero icons; as Adams notes, such immediately identifiable cinematic images act as "prior texts for processing travelers' adventures in dangerous destinations" ("Global Cities"). It is interesting to note that *The Beach* itself—both novel and film—has now successfully inserted itself into this highly commodified image repertoire.

Chapter Four

1. See, for example, Huyssen: "The mode of memory is recherche rather than recuperation. The temporal status of any act of memory is always the present and not, as some naïve epistemology might have it, the past itself, even though all memory in some ineradicable sense is dependent on some past event or experience. It is this tenuous fissure between past and present that constitutes memory, making it powerfully alive and distinct from the archive or any other mere system of storage and retrieval" (3).

2. Again, it is worth quoting Huyssen at length. "Rather than leading us to some authentic origin or giving us verifiable access to the real, memory, even and especially in its belatedness, is itself based on representation. The past is not simply there in memory, but it must be articulated to become memory. The fissure that opens up between experiencing an event and remembering it in representation is unavoidable. Rather than lamenting or ignoring it, this split should be understood as a powerful stimulant for cultural and artistic creativity" (2–3).

3. In his famous 1963 essay, Frank notes that the spatialization of form in the modern novel creates the impression of *synchronicity,* of "simultaneous activity occurring in different places" (17). Synchronicity is a common feature of Chatwin's and Sebald's work, often being allied, particularly in Sebald's, to an uncanny chain of coincidences (see, especially, *Vertigo*). Synchronicity is counter-

balanced, however, by an equally strong awareness of *untimeliness.* Probably the most startling apprehension of untimeliness in Sebald's work is in the following lengthy passage in *Austerlitz:* "It does not seem to me . . . that we understand the laws governing the return of the past, but I feel more and more as if time did not exist at all, only various spaces interlocking according to the rules of a higher form of stereometry, between which the living and the dead can move back and forth as they like, and the longer I think about it the more it seems to me that we who are still alive are unreal in the eyes of the dead, that only occasionally, in certain lights and atmospheric conditions, do we appear in their field of vision. As far as I can remember . . . I have always felt as if I had no place in reality, as if I were not there at all" (261). Other interesting parallels between Chatwin's and Sebald's work include their exoticist fascination with arcane knowledge, etymology, the history of art, and the social life of museum/antiquarian relics; their exploration of the metaphysical dimensions, as well as material conditions, of expatriation and exile; their romantic sympathy with the underdog and their attempt to rehabilitate the lives of the unjustly forgotten, the self-acknowledged failures, the oppressed; their highly developed sense of the "literariness" of travel and the tradition of the *voyage imaginaire;* and their use of modernist (not postmodernist) techniques of symbolic association. This is not to deny the many obvious differences between these two highly gifted, and undoubtedly idiosyncratic, writers, neither of whom would have been likely to call himself a travel writer; it is rather to stress that both are working within well-known conventions of travel writing—especially the conventions attached to the "literary traveler"—that make their work possibly less original than it might appear at first sight.

4. Much of Sebald's work resonates with Freud's, particularly the well-known essays "Mourning and Melancholia" (1915) and "The Uncanny" (1919). Sebald's associative style also draws on Freudian techniques, e.g., those used in *The Interpretation of Dreams,* and it is certainly tempting to see works like *Vertigo* and *The Rings of Saturn,* in which the narrator's neuroses are writ large, as extended case studies. Sebald stops short, however, of deploying a full-blown Freudian vocabulary, and it is often his deliberately anachronistic (pre-Freudian) treatment of mental illness that comes to the fore.

5. For a more detailed analysis of originary displacement, and its connection to the phenomenon of the "haunted journey," see Porter, especially the chapter on Naipaul.

6. Sebald's landscape and architectural photographs, in particular, are a sustained exercise in the objective correlative, the romantic melancholic's attempt to find "un paysage qui [lui] ressemble" (Baudelaire).

7. Sebald's indebtedness to Proust is obvious, although the great French writer, perhaps surprisingly, is not given a cameo appearance in Sebald's pages. Analogies can certainly be made between Proust's and Sebald's sinuous syntax, their carefully managed detours and divagations, and between both authors' enormously wide-ranging efforts to investigate, through the multiple transpositions of memory, the uncanny effect of time on place. A crucial distinction, however, is between Proust's "optimistic" conception of time as, in the critic

Malcolm Bowie's words, "a connection-making and irrepressible potentiality" (64) and Sebald's "pessimistic" view of irreversibly degenerative historical processes and his apparently unredemptive foreshadowing of the apocalyptic "end of time" itself.

8. It is worth noting that all of Sebald's works were originally written in German, nominally his native language, even though his literary reputation, right up until his untimely death in 2001, seemed to be notably higher in the English-speaking world than it was in the country he had left behind several decades ago. Michael Hulse's superb translations not only capture the anachronism of Sebald's mannered language, but also the atmosphere of untimeliness he wishes to create, which, despite his work's wealth of historical references, is curiously unanchored from any specific time or place.

9. On the connections between memory and amnesia, see Huyssen; also LaCapra.

10. As Derrida points out, ghosts cause anxiety, not only because they appear to watch us (cf. the sawn-off portraits in *Vertigo,* some reduced to eyes that implacably stare down the viewer), but because they do so *repeatedly*. The spectral, in fact, is an effect of repetition: an effect well captured in Sebald's work, where ghostly figures, sometimes linked in groups, either drift in and out of or semi-permanently hover behind the text. Some of these figures are actively conjured by the narrator, others intrude against his will. The "spectrality" of Sebald's work arguably consists, however, less in the frequency with which ghosts appear or the specific conditions governing their appearance, but rather in the general uncertainty they raise over the passage, or even the nature, of time (cf. the narrator's perception of himself as a ghost).

11. Melancholy dialectics, in Sebald's work, goes well beyond a Freudian process of dysfunctional mourning (see Freud, "Mourning"; also LaCapra). It also involves the active desire to be haunted; the perpetuation of haunting is the perpetuation of a condition one embraces. Within this self-perpetuating context, the work of melancholy in the melancholic text (see the previous discussion of Chambers) is never finished; but, at the same time, the melancholic writer cannot help but imagine that his condition, anid the dark vision of the world that condition reflects, might one day come to an end.

12. See here the related idea of "traveling theory," associated primarily with Edward Said's chapter of the same name in *The World, the Text, and the Critic* (1983). For Said, it is not just words but the ideas they enshrine that "travel," gaining or losing strength and sometimes changing altogether as they move, and that are accordingly translated, across time and space (226). The idea of the Holocaust also travels—not that this makes it any less real—and is principally mediated through (post)memory; its multiple movements, and the translations they occasion, are the subject of Michaels's text.

13. Frow suggests, with obvious relevance here to the work of Gilbert and, especially, Michaels, that "texts are . . . not structures of presence but traces and tracings of otherness, [and] are shaped by the repetition and transformation of other textual structures" (45).

14. Said died in 2003 after a long struggle with leukemia.

Postscript

1. See also Diller and Scofidio, who claim that tourists and soldiers "assume a similar representation role on foreign soil: they are both embodiments of another nationalism. Each one is seen as a performative body, measured against the image of its national stereotype" (24; also quoted in Phipps, 78).

2. The analogy can of course easily be taken too far, as in, for example, Phipps's otherwise persuasive essay, in which he makes a strained comparison between the "undercover" operations of the tourist and the terrorist, even coining the portmanteau term *tourorist* to emphasize his point that "the differences between tourists and terrorists, war and peace, may well be less than imagined" (75). For a more balanced discussion of the relations between tourism and terrorism, see Sönmez.

3. Unsurprisingly, the company has been adept at marketing/mythologizing its own history, with strategic anecdotes about dire impoverishment, shoestring travel, and—in the case of the first book, literal—kitchen-table production values looming large in the company's promotional materials, helping to add to the series' vaguely countercultural cachet. For an interesting overview essay on the foundation and rapid expansion of the Lonely Planet empire, see Krakauer, "All They Really Wanted"; for a more critical view, see Hatcher, who also points out the inevitable backlash that has accompanied the company's astonishing success: "Among a hard core of embittered, alienated 'travellers' Lonely Planet has become a symbol for everything wrecking their world. Having seen backpacker hangouts from Kuta to Boracay taken over, packaged and commodified by the mainstream tourist industry, their mantra has become 'For God's sake don't tell Lonely Planet'. But of course people always do, now increasingly on-line on Lonely Planet's sophisticated internet website, where, with a million visitors a month, the old travellers' grapevine has dematerialised and quickened to the speed of light" (134).

4. See, for example, the mission statement on Lonely Planet's Web site: "Travel can be a powerful force for tolerance and understanding. As part of a worldwide community of travellers, we want to enable everyone to travel with awareness, respect and care" (www.lonelyplanet.com).

5. It is worth comparing this statement, however, to another interview in 1999, in which Wheeler—forced back on the defensive—claims that Bali is a fine example of the positive effects of tourism: "In Bali tourism has contributed to change but this change has certainly not ruined the place. The dancers may be performing for tourists in hotels rather than the nobility in the palaces but they are still dancing. Quite possibly they wouldn't be if there weren't such a high demand among visitors" ("Philosophy," 55).

6. Tourists and refugees are clearly on opposite ends of the modern travel spectrum. But their fates are also arguably linked insofar as refugees are the negative counterpart to the cosmopolitan (touristic?) ideal of unrestricted global movement. As Don McMaster, in his book on Australian asylum seekers, puts it: "In contemporary times refugees represent a symptom of the homelessness and uprootedness of the modern and (so-called) postmodern age. The refugee, in many cases, is denied not only a homeland but also the possibility of establishing a home, of making roots and securing identity (20–21). See also chap. 1, note 3.

Works Cited

Adams, Jonathan S., and Thomas O. McShane. *The Myth of Wild Africa: Conservation without Illusion.* New York: Norton, 1992.

Adams, Kathleen. "Danger-Zone Tourism: Prospects and Problems for Tourism in Tumultuous Times." In *Interconnected Worlds: Tourism in Southeast Asia,* ed. Peggy Teo, T. C. Chang, and K. C. Ho, 265–80. Oxford: Pergamon, 2001.

Adams, Kathleen. "Global Cities, Terror and Tourism: The Ambivalent Allure of the Urban Jungle." In *Postcolonial Urbanism: Southeast Asian Cities and Global Processes,* ed. Ryan Bishop, John Phillips, and Wei-Wei Yo, 37–62. London: Routledge, 2003.

Altman, Dennis. *Global Sex.* Chicago: University of Chicago Press, 2001.

Appadurai, Arjun. "Dead Certainty: Ethnic Violence in the Age of Globalization." In *Genocide: An Anthropological Reader,* ed. Alexander Laban Hinton, 254–85. Oxford: Blackwell, 2002.

Appadurai, Arjun. *Modernity at Large: Cultural Aspects of Globalization.* Minneapolis: University of Minnesota Press, 1996.

Armbruster, Karla. "Creating the World We Must Save: The Paradox of Television Documentaries." In *Writing the Environment: Ecocriticism and Literature,* ed. Richard Kerridge and Neil Sammells, 218–38. London: Zed Books, 1998.

Ashcroft, Bill, Gareth Griffiths, and Helen Tiffin. *The Empire Writes Back: Theory and Practice in Post-Colonial Literatures.* London: Routledge, 1989.

Ashcroft, Frances. *Life at the Extremes: The Science of Survival.* Berkeley: University of California Press, 2000.

Atkinson, Alan. *Three Weeks in Bali: A Personal Account of the Bali Bombing.* Sydney: ABC Books, 2002.

Bal, Mieke, Jonathan Crewe, and Leo Spitzer, eds. *Acts of Memory: Cultural Recall in the Present.* Hanover, NJ: University of New England Press (Dartmouth College), 1999.

Bandy, Joe. "Managing the Other of Nature: Sustainability, Spectacle, and Regimes of Global Capital in Ecotourism." *Public Culture* 8 (1996): 539–66.

Barcott, Bruce. "Cliffhangers: The Fatal Descent of the Mountain-Climbing Memoir." *Harper's Magazine,* August 1996, 64–68.

Bate, Jonathan. *Romantic Ecology: Wordsworth and the Environmental Tradition.* London: Routledge, 1991.

Bauman, Zygmunt. "Reconnaissance Wars of the Planetary Frontierland." *Theory, Culture and Society* 19, no. 4 (2002): 81–90.

Bayer, Julia. "Dennis O'Rourke." Interview with the filmmaker. Essay, 2005.

Beck, Ulrich. *Risk Society: Towards a New Modernity.* London: Sage, 1992.

Beck, Ulrich. "World Risk Society as Cosmopolitan Society? Ecological Questions in a Framework of Manufactured Uncertainties." *Theory, Culture and Society* 13, no. 4 (1996): 1–32.

Behdad, Ali. *Belated Travelers: Orientalism in the Age of Colonial Dissolution.* Durham, NC: Duke University Press, 1994.

Bell, Claudia, and John Lyall. *The Accelerated Sublime: Landscape, Tourism, and Identity.* Westport, CT: Praeger, 2002.

Benjamin, Walter. "The Task of the Translator." In *Illuminations,* trans. Harry Zohn, 69–82. London: Jonathan Cape, 1970.

Benz, Stephen. *Green Dreams: Travels in Central America.* Melbourne: Lonely Planet Publications, 1998.

Berger, John. "Why Look at Animals?" In *About Looking,* 1–26. New York: Pantheon, 1980.

Berry, Chris, Annette Hamilton, and Laleen Jayamanne, eds. *The Filmmaker and the Prostitute: Dennis O'Rourke's The Good Woman of Bangkok.* Sydney: Power Publications, 1997.

Bhabha, Homi. "Double Visions." *Artforum,* January 1992, 82–90.

Blanchot, Maurice. *The Writing of the Disaster.* Trans. A. Smock. Lincoln: University of Nebraska Press, 1995.

Bonyhady, Tim. *The Colonial Earth.* Melbourne: Melbourne University Press, 1998.

Bowie, Malcolm. *Proust Among the Stars.* New York: Columbia University Press, 1998.

Boym, Svetlana. *The Future of Nostalgia.* New York: Basic Books, 2001.

Breckenridge, Carol A., Sheldon Pollock, Henri K. Bhabha, and Dipesh Chakrabarty, eds. "Cosmopolitanism." Special issue of *Public Culture,* 12, no. 3 (2000): 577–786.

Brennan, Timothy. *At Home in the World: Cosmopolitanism Now.* Cambridge: Harvard University Press, 1997.

Bronfen, Elisabeth. "Faultlines: Catastrophe and Celebrity Culture." In *Britain at the Turn of the Twenty-First Century,* ed. Ulrich Broich and Susan Bassnett, 117–39. Special Issue of *European Studies,* 16. New York: Rodopi, 2000.

Bronfen, Elisabeth. *Over Her Dead Body: Death, Femininity, and the Aesthetic.* Manchester: Manchester University Press, 1992.

Broszat, Martin, and Saul Friedländer. "A Controversy about the Historicization of National Socialism." In *Reworking the Past: Hitler, the Holocaust, and the Historians' Debate,* ed. Peter Baldwin. Boston: Beacon, 1990.

Browne, Stephen. *Aid and Influence: Do Donors Help or Hinder?* London: Earthscan, 2006.

Bruner, Edward M. *Cultures on Tour: Ethnographies of Travel.* Chicago: University of Chicago Press, 2005.

Buell, Lawrence. *The Environmental Imagination: Thoreau, Nature Writing, and the Formation of American Culture.* Cambridge: Harvard University Press, 1995.

Buettner, Angelika. "Animal Holocausts." *Cultural Studies Review* 8, no. 1 (2002): 28–44.

Buzard, James. *The Beaten Track: European Tourism, Literature and the Ways to Culture, 1800–1918.* Oxford: Clarendon, 1993.

Callicott, J. Baird. *In Defense of the Land Ethic: Essays in Environmental Philosophy.* Albany: New York State University Press, 1989.

Campbell, Mary B. *The Witness and the Other World: Exotic European Travel Writing, 400–1600.* Ithaca: Cornell University Press, 1988.

Carter, Paul. *Living in a New Country: History, Travelling and Language.* London: Faber and Faber, 1992.

Chambers, Ross. *The Writing of Melancholy: Modes of Opposition in Early French Modernism.* Trans. Mary Seidman Trouville. Chicago: University of Chicago Press, 1987.

Chowdhury, Bernie. *The Last Dive: A Father and Son's Fatal Descent into the Ocean's Depths.* London: Headline, 2000.

Clifford, James. "On Ethnographic Allegory." In *Writing Cultures: The Poetics and Politics of Ethnography,* ed. James Clifford and George Marcus, 98–121. Berkeley: University of California Press, 1986.

Clifford, James. *Routes: Travel and Translation in the Late Twentieth Century.* Cambridge: Harvard University Press, 1997.

Cohen, Erik. "Thai Girls and Farang Men: The Edge of Ambiguity." *Annals of Tourism Research* 9, no. 4 (1982): 403–28.

Conrad, Joseph. *Heart of Darkness.* New York: Norton Critical Editions, 1988 [1899].

Couch, Stephen R., and J. Stephen Kroll-Smith, eds. *Communities at Risk: Collective Responses to Technological Hazards.* New York: Peter Lang, 1991.

Crick, Malcolm. "The Anthropologist as Tourist: An Identity in Question." In *International Tourism: Identity and Change,* ed. M.-F. Lanfant, J. B. Allcock, and E. M. Bruner, 205–23. London: Sage, 1995.

Crosby, Alfred. *Ecological Imperialism: The Biological Expansion of Europe, 900–1900.* Cambridge: Cambridge University Press, 1986.

Curtin, Deane. *Chinnagounder's Challenge: The Question of Ecological Citizenship.* Bloomington: Indiana University Press, 1999.

Davis, Mike. *The Ecology of Fear.* New York: Vintage, 1998.

Deleuze, Gilles, and Félix Guattari. *A Thousand Plateaus: Capitalism and Schizophrenia.* Trans. B. Massumi. Minneapolis: University of Minnesota Press, 1988.

Derrida, Jacques. *Specters of Marx: The State of the Debt, the Work of Mourning, and the New International.* Trans. Peggy Kamuf. New York: Routledge, 1994.

Destexhe, Alain. *Essai sur le génocide.* Brussels: Éditions Complexe, 1994.

Devall, Bill, and George Sessions. *Deep Ecology: Living as if Nature Mattered.* Salt Lake City: Peregrine Smith Books, 1985.

Diller, Elizabeth, and Richard Scofidio. *Back to the Front: Tourisms of War.* Basse-Normandie: FRAC, 1994.

Dixon, Wheeler Winston. *Disaster and Memory: Celebrity Culture and the Crisis of Hollywood Cinema.* New York: Columbia University Press, 1999.

Dobson, Andrew. *Green Political Thought: An Introduction.* London: Unwin Hyman, 1990.

Dugard, Martin. *Knockdown: The Harrowing True Account of a Yacht Race Turned Deadly.* New York: Pocket Books, 1999.

During, Simon. "Postcolonialism and Globalisation: A Dialectical Relation After All?" *Postcolonial Studies* 1, no. 1 (1998): 31–47.

Elegant, Simon. "The Jihadis' Tale: The Confessions of Two Bali Bombers Tell of Their Hatred for the West—and Their Ties to Osama bin Laden." *Time International* 161 (Jan. 27, 2003): 1–5.

Elsrud, Torun. "Risk Creation in Traveling: Backpacker Adventure Narration." *Annals of Tourism Research* 28, no. 3 (2001): 597–617.

Emmanuel, Greg. *Extreme Encounters: How It Feels to Be Drowned in Quicksand, Shredded by Piranhas, Swept Up in a Tornado, and Dozens of Other Unpleasant Experiences.* Philadelphia: Quirk Books, 2002.

Erikson, Kai. "A New Species of Trouble." In *Communities at Risk: Collective Responses to Technological Hazards,* ed. Stephen J. Couch and J. Stephen Kroll-Smith, 11–29. New York: Peter Lang, 1991.

Feifer, Maxine. *Going Places: The Ways of the Tourist from Imperial Rome to the Present Day.* London: Macmillan, 1985.

Fennell, David. *Ecocriticism: An Introduction.* London: Routledge, 1999.

Finkelstein, Norman G. *The Holocaust Industry: Reflections on the Exploitation of Jewish Suffering.* London: Verso, 2001.

Frank, Joseph. *The Widening Gyre: Crisis and Mastery in Modern Literature.* New Brunswick: Rutgers University Press, 1963.

Freeman, Barbara. *The Feminine Sublime: Gender and Excess in Women's Fiction.* Berkeley: University of California Press, 1995.

Freud, Sigmund. "Mourning and Melancholia." In *The Standard Edition of the Complete Psychological Works of Sigmund Freud,* vol. 14, trans. and ed. J. Strachey, 243–58. London: Hogarth Press, 1957 [1915].

Freud, Sigmund. *The Interpretation of Dreams.* Ed. A. Richards. London: Penguin, 1991 [1900].

Freud, Sigmund. "The Uncanny." In *The Standard Edition of the Complete Psychological Works of Sigmund Freud,* vol. 17, trans. and ed. J. Strachey, 217–52. London: Hogarth Press, 1955 [1919].

Frow, John. "Intertextuality and Ontology." In *Intertextuality: Theories and*

Practices, ed. M. Worton and J. Still, 45–55. Manchester: Manchester University Press, 1990.

Fussell, Paul. *Abroad: British Literary Traveling Between the Wars.* New York: Oxford University Press, 1990 [1980].

Gallmann, Kuki. *I Dreamed of Africa.* London: Penguin, 1991.

Garland, Alex. *The Beach.* London: Penguin, 1997 [1996].

Geertz, Clifford. "Blurred Genres: The Refiguration of Social Thought." *American Scholar* 49, no. 2 (1979): 165–79.

Gilbert, Helen. "Belated Journeys: Ecotourism as a Style of Travel Performance." In *In Transit: Travel, Text, Empire.* ed. Helen Gilbert and Anna Johnston. New York: Peter Lang, 2002.

Gilbert, Martin. *Holocaust Journey: Travelling in Search of the Past.* London: Phoenix, 2001 [1997].

Gilmore, Leigh. *The Limits of Autobiography: Trauma and Testimony.* Ithaca: Cornell University Press, 2001.

Gilroy, Paul. *After Empire: Melancholia or Convivial Culture?* London: Routledge, 2004.

Glotfelty, Cheryll, and Harold Fromm, eds. *The Ecocriticism Reader.* Athens: University of Georgia Press, 1996.

Gluckman, Ron. " 'On the Beach' with Alex Garland." *Asian Wall Street Journal,* Feb. 19–20, 1999, 13.

Goldie, Terry. *Fear and Temptation: The Image of the Indigene in Canadian, Australian, and New Zealand Literatures.* Montreal: McGill-Queen's University Press, 1989.

Goldstone, Patricia. *Making the World Safe for Tourism.* New Haven: Yale University Press, 2001.

Goodwin, Sarah Webster, and Elisabeth Bronfen, eds. *Death and Representation.* Baltimore: Johns Hopkins University Press, 1993.

Gourevitch, Philip. *We wish to inform you that tomorrow we will be killed with our families: Stories from Rwanda.* New York: Picador, 1998.

Grove, Richard. *Green Imperialism: Colonial Expansion, Tropical Island Edens and the Origins of Environmentalism, 1600–1860.* Cambridge: Cambridge University Press, 1995.

Hammond, Dorothy, and Alta Jablow. *The Myth of Africa.* New York: Library of Social Sciences, 1975.

Hannerz, Ulf. *Transnational Connections: Culture, People, Places.* New York: Routledge, 1996.

Harvey, David. *The Condition of Postmodernity: An Enquiry into the Origins of Cultural Change.* Oxford: Blackwell, 1989.

Hatcher, John. "Lonely Planet, Crowded World: Alex Garland's *The Beach.*" *Studies in Travel Writing* 3 (1999): 131–47.

Hayter, Teresa. *Aid as Imperialism.* London: Penguin, 1971.

Herr, Michael. *Dispatches.* New York: Avon, 1978 [1968].

Hertsgaard, Mark. *Earth Odyssey: Around the World in Search of Our Environmental Future.* New York: Broadway Books, 1999.

Hilberg, Raul. *The Destruction of the European Jews.* Teaneck, NJ: Holmes and Meier, 1985.

Hirsch, Marianne. *Family Frames: Photography, Narrative, and Postmemory.* Cambridge: Harvard University Press, 1997.

Hobsbawm, Eric. *Age of Extremes: The Short Twentieth Century, 1914–1991.* London: Michael Joseph, 1994.

Holland, Patrick, and Graham Huggan. *Tourists with Typewriters: Critical Reflections on Contemporary Travel Writing.* Ann Arbor: University of Michigan Press, 1998.

Huyssen, Andreas. *Twilight Memories: Marking Time in a Culture of Amnesia.* London: Routledge, 1995.

Ignatieff, Michael. "An Interview with Bruce Chatwin." *Granta* 21 (spring 1987): 23–37.

Iyer, Pico. *The Global Soul: Jet Lag, Shopping Malls, and the Search for Home.* New York: Knopf, 2000.

Iyer, Pico. *Video Night in Kathmandu, and Other Reports from the Not-So-Far East.* New York: Vintage, 1988.

Jenkins, McKay. *The White Death: Tragedy and Heroism in an Avalanche Zone.* New York: Flamingo, 2000.

Junger, Sebastian. *The Perfect Storm.* New York: HarperPerennial, 1999 [1997].

Kane, Joe. *Savages.* New York: Vintage, 1996.

Kaplan, Caren. *Questions of Travel: Postmodern Discourses of Displacement.* Durham: Duke University Press, 1996.

Kaur, Raminder, and John Hutnyk, eds. *Travel Worlds: Journeys in Contemporary Cultural Politics.* London: Zed Books, 1999.

Keay, John, ed. *The Mammoth Book of Travel in Dangerous Places.* London: Constable and Robinson, 2002.

Kenny, Gillian. "'Our Travelers' Out There on the Road: *Lonely Planet* and Its Readers, 1973–1981." In *Jumping the Queue,* ed. Gabriella Espak, Scott Fatnowna, and Denise Woods, 111–19. St Lucia: University of Queensland Press, 2002.

Kerridge, Richard. "Ecologies of Desire: Travel Writing and Nature Writing as Travelogue." In *Travel and Empire: Postcolonial Theory in Transit,* ed. Steve Clark, 164–82. London: Zed Books, 1999.

Khouri, Norma. *Forbidden Love: A Harrowing True Story of Love and Revenge in Jordan.* Sydney: Bantam, 2003.

Kimerling, Judith, Susan Henriksen, and Robert F. Kennedy, eds. *Amazon Crude.* New York: Natural Resources Defense Council, 1991.

Klein, Naomi. *The Shock Doctrine: The Rise of Disaster Capitalism.* London: Penguin, 2007.

Klein, Sherwin Lee. "The Emergence of Memory in Historical Discourse." *Representations* 69 (2000): 127–48.

Krakauer, Jon. "All They Really Wanted Was to Travel." *Smithsonian* 25, no. 7 (1994): 132–44.

Krakauer, Jon. *Into the Wild.* New York: Anchor, 1997 [1996].

Krakauer, Jon. *Into Thin Air.* New York: Anchor, 1997.

Kristeva, Julia. *Black Sun: Depression and Melancholia.* New York: Columbia University Press, 1989.

Kruhse-MountBurton, S. "Sex Tourism and the Traditional Australian Male." In *International Tourism: Identity and Change,* ed. M. F. Lanfant, J. B. Allcock, and E. M. Bruner, 192–203. London: Sage, 1995.

Kumar, Amitava. *Bombay London New York.* New York: Routledge, 2002.

LaCapra, Dominick. *Representing the Holocaust: History, Theory, Trauma.* Ithaca: Cornell University Press, 1994.

Laqueur, Walter. *The New Terrorism: Fanaticism and the Arms of Mass Destruction.* London: Phoenix, 1999.

Lazarus, Neil. *Nationalism and Cultural Practice in the Postcolonial World.* Cambridge: Cambridge University Press, 1999.

Leed, Eric. *The Mind of the Traveler: From Gilgamesh to Global Tourism.* New York: Basic Books, 1991.

Lemarchand, René. "The Apocalypse in Rwanda." *Cultural Survival Quarterly* (1994): 29–39.

Lennon, John, and Malcolm Foley. *Dark Tourism: The Attraction of Death and Disaster.* London: Continuum, 2000.

Lévi-Strauss, Claude. *Tristes Tropiques.* Trans. D. Weightman and J. Weightman. New York: Atheneum, 1984 [1955].

Lisle, Debbie. "Consuming Danger: Re-imagining the War-Tourism Divide." *Alternatives* 25, no. 1 (2000): 91–116.

Lisle, Debbie. *The Global Politics of Contemporary Travel Writing.* Cambridge: Cambridge University Press, 2006.

Luttwak, Edward. *The Endangered American Dream.* New York: Simon and Schuster, 1993.

Lutz, Catherine A., and Jane L. Collins. *Reading National Geographic.* Chicago: University of Chicago Press, 1993.

Lyon, James, Paul Greenway, and Tony Wheeler. *Lonely Planet: Bali and Lombok.* Melbourne: Lonely Planet Publications, 2001.

Lyon, Thomas J. "A Taxonomy of Nature Writing." In *The Ecocriticism Reader,* ed. Cheryll Glotfelty and Harold Fromm, 276–81. Athens: University of Georgia Press, 1996.

MacCannell, Dean. *Empty Meeting Grounds: The Tourist Papers.* New York: Routledge, 1992.

MacCannell, Dean. *The Tourist: A New Theory of the Leisure Class.* New York: Schocken, 1989 [1976].

MacInnes, John. *The End of Masculinity: The Confusion of Sexual Genesis and Sexual Difference in Modern Society.* Buckingham: Open University Press, 1998.

Maier, Charles. *The Unmasterable Past.* Cambridge: Harvard University Press, 1988.

Malkki, Liisa H. "Speechless Emissaries: Refugees, Humanitarianism, and Dehistoricization." In *Genocide: An Anthropological Reader,* ed. Alexander Laban Hinton, 344–67. Oxford: Blackwell, 2002.

MacDougall, David. *Transcultural Cinema.* Princeton: Princeton University Press, 1998.

McDowell, William. "The Bakhtinian Road to Ecological Insight." In *The Ecocriticism Reader,* ed. Cheryll Glotfelty and Harold Fromm, 371–92. Athens: University of Georgia, 1996.

McKibben, Bill. *The Age of Missing Information.* New York: Random House, 1992.

McLaren, Deborah. *Rethinking Tourism and Ecotravel: The Paving of Paradise and What You Can Do to Stop It.* West Hartford, CT: Kumarian Press, 1998.

McLynn, Frank. *Hearts of Darkness: The European Exploration of Africa.* London: Pimlico, 1993.

McMaster, Don. *Asylum Seekers: Australia's Response to Refugees.* Melbourne: Melbourne University Press, 2002.

Meeker, Joseph W. "The Comic Mode." In *The Ecocriticism Reader,* ed. Cheryll Glotfelty and Harold Fromm, 155–69. Athens: University of Georgia Press, 1996.

Meethan, Kevin. *Tourism in Global Society.* Basingstoke: Palgrave, 2001.

Mehta, Suketu. *Maximum City: Bombay Lost and Found.* Delhi: Penguin India, 2004.

Meier, Christian. "Obituary: Martin Broszat." *Vierteljahrshefte für Zeitgeschichte* 38, no. 1 (1990): 37.

Merchant, Carolyn. *Radical Ecology: The Search for a Livable World.* New York: Routledge, 1992.

Meštrović, Stjepan. *Postemotional Society.* London: Sage, 1997.

Michaels, Anne. *Fugitive Pieces.* Toronto: McClelland and Stewart, 1996.

Middleton, Nick. *Going to Extremes.* London: Channel Four Books, 2001.

Mignolo, Walter. "The Many Faces of Cosmopolis: Border Thinking and Critical Cosmopolitanism." *Public Culture* 12, no. 3 (2000): 721–48.

Moeller, Susan D. *Compassion Fatigue: How the Media Sell Disease, Famine, War and Death.* London: Routledge, 1999.

Morris, Meaghan. "Tooth and Claw: Tales of Survival and Crocodile Dundee." In *The Pirate's Fiancée: Feminism, Reading, Postmodernism,* 241–69, 284–87. London: Verso, 1988.

Mulvey, Laura. "Visual Pleasure and Narrative Cinema." *Screen* 16, no. 3 (1975): 6–18.

Nash, Roderick. *Wilderness and the American Mind.* 3d ed. New Haven: Yale University Press, 1982.

Nichols, Bill. *Introduction to Documentary.* Bloomington: Indiana University Press, 2001.

Nixon, Rob. *London Calling: V. S. Naipaul, Postcolonial Mandarin.* New York: Oxford University Press, 1992.

Nolan, Maggie, and Carrie Dawson. "Who's Who? Hoaxes, Imposture, and Identity Crisis in Australian Literature." Special issue of *Australian Literary Studies* 21, no. 4 (2004): 1–178.

Nora, Pierre. "Between Memory and History: Les Lieux de Mémoire." *Representations* 26 (1989): 7–25.

Nora, Pierre, ed. *Les Lieux de Mémoire*. Paris: Gallimard, 1984–93. (7 vols.)

Norton, Bryan. "The Cultural Approach to Conservation Biology." In *Environmental Ethics*, ed. John Benson, 143–52. London: Routledge, 2000.

O'Brien, Susie. "'Back to the World': Reading Ecocriticism in a Postcolonial Context." In *Five Emus to the King of Siam*, ed. Helen Tiffin, 177–200. Amsterdam: Rodopi, 2007.

O'Reilly, James, ed. *Danger! True Stories of Trouble and Survival*. New York: Travelers' Tales, 2000.

O'Rourke, Dennis (writer and director). *Cannibal Tours*. Institute of Papua New Guinea Studios, 1988.

O'Rourke, Dennis (writer and director). *The Good Woman of Bangkok*. Australia: O'Rourke and Associates Filmmakers Pty. Ltd., 1991.

Ortner, Sherry. "Thick Resistance: Death and the Cultural Construction of Agency in Himalayan Mountaineering." *Representations* 59 (1997): 135–62.

O'Tuathail, Gearoid. *Critical Geopolitics: The Politics of Writing Global Space*. Minneapolis: University of Minnesota Press, 1996.

Pelton, Robert Young, Coskun Aral, and Wink Dulles, eds. *The World's Most Dangerous Places*. Redondo Beach, CA: Fielding Worldwide, 1998.

Pensky, Max. *Melancholy Dialectics: Walter Benjamin and the Play of Mourning*. Amherst: University of Massachussetts Press, 1993.

Pepper, David. *Eco-Socialism: From Deep Ecology to Social Justice*. London: Routledge, 1993.

Phillip, Joan, and Graham Dann. "Bar Girls in Central Bangkok: Prostitution as Entrepreneurship." In *Sex Tourism and Prostitution: Aspects of Leisure, Recreation, and Work*, ed. M. Oppermann, 60–72. New York: Cognizant Communication Offices, 1998.

Phipps, Peter. "Tourists, Terrorists, Death and Value." In *Travel Worlds: Journeys in Contemporary Cultural Politics*, ed. Raminder Kaur and John Hutnyk, 74–93. London: Zed Books, 1999.

Pinney, Christopher. "Future Travel: Anthropology and Cultural Distance in an Age of Virtual Reality Or, A Past Seen From a Possible Future." In *Visualizing Theory: Selected Essays from V.A.R. 1990–1994*, ed. Lucien Taylor, 409–28. New York: Routledge, 1994.

Pitts, W. J. "Uprising in Chiapas, Mexico: Zapata Lives: Tourism Falters." In *Tourism, Crime, and International Security Issues*, ed. A. Pizam and Y. Mansfeld, 215–27. New York: Wiley, 1996.

Piven, Joshua, and David Borgenicht. *The Worst-Case Scenario Survival Handbook*. San Francisco: Chronicle Books, 1999.

Plett, Heinrich. *Intertextuality*. New York: de Gruyter, 1991.

Porritt, Jonathan. *Seeing Green*. Oxford: Blackwell, 1990.

Porter, Dennis. *Haunted Journeys: Desire and Transgression in European Travel Writing*. Princeton: Princeton University Press, 1991.

Pratt, Mary Louise. "Fieldwork in Common Places." In *Writing Culture: The Poetics and Politics of Ethnography*, ed. James Clifford and Goerge Marcus, 27–50. Berkeley: University of California Press, 1986.

Pratt, Mary Louise. *Imperial Eyes: Travel Writing and Transculturation.* New York: Routledge, 1992.

Pruner, Gérard. *The Rwandan Crisis: History of a Genocide.* New York: Columbia University Press, 1995.

Pye-Smith, Charlie. *Travels in Nepal.* London: Penguin, 1988.

Rachowiecki, Rob. *Costa Rica.* Melbourne: Lonely Planet Publications, 1997 [1991].

Richmond, Anthony. "Reactive Migration: Sociological Perspectives on Refugee Movements." *Journal of Refugee Studies* 6, no. 1 (1993): 7–24.

Richter, L. K., and W. L.Waugh Jr. "Terrorism and Tourism as Logical Companions." *Tourism Management* 7 (1986): 230–38.

Ridgeway, Rick. *The Shadow of Kilimanjaro.* London: Flamingo, 2000 [1998].

Ritzer, George, and Allan Liska. "'McDisneyization' and 'Post-Tourism': Complementary Perspectives on Contemporary Tourism." In *Touring Cultures: Transformations of Travel and Theory,* ed. Chris Rojek and John Urry, 96–109. London: Routledge, 1997.

Robertson, Roland. *Globalization: Social Theory and Global Culture.* London: Sage, 1992.

Roderick, Daffyd, Kho Phi Phi, Jeremy Walden-Schertz, and Kho Pha-Ngan. "The 'Explorers' Who Swallowed the World: Backpackers Are a Long Way from the Kinder, Gentler Tourists They Set Out to Be." *Time International* 158 (Aug. 20, 2001): 7–8.

Rojek, Chris. *Ways of Escape: Modern Transformations in Leisure and Travel.* Lanham, MD: Rowman and Littlefield, 1993.

Rosaldo, Renato. *Culture and Truth: The Remaking of Social Analysis.* London: Routledge, 1993 [1989].

Ross, Andrew. *Strange Weather: Culture, Science, and Technology in the Age of Limits.* New York: Verso, 1991.

Ryan, Chris, and C. Michael Hall. *Sex Tourism: Marginal People and Liminalities.* London: Routledge, 2001.

Said, Edward W. *Orientalism.* London: Penguin, 2003 [1978].

Said, Edward W. *Out of Place: A Memoir.* London: Granta, 1999.

Said, Edward W. *The World, the Text, and the Critic.* London: Vintage, 1991 [1983].

Schaffer, Kay, and Sidonie Smith. "Conjunction: Life Narratives in the Field of Human Rights." *Biography* 27, no. 1 (2004): 1–24.

Schama, Simon. *Landscape and Memory.* New York: HarperCollins, 1995.

Schwartz, B. "The Social Context of Commemoration: A Study of Collective Memory." *Social Forces* 61, no. 2 (1982): 327–401.

Seabrook, Jeremy. *Travels in the Skin Trade.* London: Pluto Books, 1996.

Seaton, A. V. "Guided by the Dark: From Thanatopsis to Thanatourism." *International Journal of Heritage Studies* 2, no. 4 (1996): 234–44.

Sebald, W. G. *Austerlitz.* Trans. Anthea Bell. London: Harvill Press, 2001.

Sebald, W. G. *The Emigrants.* Trans. Michael Hulse. London: Harvill Press, 1997 [1992].

Sebald, W. G. *The Rings of Saturn.* Trans. Michael Hulse. London: Harvill Press, 1998 [1995].

Sebald, W. G. *Vertigo.* Trans. Michael Hulse. London: Harvill Press, 1999 [1990].

Seltzer, Mark. *Serial Killers: Death and Life in America's Wound Culture.* New York: Routledge, 1998.

Short, John Rennie. *Global Metropolitan: Globalizing Cities in a Capitalist World.* New York: Routledge, 2004.

Singer, Peter. *Animal Liberation.* New York: Random House, 1975.

Slater, Candace. *Dance of the Dolphin: Transformation and Disenchantment in the Amazonian Imagination.* Chicago: University of Chicago Press, 1994.

Slemon, Stephen. "Climbing Mount Everest: Postcolonialism in the Culture of Ascent." *Ariel* 158 (1998): 15–35.

Smith, Valene. "War and Its Tourist Attractions." In *Tourism, Crime, and International Security Issues,* ed. Abraham Pizam and Yoel Mansfeld, 249–64. New York: John Wiley and Sons, 1996.

Sönmez, Sevil. "Tourism, Terrorism, and Political Instability." *Annals of Tourism Research* 25, no. 2 (1998): 416–56.

Sontag, Susan. *On Photography.* New York: Dell, 1977.

Soper, Kate. *What Is Nature? Culture, Politics and the Non-Human.* Oxford: Blackwell, 1995.

Spanos, William. "Bill Spanos in Conversation." With Robert Kroetsch and Dawn McCance. *Mosaic* 34, no. 4 (2001): 1–19.

Spivak, Gayatri C. *A Critique of Postcolonial Reason: Toward a History of the Vanishing Present.* Cambridge, MA: Harvard University Press, 1999.

Spivak, Gayatri C. "Can the Subaltern Speak?" In *Marxism and the Interpretation of Culture,* ed. C. Nelson and L. Grossberg, 271–313. Houndmills, UK: Macmillan, 1988.

Spivak, Gayatri C. "Three Women's Texts and Circumfession." In *Postcolonialism and Autobiography,* ed. A. Horning and E. Ruhe, 7–22. Amsterdam: Rodopi, 1998.

Stone, Rob. "Social Theory, Documentary Film and Distant Others: Simplicity and Subversion in *The Good Woman of Bangkok.*" *European Journal of Cultural Studies* 5, no. 5 (2002): 217–37.

Strain, Ellen. *Public Places, Private Journeys: Ethnography, Entertainment, and the Tourist Gaze.* New Brunswick: Rutgers University Press, 2003.

Sturken, Marita. *Tourists of History: Memory, Kitsch, and Consumerism from Oklahoma to Ground Zero.* Durham: Duke University Press, 2008.

Taussig, Michael. *Mimesis and Alterity: A Particular History of the Senses.* New York: Routledge, 1993.

Taussig, Michael. *Shamanism, Colonialism, and the Wild Man: A Study in Terror and Healing.* Chicago: University of Chicago Press, 1987.

Taylor, Bron, ed. *Ecological Resistance Movements: The Global Emergence of Radical and Popular Environmentalism.* Albany: State University of New York Press, 1995.

Thanh-Dam, T. "The Dynamics of Sex-Tourism: The Cases of Southeast Asia." *Development and Change* 14, no. 4 (1983): 533–53.

Tomlinson, J. *Globalization and Culture.* Cambridge: Polity Press, 1999.

Urry, John. "The Global Complexities of September 11th." *Theory, Culture and Society* 19, no. 4 (2002): 57–69.

Walkowitz, Rebecca. *Cosmopolitan Style: Modernism Beyond the Nation.* New York: Columbia University Press, 2006.

Walter, Jonathan, ed. *World Disasters Report 2001: Focus on Recovery.* Geneva: International Federation of the Red Cross and the Red Crescent Societies, 2001.

Waugh, Evelyn. *When the Going Was Good.* London: Duckworth, 1946.

Weinberger, Eliot. "The Camera People." *Transition* 55 (1992): 24–54.

Weiner, Justus Reid. " 'My Beautiful Old House' and Other Fabrications by Edward Said." *Commentary* 108, no. 2 (1999): 23–31.

Wheeler, Tony. "Philosophy of a Guidebook Guru." *UNESCO Courier,* July–August 1999, 54–55.

Wheeler, Tony, et al., eds. *Unpacked: Travel Disaster Stories.* Melbourne: Lonely Planet, 1999.

Wheeler, Tony, and Maureen Wheeler. *South-East Asia on a Shoestring.* Melbourne: Lonely Planet, 1975.

Whitlock, Gillian. "Tainted Testimony: The Khouri Affair." *Australian Literary Studies* 21, no. 4 (2004): 165–77.

Willis, Clint, ed. *Wild: Stories of Survival from the World's Most Dangerous Places.* Edinburgh: Mainstream Publishing, 1999.

Wilson, Alexander. *The Culture of Nature: North American Landscape from Disney to the Exxon Valdez.* Cambridge, MA: Blackwell, 1992 [1991].

Wilson, Edward O. *The Diversity of Life.* New York: Norton, 1999 [1992].

Worster, Donald. *Nature's Economy: A History of Ecological Ideas.* Cambridge: Cambridge University Press, 1997.

Yates, Frances. *The Art of Memory.* London: Routledge and Kegan Paul, 1966.

Yeğenoğlu, Meyda. *Colonial Fantasies: Towards a Feminist Reading of Orientalism.* Cambridge: Cambridge University Press, 1998.

Young, James E. "Interpreting Literary Testimony: A Preface to Rereading Holocaust Diaries and Memoirs." *New Literary History* 18, no. 2 (1987): 403–23.

Zipes, Jack, and Leslie Morris, eds. *Unlikely History: The Changing German Jewish Symbiosis, 1941–2000.* Basingstoke: Palgrave Macmillan, 2002.

Index